Books by Fred Powledge

Black Power/White Resistance:
Notes on the New Civil War (1967)
To Change a Child: A Report on the Institute
for Developmental Studies (1967)
Model City (1970)

MODEL CITY

A Test of American Liberalism:
One Town's Efforts to Rebuild Itself

BY

FRED POWLEDGE

Simon and Schuster · New York

ACKNOWLEDGMENTS

A good number of people, most of them New Haveners, were generous with their time and patience when I came asking questions; some were generous even when they suspected I was not on their side. I would like to thank them:

Melvin Adams, James Ahern, Ivan Allen, Peter Almond, Arthur Barbieri, Richard Belford, Milton Brown, Jerome Cavanagh, Joel Cogen, Willie Counsel, Joel Fleishman, Robert Giaimo, James Gilbert, Joseph Goldman, Fred Harris, Rose Harris, Reuben Holden, Ronald Johnson, William Jones, Richard Lee, Frank Logue, Marion Morra, Arthur Naftalin, Ernest Osborne, Hugh Price, Dennis Rezendes, Phyllis Ryan, William Ryan, Bernard Shiffman, Dick Snyder, Kerry Snyder, Lawrence Spitz, Mitchell Sviridoff, Jay Talbot, Joan Thornell, and Richard Thornell.

There were others who will be just as happy not to have their names printed, and I thank them, too. And there were those who helped in other ways—Dave Maness and Willie Morris, to name just two. Most of all there was Tabitha, who kept saying it could be done.

TO POLLY, WHO WAS BORN THERE

Contents

1

The End of an Era

Sixteen years is a long time.
—Mayor Richard Lee of New Haven

ON A WARM Monday morning in July 1969, employees of Mayor Richard C. Lee of New Haven, Connecticut, summoned reporters to City Hall. The mayor was going to make an important statement.

Almost everybody thought they knew what it would be. Richard Lee was going to announce that he was running again for mayor, for the position he had held since 1953 and that he had successfully defended against Republican challengers on eight separate occasions, including one in which he was too sick to campaign.

That he was going to run again was a foregone conclusion. Some politician-watchers reported seeing him at lunch with Arthur Barbieri, the chairman of the local Democratic machine and, ordinarily, a political enemy of Lee's. Others had noticed that Lee was being seen more frequently in public. "When a man starts cutting ribbons at the dedication of shoe stores," said one sage, "you know he's running."

Lee would talk, on that warm Monday morning, about how others had called New Haven a Model City, and he would say that that was not true, that there were no Model Cities; and then he would add that that was no excuse; that New Haven had to try, nevertheless, because cities could not just give up and go away, because cities were the only hope for society. And he would say that he thought he knew how to do the job.

Richard Lee said none of this, however. Instead of announcing his entry into the race, he read a two-page typewritten statement. He said:

> There is never, ever, a right time in these perilous and troubled days to make a statement or launch a project. There is never, ever, a right time to build, or a right time even to arrive at a decision which involves the life of a city or the life of all those among us who can be classed as political leaders.
>
> Therefore, what I am about to say I have delayed saying because of the important urban legislation before the General Assembly of 1969—now ended—and other important negotiations which I am still carrying out involving the vitality and the future of our community. However, recognizing all of those things, I want now to say just this to all of you:
>
> Today I am here to tell you I will not be a candidate for mayor in the coming election. This is a decision reached many months ago, but one which has been withheld publicly because there are so many things at stake for our city in a number of areas— the General Assembly and the Board of Aldermen, to name just two.
>
> Why this decision now, you may ask? I shall tell you why:
>
> Sixteen years is a long time. For me, it covers the lifetime of a child from birth through her junior year in high school. It covers portions of the span of life of four Presidents of the United States, and in Connecticut of three governors; and it has taken me from the age of 37 to the age of 53.
>
> New Haven in the past sixteen years has become an exciting city. Just as its liabilities are still evident and constantly underscored, so are its many, many accomplishments—advancements in education, advancements in housing, in people-programs and in magnificent new buildings which now grace the skyline of our community.
>
> These past sixteen years have been the most exciting years in all of my life. I am sure that never again will I do anything so important as running a city, for this is where all the problems of my generation are focused—the problems of unequality, of crime, of education, of equal employment opportunities, of poor housing —the problems of the inner city in America.
>
> I have enjoyed life in City Hall and I know I will enjoy life when I leave City Hall. But there always arrives a time in a man's

political career when he should do other things, pursue other challenges, and mine is now.

I am grateful to my thousands of friends and supporters who have helped me over the years. I am grateful to God for the opportunity which has been mine to lead the city. I am grateful to the Democratic Party which first nominated me and which has supported me all of this long period of time.

God bless this city to which, literally, I have given my adult life. But, life must go on, and it will go on, not only for me, but also for the city.

Outside City Hall and a few doors down Church Street, at the drab, fluorescent-lit tables of Lindy's luncheonette, where the lawyers and politicians gathered for their coffee, the significance of all this was endlessly explored. Young and middle-aged white men, most of them a few pounds overweight, men with tentative sideburns but hair cut short enough to pass muster in a courtroom, put their briefcases down on Lindy's floor, shucked their muted gray, green, and brown suit jackets, exposing their short-sleeved white dress shirts, and tried to figure out what would happen:

Lee did it because he wanted the Democratic Party, and the citizens of New Haven generally, to draft him for the job.

No, if that's what he wanted, he would have phrased it differently.

Would this mean a law-and-order candidate would have a chance to become the next mayor of New Haven? It had happened elsewhere. Look at Minneapolis—a cop was already mayor. Look at the troubles Lindsay was having in New York. Look at Yorty in Los Angeles.

Would this mean a *Republican* would have a chance to become the next mayor of New Haven? The Republicans had been out of office so long they had almost forgotten how to campaign. But there was a nice, young fellow, a member of the Yale staff, who wanted to be mayor, and who didn't talk all the time about fiscal irresponsibility, and who seemed fairly moderate. Could he beat a Democrat? The Democrats, all of them except Lee, had almost forgotten how to campaign, too.

Would this mean a *black* man—a black man was already in the race. He had announced, as a Democrat, some weeks before Lee's withdrawal, and it looked as if he was committed to challenging Lee in a primary, if necessary. For the first time in a very long time, some of the lawyers and politicians in Lindy's started trying to remember what percentage of the voting-age people in New Haven were black.

What of Lee? Was he getting out because his polls showed he would lose? Lee had always placed great reliance on polls. He used them, although not everybody knew this, to determine in advance what the public would think of the urban renewal projects he was about to unveil. Was it the riot? New Haven had had one in the summer of 1967, although it was called a "disturbance." The riot had been crushing for Lee at first. He had said, at the time, that he really hadn't thought it would happen here. Later, of course, he started saying that it was happening everywhere in urban America.

Lee's health? It had been bad, very bad for a politician. He hadn't campaigned at all in 1967. Was he plotting a future race for governor? What had he said?—"a time in a man's political career when he should do other things . . ." Was he after the Senate seat of Thomas Dodd, who had been censured by his colleagues for using campaign funds for his personal benefit, but who had not had the grace to resign?

And, perhaps the biggest question of them all: What would happen to New Haven? Richard Lee had done more than any other mayor in New Haven's history—perhaps even in America's history—to renew, rebuild, and rehabilitate his city. He had been more than a step ahead of everybody else, first in physical renewal, then in human renewal, which he had called "people-programs" in his announcement of retirement. He had brought millions in from the federal government, millions in from the foundations, millions in from private business, and he had spent it on rebuilding a rotten downtown; on building housing that was, often, pleasing to the eye; on cutting red tape; on pioneering in the field of city-rebirth.

The little mayor (he was only five feet, seven inches tall, and he weighed only 130 pounds, and it was almost impossible to avoid describing him as "bandy-legged," whether he actually was or not) had caused New Haven to be called a Model City, and although he had denied it, the citizens and Mayor Lee nevertheless had derived some degree of pleasure out of seeing delegations from other cities step off the seedy New Haven Railroad trains, walk through the pastures of old bricks and the other shrapnel of urban renewal, ask how it was done; could they do it themselves, once they returned to their own cities? What was the secret?

A cab driver, one of the most frequently quoted sources of misinformation in the nation, said things would be all right; that it was time for a change anyway; and that, besides, all politicians were the same. A black militant (there *were* no black militants in New Haven back when Richard Lee became mayor, and there were surprisingly few of them during most of his term in office) agreed in part with the cab driver: It didn't matter, because one mayor was as big a racist as another.

An official at Yale University said he was honestly worried. Yale had gotten along well with Mayor Lee; he feared that any replacement would not be as kind to the university.

A lawyer, drinking his coffee in Lindy's, said he didn't know what would happen. "All I know," he said, "is that this is the end of an era. And I'm not quite sure what kind of an era it's been."

II

A Massive Dose of Opportunity

Why, the smell of this building . . . It was just awful and I got sick. And there, there I really began. . . .
—Richard Lee, after campaigning on Oak Street in 1951

WHAT NEW HAVEN had as the sixties ended, in addition to the abundant physical evidence of its efforts to improve and rehabilitate itself, was something that few cities have—a good reputation. It was a reputation, built over fifteen years, for being one of the most exciting cities in the nation.

It was certainly not an exciting city in the sense that San Francisco was exciting, or New York, or Los Angeles, or even Philadelphia or Washington or Atlanta. New Haven's climate was harsh and punishing to those who lived there. No one would travel to New Haven to take advantage of either its weather or its scenery, or for many of the other usual reasons for visiting a city.

Some of the cities of America have built airports capable of making you feel like a member of the international jet set. You stride along modern concourses in step with the Muzak and it is not difficult to imagine an air of success, even of mystery and intrigue, about yourself. New Haven's airport was more like some-

16

thing left over from World War II. Its main facility, not counting the runways and control tower, was a luncheonette. Hardly anybody flew from New Haven. To leave the city in style, you took the limousine to the New York airports.

The city could not be called quaint, nor was it sophisticated. Even with Yale University in its center, there were not many bookstores or exciting restaurants. New Haven was not even refreshingly dangerous, in the sense that some cities, such as Chicago or Atlanta or San Francisco, can provide for the conventioneer and visitor a little *danger,* mixed in with, and contributing to, his bawdiness. New Haven was a square city.

People in New Haven seemed to go to work, eat inexpensive and fairly dry lunches, and go home, and sometimes they would go to the movies or they shopped downtown or in the shopping centers and then they went home. When they wanted relaxation and real entertainment they would go somewhere else—up the coast to Hammonassett State Park, on the Sound, for swimming; to Vermont or New Hampshire for skiing. And when they wanted intrigue, bawdiness, and danger, they drove down the Merritt Parkway or the Connecticut Turnpike to New York City.

Excitements of the flesh, the mind, and the eyes were not very much a part of life in New Haven, or in Connecticut, for that matter. The land was originally dominated by puritanical people who seemed to feel that civil liberties were and should be subservient to a code of half-public, half-religious morals. The phrase "blue laws" originated in the Connecticut Colony, which printed such rules and regulations and bound them within blue covers. Although the Puritans long since have been submerged by successive waves of Irish, Italian, and now black, immigrants, the region continues to allow its police to regulate public and private morals to a degree approaching, and sometimes attaining, repression.

What made New Haven exciting was none of these usual excitements, but the knowledge, among those who cared about such things, that New Haven had the talent, the money, the leadership, and the energy—and therefore the potential—to become the Model City. Urban experts—architects, city planners, corporate execu-

17

tives, consultants, labor leaders, demographers—were experimenting elsewhere with the construction of "new towns," places like
Reston, Virginia, and Columbia, Maryland, which were started
from scratch. But in New Haven there was an effort under way
to make a new town out of a very old, decayed, dying, or—as some
said—already dead one.

And the effort did not consist merely of the unleashing of teams
of bulldozers, to be followed by teams of unimaginative and estheti-
cally boring architects, although there was some of that. The effort
included the work of the best, the most exciting, and the most
experimental planners and architects, people like Eero Saarinen
and Paul Rudolph, who shared with critics such as Jane Jacobs
and Lewis Mumford a displeasure over the way cities had made
living so difficult.

The best of the "art and science of city planning," as Miss
Jacobs called it, went into the effort in New Haven. The city was
a showcase for architectural talent, and a designer of buildings
who wanted to erect a memorial to his ideas couldn't have picked
a better place in which to work. Many of the new buildings were
designed so that they would be warm and comfortable and attractive, but most of all *interesting,* to people. Old buildings which
were still useful and attractive were retained. Neighborhoods, too,
were being preserved. And leaders of other American cities, watching what was happening in New Haven, were impressed with what
they saw there. They were also a little jealous, and they were influenced to upgrade their own planning and architecture. They
called New Haven a Model City. The result of all this was excitement—excitement in New Haven and in urban America—for things
were being done that had needed doing for a long, long time.

One thing that contributed mightily to this excitement, in New
Haven at least, was money. For years—a good number of years
longer than most other cities—New Haven had been asking for,
and getting, vast amounts of federal and private money to use in
rebuilding itself.

By 1967, around the time Washington's involvement in poverty
and other urban problems was at its height, it was estimated that

federal urban renewal allocations to New Haven were equivalent to $790 for each man, woman, and child. By contrast, Newark, New Jersey, which was being heralded (before its tragic riot) as another "Model City," was getting $286 per capita; Boston had $268, and New York City had $42.[1] William F. Buckley, Jr., the conservative writer, had pointed out before that if New Haven's per capita success at getting money were shared by all other U.S. cities, the nation would have been spending $146 billion on urban programs.

There was no deep mystery, nor even a convenient conspiracy, involved in New Haven's success at getting money. Any city could have done it with the same mixture of leadership, politics, and intelligence.

Before the late fifties and early sixties, American city halls did not have much of a reputation for either leadership or intelligence. Cities, by and large, were merely political jurisdictions through which services, such as police protection and garbage pickup, could best be provided for an area where the population was relatively dense. They also were centers of shopping activity, although parking was becoming more difficult and the suburban shopping centers were successfully competing with downtown districts.

There were few mayors who exhibited any inclination to see beyond these mundane boundaries. But eventually there arrived on the scene a number of mayors who saw things differently, who rejected the traditional limitations, who pushed aside the old boundaries and hired bright young assistants who could formulate urban programs. Richard Lee, of New Haven, was one of the first of these mayors.

Such an infusion of vitality into city hall would have gone to waste if there had not been a place outside the city where the bright, aggressive mayors could get their money. The cities themselves certainly could not provide the funds necessary for their own reconstruction. They never *had* been able to do so before, and

---

[1] Bernard Asbell, "Dick Lee Discovers How Much Is Not Enough," *The New York Times Magazine,* September 3, 1967.

already in the late fifties and early sixties there were signs that the cities' tax bases were shrinking badly. Fortunately, for Richard Lee and his colleagues, there was a source of income—unprecedented amounts of income, as it turned out.

A new administration had come into office in Washington at the beginning of the decade of the sixties. It was an administration vitally interested in urban America, for urban America had elected it. The Kennedy Administration wanted to do things for and with cities. And in many cases the mayors and the bright young assistants to mayors, the ones who could formulate programs, formulated them, sold them to the officials in Washington, and then appeared at the front of the line with their hands outstretched when the time came for the money to be handed out.

Richard Lee became a master at this. He thought up programs on his own; he hired assistants who were comfortable with the mathematical and legal aspects of the federal funding apparatus. He even figured out intricate maneuvers whereby the city could avoid largely or altogether paying its share—one-third or one-tenth, in most cases—of federally funded projects, usually by including public improvements, such as schools, in a redevelopment plan. And Lee was friendly with the Kennedys; he was a supporter of their new form of Democratic politics, while at the same time he understood the older New England form of politics.

The combination of leadership, politics, and intelligence worked to get New Haven established as a prime recipient of federal funds, and after its establishment, additional funds were assured by the snowballing effect of Lee's earlier successes. Soon other cities were watching closely what New Haven was accomplishing, and they were lining up for funds, too. In Detroit, which frequently has been compared with New Haven, Mayor Jerome Cavanagh fashioned a technique largely after Lee's. Much later, he recalled in an interview how it worked:

". . . a lot of federal programs were not the products of any fertile federal mind, by any chance," he said. They were "the products of some of these new mayors, and some of the mayors' offices, including my own. I could identify a whole series of programs that we helped to shape in terms of legislation. We had a very receptive administration in Washington, and one that was looking for programs that would make them look good.

"People used to say, 'What's the trick? How do you get all that federal money?' Well, what we used to do is come up with an idea, take it to Washington, sell it to the administration, help draft the legislation, write the rules and regulations, and at the same time have a stack of applications ready on their desk for the moment the legislation was passed. The idea was to get there firstest with the mostest. Dick Lee and I used to have footraces to see who was going to get to Washington first."

There was money, too, from private sources. In 1962, the Ford Foundation gave New Haven $2.5 million so that it might try its hand at human, as well as physical, renewal. The result was the establishment of an organization called Community Progress, Incorporated. CPI turned out to be the forerunner of the national war on poverty that was declared in 1964 with the passage of the Economic Opportunity Act.

With the arrival of the money, it became possible for men to identify the challenges that faced them and to start designing solutions to the city's problems, both physical and human. There were some designs lying around from before—such as the one Maurice Rotival, the city planner, had done when he was a member of the Yale faculty in 1941. Rotival had recommended, among other things, that New Haven utilize its natural harbor setting as its "front door," funnelling in traffic that way rather than through the congested back streets; that the Central Green[2] be incorporated into the plan, and that everyone involved recognize that the automobile

---

[2] The Central Green, which remains as New Haven's centerpiece, was part of an even earlier plan for the city. In 1640 John Brockett, a surveyor, laid out nine orderly squares. In the center was a public market, which later became the Green. New Haven, as the Redevelopment Agency liked to point out, was "America's first town planned by Europeans in the New World." Later, in 1910, architects Cass Gilbert and Frederic Law Olmstead presented another plan which sought to maintain green belts around New Haven's perimeter, along with a new traffic system. Not much attention was paid to their proposals.

was here to stay. The plan had failed to excite many of those whose support would have been necessary, and Rotival had gone on to other things.

Now, though, with Lee in office and redevelopment an increasingly important issue, talent began to arrive again—men like Edward C. Logue and, later, Mitchell Sviridoff, who were pioneers in a field that *Time* magazine was later to dub "urbanology." Rotival himself returned to help combine the construction of the Connecticut Turnpike—along the harbor, as he had suggested—with a program of slum clearance that would give a projected 34,000 motorists from surrounding towns someplace to park once they had entered the city's front door in search of shopping bargains.

Urbanology was a field in which educated, articulate men, who had training or experience, or both, in such fields as sociology, political science, the law, architecture, or other disciplines among or bordering on the behavioral sciences, along with an appreciation for and understanding of practical politics, were able to accumulate and to use power in rebuilding cities. They did not need to be politicians, although it was inevitable that before they were long in the job, they would *become* politicians to a greater degree than before.

They became partners with politicians—and especially with Mayor Lee (who appreciated and understood *them*)—in rebuilding the city. As Robert A. Dahl put it in his classic 1961 study of power and decision-making in New Haven, "The new men in local politics may very well prove to be the bureaucrats and experts— and politicians who know how to use them."[3]

Logue, a Yale law graduate who had worked under Governor (later Ambassador) Chester Bowles, was development administrator of New Haven from 1955 to 1961, when he went to Boston to head the redevelopment effort there. He ran unsuccessfully for mayor of Boston, and then moved to New York to become the head of Governor Nelson Rockefeller's $6-billion Urban Develop-

---

[3] Robert A. Dahl, *Who Governs?* (New Haven and London: Yale University Press, 1961), paperback edition, p. 62.

ment Corporation. Sviridoff, who was the executive director of Community Progress, Incorporated, from its inception in 1962 to 1966, went to New York City to become its administrator of human resources, then to the Ford Foundation as its vice-president in charge of the division of national affairs.

While men such as these—and especially Logue, since he was among the first—were in New Haven, they helped to attract talent from all over the nation. They had their own reputations, which were already good in the emerging field of urbanology, and which were growing with each experimental program that was announced. For students of urban change looking for a job, the combination of someone like Logue and someone like Lee was almost impossible to pass up. Wrote Allan Talbot, another observer, who saw things from inside City Hall:

> Those were the Eisenhower years, and federal service seemed stodgy and unexciting. Certainly there were no state governments offering the innovative spirit that such states as New Jersey and North Carolina have seen in recent years. Yet in New Haven, the most unlikely of places, there were two men—a strong, liberal Mayor and a tough, intelligent administrator—who were pioneering a new domestic program called urban renewal. The applications came pouring in. . . .
>
> The result of the process was an unusual group of high-strung, brilliant, humorous, often naive, arrogant but friendly, ambitious hard workers.[4]

Lee, Logue, and the others, as they arrived and set up shop, were able to offer a few other inducements: the promise of programs that already were looking like winners, and that therefore would continue to attract a disproportionate amount of money, interest, and talent; the city's geographical location, close to New York City in a setting along the main line of the Eastern megalopolis; and Yale University.

---

[4] Allan R. Talbot, *The Mayor's Game* (New York: Harper & Row, 1967), pp. 41–42.

New Haven's proximity to New York City may not, by itself, have served as the crucial factor in any apprentice urbanologist's decision to go there to work, but a comparison of the city's problems with those of the huge, uncontrolled (and apparently uncontrollable) giant 80 miles to the south may have. New Haven, with a population of around 150,000, seemed to be a place small enough so that it was possible to live there, to study it, and to execute controllable programs of social change. The new urbanologists were, for the most part, at least half social scientist in their thinking and technique; they needed control groups and they needed test groups, both small enough to comfortably manipulate. It helped, too, that the question of solving some of the city's problems by annexation or other expansion was out of the question; New Haven was hemmed in on one side by Long Island Sound and on the others by well-established suburbs.

New Haven's problems of housing, transportation, health, education, and race relations may have been enormous, but they were not *infinitely* enormous as were those of New York City, or Chicago, or Los Angeles. While even in the fifties a good case could be made for the argument that those larger cities were becoming ungovernable, there was no clear basis for applying the same sort of pessimism to New Haven.

As Jane Jacobs put it in her 1961 classic, *The Death and Life of Great American Cities,* New Haven was small enough so that administrators and staff members could communicate with one another. Also, they could absorb a great deal of information about the city in general from other people in and outside the government. "New Haven is understandable," she wrote, "by combinations of all these means, to normally bright intellects . . . In short, New Haven, as an administrative structure, has a relative coherence built right into it, as one factor of its size."[5]

Yale, the comfortable haven for many of those who came to study, survey, and manipulate, was not able to decide, until very

---

[5] Jane Jacobs, *The Death and Life of Great American Cities* (New York: Random House, 1961), p. 412.

late in the sixties, whether it was proper for an Ivy League school to condescend to involve itself as an institution in the affairs of the city. It was considered sufficient that the faculty members were allowed to sell or donate their talents to the city. Political scientists might want to run for the Board of Aldermen, city planners might want to devise new traffic patterns, and architects might want to accept commissions to design new buildings and other memorials to themselves. But beyond that, and beyond frequent scrapes between the students and the townspeople, Yale had little to do with the city around it.

Town-gown relations were notoriously bad. The poorly trained and poorly disciplined New Haven police seemed to relish outbreaks of collegiate violence, such as that which occurred one Saint Patrick's Day in the early sixties, for that gave them an opportunity to release their stored-up hatred against the privileged Yalies; and the students had plenty of their own hatred, too. Yale as an institution was not having much to do with New Haven as a city, and it certainly was not having much to do with New Haven's problems of poverty and race relations. But Yale did offer a community of scholars, architects and planners, and that meant bookstores and newsstands where one might buy *The New York Times* on the morning of its publication, and *The New Republic,* and *The Economist,* and *Architectural Forum,* and that made living in New Haven less painful for some of the young, talented urbanologists who were invited to come help rebuild the city.

Most of all, though, New Haven had Richard C. Lee.

In recent years, the magazines have been full of success stories about New Haven. (The public information office of the Redevelopment Agency handed to inquisitive visitors an eighteen-page mimeographed bibliography containing citations for 242 articles in general and trade periodicals, ranging from a *Saturday Evening Post* piece titled "He Is Saving a Dead City" to "Tree Stump Removal" in *American City,* and for eight books.) Almost all the stories and books have been about the success of Richard

Lee as well.[6] As one of the articles listed in the bibliography put it:

> When Lee alighted from the Cadillac, he left more than an empty seat behind. The limousine became just another car. Nobody waved from the sidewalk.
> And one has the same feeling about New Haven itself.
> Without Lee, it would be just another city. A city on the move, perhaps. Rejuvenated. Bustling. But with something definitely, irrevocably missing.[7]

Success stories about New Haven and her mayor generally start something like this: "Born in a cold-water flat . . ." Lee's origins, and his somewhat painful rise to power, are intriguing for journalists, many of whom are from middle- or lower-middle-class backgrounds themselves and almost all of whom would rather write a Horatio Alger story than spend a weekend drinking and talking with a Nelson Rockefeller. Lee *was* born in relative poverty, on March 12, 1916, in a cold-water flat in New Haven, to a Catholic working-class family that traced its origins to England, Scotland, and Ireland. In public appearances, noted Dahl, he "chose to emphasize his Irish forebears,"[8] and those who have called on the mayor have gone away convinced that they have been talking to a *bona fide* full-blooded New England Irish politician.

---

[6] New Haven has been inordinately written about and reported on, partly because Yale was there and the professors have wanted to write about something close at hand. Robert A. Dahl, whose book, *Who Governs?* has been previously cited and who will be cited frequently again here, was a political scientist at Yale. In the preface to his book he commented: "The community I chose to study was New Haven, Connecticut, and I chose it for the most part because it lay conveniently at hand." In addition, he said, New Haven was fairly typical of other American cities. Allan R. Talbot's book, *The Mayor's Game,* is another indispensable volume for someone interested in the city and in Lee. Talbot was director of administration for Community Progress, Incorporated, in New Haven, during the early sixties. *The Fifteenth Ward and the Great Society,* by William Lee Miller (Boston: Houghton Mifflin, 1966), is an account of Miller's encounter with New Haven politics; the author, who was an associate professor of social ethics at Yale Divinity School, also was an alderman from the Fifteenth Ward. Together, these books provide an excellent history of the Lee administration in its first several years.
[7] Robert Cormier, "A City on the Way Up," *The Sign,* November 1966.
[8] Dahl, *op. cit.,* p. 118.

Someone once called Lee a cross between the New Frontier and the Last Hurrah, a characterization which Lee did not encourage, but which seemed to fit him well.

From the time he was twelve years old, Richard Lee worked—as a grocery clerk, a soda jerk, a pin-boy in a bowling alley, a messenger, a professional pallbearer, an usher at sporting events at Yale. He graduated from Hillhouse High School, and after that he went not to college but to work for the *Journal-Courier,* the morning paper in New Haven (and sister to the much fatter evening *Register*) as a reporter. He covered police and fire news, and was eventually promoted to the City Hall beat.

In 1939, at the age of 23, Lee ran for alderman and was elected. He said, much later, that his being on the scene for the *Journal-Courier* had helped whet his appetite for the job. "I'd been around City Hall for five years," he said, "and I could see in government the kind of challenge I thought was open for a person like me. I thought it would be kind of fun, and it would be educational, and I felt I wanted to participate. I guess that's what it amounted to."

The young alderman asked to be assigned to the City Plan Commission, which, until then, had been doing relatively little. According to an account of the history of renewal in New Haven compiled later by Lee's Redevelopment Agency, Lee was instrumental in seeing to it that the city hired Maurice Rotival in 1941 to come up with the plan that met with such widespread lack of enthusiasm.

In 1942 Lee was inducted into the Army, but he soon was discharged because of a difficulty that has plagued him most of his life, and most noticeably since he entered the public arena—frail health. He came down with measles, pneumonia, and ulcers, and was a civilian again by 1943. He resumed his duties as a city alderman, and in 1944 he became the director of the Yale News Bureau, the university's public relations outlet. It was a job that was to last for a decade and that was to put Lee in touch with many of those whom the poor boy, born in a cold-water flat and confined to a high school education, might never have otherwise aspired to meet.

By 1947 he had served four terms on the Board of Aldermen,

and had become its Democratic minority leader. In the next year he married the former Ellen Griffin, and he started thinking about more exciting politics. In 1949 he ran for mayor.

Lee lost that election, in which he challenged the Republican incumbent (William Celentano, an undertaker who had held the job since 1945), by 712 votes, 34,923 to 34,211. Two years later he ran against Celentano again, and again he lost. The final vote was challenged, and a court later ruled that Lee had missed by two votes.

There was little reason, in 1949 or 1951, to believe that Richard Lee was going to be the man whose name, and whose hometown's name, would become for some observers synonymous with the term "Model City." Allan Talbot, writing about the two unsuccessful campaigns, noted that in 1949, Lee's effort "was a series of promises to do better the things that Mayor Celentano was already doing," and that in 1951 his attraction again "was not a positive issue or a clear-cut alternative to Celentano but the magnetism of his own personality. However, such magnetism was not enough to attract the support he needed. . . . He needed to attach his personal dynamism to a public cause. . . . The reformer within Lee manifested itself hardly at all in 1949 and 1951."[9]

But perhaps Lee had learned something from those unsuccessful (and, especially for the latter one, heartbreaking) campaigns. During the 1951 effort his managers had arranged for him to visit various gathering places and private homes, in the manner of most politicians. One of the visits was to Oak Street, then the center of the worst of New Haven's slum areas. Out of that came a recollection of Lee's that has been quoted frequently by those who have written about Lee and New Haven, including Dahl:

> . . . I came out from one of those homes on Oak Street, and I sat on the curb and I was just as sick as a puppy. Why, the smell of this building; it had no electricity, it had no gas, it had kerosene lamps, light had never seen those corridors in generations. The smells . . . It was just awful and I got sick. And there, there

---

[9] Talbot, *op. cit.,* pp. 9–11.

I really began . . . right there was when I began to tie in all these ideas we'd been practicing in city planning for years in terms of the human benefits that a program like this could reap for a city. . . . In the two-year period (before the 1953 election) I began to put it together with the practical application . . . And I began to realize that while we had lots of people interested in doing something for the city *they were all working at cross purposes. There was no unity of approach.*[10]

Perhaps because of his somewhat nervous stomach, Lee had learned how to "attach his personal dynamism to a public cause." In 1953, with two defeats behind him and a history of bad health —health which seemed to go especially bad during crises—Lee decided to run again. On September 29, 1953, in accepting the nomination that the Democratic Party had, for the third time, bestowed upon him, he declared that if he were elected he would appoint within 60 days a committee of citizens to study the city's problems and to work out possible solutions to them. "We must take the public of New Haven into partnership with the city government," he said.

On election day 1953 the voters of New Haven elected Richard Lee their mayor, over Mayor Celentano. Lee won by 3,582 votes, 39,526 to 35,944. He was 37 years old when he was elected, which was pretty young for a mayor, but he had, now, quite a mature cause. Wrote Talbot:

It is quite likely that if Lee had not lost in 1951 he, too, would have continued to take a limited view of what was wrong and what could be done. But, rejected twice and forced into a painful process of self-definition, he could now look at his city from a new perspective—that of a man who felt alienated, who was a stranger to himself and to his city—and from that fresh vantage point he could see that there was indeed a local position available for one of his hybrid development, the post not of mayor but of community leader. He could also see that there was a fundamental issue for a political campaign in New Haven, and that the issue was as pervasive and as basic as the sorry state

---

[10] Dahl, *op. cit.,* p. 120.

of New Haven, which affected everyone who lived there. Thus he had found the vital cause which he needed, the cause he was later to call "the rebirth of New Haven."[11]

Lee had his cause, and the voters had responded to it, and he was the mayor of New Haven. But during his second year in office he was in the hospital three times.

The citizens' group that Mayor Lee had promised took nine months, not 60 days, to organize. It was perhaps the wisest political move he ever made; had Lee chosen to inaugurate his plans for the city's rebirth from a position inside the Democratic Party, he could (and certainly would) have been accused of playing politics, and his programs might have taken longer to get off the ground. Instead he drafted a group of diverse citizens and got them behind his dreams, and it became more difficult to allege partisanship.

After an initial reluctance on the part of civic leaders to become involved in the committee, more than 400 of them were finally brought together and put to work finding out what was wrong with the city and figuring out what to do about it (or, at least, that was their theoretical job; Lee, Logue, and their lieutenants did most of the actual work). The Citizens Action Commission, as the organization was called, was headed by a bank president. It contained representatives of almost all walks of New Haven life. (The "almost" is there because there were apparently no members who would fit a current-day definition of "the poor" and very few who could be properly classified as "representatives of the poor.")

"The members had been shrewdly selected to represent many of the major centers of influence or status in the community," reported

---

11 Talbot, *op. cit.,* pp. 11–12. Mayor Lee, asked several years later about Talbot's interpretation, replied that it must have been essentially correct. Much of the legislation that made city-rebuilding possible was not on the books at the time of the earlier campaigns. "But by the time I ran in '53," said Lee, "I had put together my own background in city planning and knowledge, along with the laws then on the books, and the experiences of some other cities, and I came up with a massive dose of opportunity."

Dahl,[12] who went on to list its members, who included three bankers, one of whom was head of the Chamber of Commerce; the president of Yale and the dean of its law school; Democratic National Committeeman John Golden; top labor leaders; manufacturers; the chairman of the board of a utility; and representatives of Italian-American and Jewish interests. A good-sized portion of the commission's members lived in New Haven's suburbs.

The question of representation on such an important body by spokesmen for the poor, or for militant black groups, was not being raised back in 1953. There is no record that anyone sought to question the claims, by Lee and the commission, that the Citizens Action Commission represented "community participation" in the finest sense.[13] What was far more important was the fact that, in assembling the group, Lee was creating an establishment that would run interference while he carried the redevelopment ball. And it was an establishment that was outside the traditional Democratic machine, which, while it might have been good at dispensing patronage and other tasks, was no good whatsoever at helping to change the status quo. The CAC's multipartisan composition meant that whatever the commission decided or agreed on could not be attacked quite so easily as the decisions of a lone Democratic mayor. The CAC determined that its purpose would be to:

—Develop public understanding of community problems.
—Promote public interest and participation in the various programs aimed at solving the problems.
—Conduct non-partisan studies of causes, effects, and cures of such problems.
—Disseminate information from the studies and other sources.
—Serve as an agency for exchange of ideas and opinions.
—Serve as a means by which citizens may offer advice and

---

[12] Dahl, *op. cit.*, p. 131.
[13] Lee was asked about this in 1969. Were poor people asking, in 1953, to be on the commission? "No," he said. What about ministers and others who claimed to represent the poor? "No." Members of the social work establishment? "No." Yet people criticized Lee in 1969 for not putting any of the poor on the commission? "Yeah, *now*," he replied.

contribute their services to the organizations and agencies concerned with their problems and solutions.

The commission obviously thought of itself as representative of all portions of New Haven life. Its 1957 annual report stated:

> The Citizens Action Commission and its Action Committees are in the best sense "grass roots" organizations which include a cross-section of community life with all its rich and varied character. The knowledge of the program goals and their support by these representative men and women are the democratic foundation on which the success of urban renewal in New Haven depends.[14]

For some political observers, however, the commission represented something distinctly different from grass-roots democracy. It had been created and sustained by Mayor Lee; the commission received funds from the city's Redevelopment Agency. A financial statement by the commission in one year, for instance, showed that the agency had provided "grants" to the CAC of $7,500, while industries had donated $5,590 and membership dues had accounted for $1,000. The Redevelopment Agency, therefore, was the prime financial backer of the Citizens Action Commission.

The commission's strategic role in assuring that redevelopment was publicly accepted, wrote Dahl, "can hardly be overestimated." He added:

> The mere fact that the CAC existed and regularly endorsed the proposals of the city administration made the program appear nonpartisan, virtually nullified the effectiveness of partisan attacks, presented to the public an appearance of power and responsibility diffused among a representative group of community notables, and inhibited criticisms of even the most daring and ambitious parts of the program as "unrealistic" or "unbusinesslike." Indeed, by creating the CAC the Mayor virtually decapitated the opposition. The presence of leading bankers, industrialists, and businessmen—almost all of whom were Republicans

---

[14] New Haven Citizens Action Commission, *Third Annual Report* (New Haven, 1957), quoted in Dahl, *op. cit.,* pp. 122–23.

—insured that any project they agreed on would not be attacked by conservatives; the presence of two of the state's most distinguished labor leaders and the participation of well-known liberal Democrats like the Dean of the Yale Law School meant that any proposal they accepted was not likely to be suspect to liberals. To sustain a charge of ethnic or religious discrimination would have required an attack on distinguished representatives of these groups. . . . Thus, properly used, the CAC was a mechanism not for *settling* disputes but for *avoiding* them altogether.[15]

By now, with the voters apparently behind him and a seemingly invincible group of prominent citizens on his side (or, perhaps, convinced that he was on *their* side), the new mayor pushed ahead with his plans for the rebirth of New Haven. Somehow, using all his skills as a politician, Lee managed to establish a municipal government that was parallel and superior to the existing one.

It had been obvious to Lee from the first weeks of his administration that the existing government—the standard municipal collection of bureaucrats, supervisors with little responsibility, patronage-holders, and officials with vague job titles—might be sufficient for business as usual, but that it was totally incompatible with city-rebirth. It was especially useless in the area of finance. "One month in office," Lee told the aldermen in his first annual address, "has convinced me that the City of New Haven is still in the horse and buggy era when it comes to managing its fiscal affairs."

For one thing, the city was floating bonds for items that should have been paid for out of the cash box—in some cases, the *petty* cash box. When, in 1951, the city had wanted to buy catalogue cases for its library, an $8,000 bond issue had been floated. Because of financial inefficiencies such as this, New Haven was spending $250,000 a year in interest payments alone.

More disconcerting to Lee was his discovery that he needed help—top-notch, professional help—in running the city. The caliber of helpers available to him through the normal channels of the Democratic Party was simply not sufficient, although he did not say that in so many words. The situation was in such an advanced

---

[15] Dahl, *op. cit.*, pp. 133, 136.

state of decay, he told the aldermen, that it required "not improvement, but invention." His major invention, as it turned out, was the Citizens Action Commission. But he also started hiring top-notch professional help.

What Lee was building, and what he soon succeeded in establishing, was a parallel city government, with himself as its head. It was essential that such a government be formed, either parallel to or in place of the existing one, for the existing one was slovenly and inefficient, and certainly unimaginative. Numerous agency boards ran their own affairs without regard for the rest of the city. And the rest of the city was run largely by bureaucrats.[16]

Slowly but surely, the parallel government began to emerge, then to take over power, then to run the city. Lee did not choose to simply dissolve the old government by firing people; that would have brought on a political revolt. But he did shift the power of City Hall, and of most of the agencies that had operated before with such flimsy ties to City Hall, out of the hands of the bureaucrats and into the hands of himself and those whom he selected.

Lee managed to do this without incurring the active wrath of the Democratic machine (although in later years the relations between the mayor and the machine would deteriorate tremendously). Soon after his election, Lee let John Golden, the grand old man of the city Democrats, know that he would continue as the senior politician. And the mayor appointed Arthur T. Barbieri, the Democratic town chairman, as director of public works, where he could, and did, dispense patronage in the classical manner of a boss. But Lee was adamant about retaining for himself the control over

---

[16] Talbot notes that the situation was so bad when Lee took office that it was absolutely necessary for the new mayor to establish a parallel way of doing things. "The bureaucratic situation he inherited on January 1, 1954, approached anarchy," wrote Talbot. "City agencies functioned like a confederation of tribes. . . . The key to unlocking these prevailing bureaucratic practices and establishing his personal authority was clear to Lee: He had to make his presence known to the isolated departments, and he had to assume control of the city budget." (Talbot, *op. cit.,* pp. 29–30.) The ways in which Lee went about achieving these goals, which really amounted to his converting New Haven from a weak- to a strong-mayor form of government, are described in interesting detail in Talbot's book.

the agency that really counted, the agency that the Citizens Action Commission was created to legitimize, the agency through which the rebirth would be carried out, and the agency that was the central component of the parallel government—the Redevelopment Agency.

The Redevelopment Agency took over many of the responsibilities that previously had been the business of other city agencies— agencies that had been more attuned to the patronage system than to the relatively new idea of redevelopment. The result was what many observers of the New Haven scene came to call a "parallel government" which was responsive to an "executive-centered coalition," or "executive-centered order," with Lee at the center. "It was the need for redevelopment that created the need for an executive-centered order," wrote Dahl, "and it was widespread agreement on the need for redevelopment that generated widespread acquiescence in the creation of an executive-centered order.[17] Largely because of his skill at creating and maintaining the coalition around redevelopment (and doing it at a time when many American mayors were still wondering if redevelopment were politically feasible), Lee maintained himself in office.

Partly because he was doing things that had not been done before, partly because he was an astute politician, and partly, undoubtedly, because of luck, Lee was able to accomplish a lot in a short period of time. By February 1955, at the completion of his first full year as mayor, Lee reported to the aldermen that "I stand before you to say how thrilled I am that my dreams and plans for 1954, almost without exception, have been realized. . . . It has been a most thrilling and exhilarating year."

He revealed the dreams he had for 1955 and subsequent years —a "revitalized business district drawing shoppers back to our downtown area like a magnet"; a regional food market on reclaimed harbor land; parking spaces, "hundreds, even thousands, of new spaces every year for many years to come"; new industrial

[17] Dahl, *op. cit.,* pp. 200–201.

land to tempt the businesses that were moving to the South and West; a "combination of slum clearance and housing code enforcement" that could "make New Haven an attractive place to live as well as to work."

> I believe that 1954 will go down in the history of our town as the year of decision—the beginning of a great new era of development into a more lovely and a more prosperous city. The things which have been started in 1954 will bear fruit in the years to come. Unhappily for the impatient ones like me, the seed takes a long time to poke its way above ground. But in the long life of our city—over 300 years of it—our waiting period will be a very brief one, indeed.

Looking back on his first year in office, Lee cited the creation of the Citizens Action Commission as "the single most important accomplishment of my administration." The CAC, he said, "is the most dynamic factor in our community life today. Completely non-partisan, drawing on suburbanites as well as city residents, it has for the first time mobilized the resources of the entire community for a comprehensive attack on the problems confronting New Haven today."

The accomplishments were many: The Board of Aldermen, in the previous summer, had approved a new housing code, which delighted Lee, and which gave him the ammunition to start thinking and talking about rehabilitation. Engineers were at work trying to solve the city's traffic and parking problems. Maurice Rotival was at work planning the city's future. Most important, and most visible, was the Oak Street Connector.

The Connector, a multi-laned spur that was to bring motorists through the city's "front door" near the harbor, where the Connecticut Turnpike ran, to the central business district (and over the land where Lee once had sat on the curb and vomited), was the first piece of major construction that the new administration performed. Lee had talked the State Highway Department into extending the Connector further than originally planned, and at state expense. Nineteen-fifty-five, Lee told the aldermen, "will see, at long last, definite action in the Oak Street Redevelopment Area

—agreements with private developers and with the Federal Government paying the way for demolition and reconstruction along what, in truth, will be New Haven's 'Miracle Mile.' "

The timing on the Oak Street project turned out to be perfect. The federal government announced its approval the week before the November 1955 election. Lee defeated his Republican opponent, who had called Lee a stooge for Yale, by 20,808 votes, and he brought his fellow Democrats into a 31 to 2 majority on the Board of Aldermen. It was obvious, by the end of his first term, that redevelopment was a hot issue in New Haven—maybe *the* issue.

The 44-acre Oak Street clearance project and the construction of the Connector involved the removal of human beings, and at the time there was relatively little controversy, or even publicity, connected with their relocation. Jeanne R. Lowe, writing in 1957 in *Harper's* about New Haven, noted that much fanfare accompanied the demolition of Oak Street buildings (sometimes acts of destruction were timed to coincide with the visits of dignitaries) and the eradication of a horde of rats that had lived in the slum. "The peaceful relocation of 881 families went unpublicized," she added, "but no effort was spared to help the former slum dwellers get a new start, to find a decent home for a large family or an elderly couple, to reassure the fearful. This is the side of Lee's work which has nothing to do with headlines, but which means the most to many of his associates and may someday be best remembered."

Miss Lowe also found that Oak Street had become a symbol of New Haven's "new pride and hope." It was the "first integrated step in a grand design which will gear the city to the automotive age, rebuild its rotten commercial core, shore up slipping neighborhoods, and draw back the disenchanted from the suburbs. In ten years, if the people stay with the program and if federal funds hold out, New Haven may be the first slumless city."[18] Oak Street

---

[18] Jeanne R. Lowe, "Lee of New Haven and His Political Jackpot," *Harper's,* October 1957.

also became a symbol of successful involvement of business in a redevelopment area. Lee talked the Southern New England Telephone Company into building its new $15-million headquarters in the project area, next to the Connector.

In the spring of 1957, with the apparently peaceful relocation of the Oak Street families under way, Lee announced the Church Street project, an $85-million effort that he called "the most important thing that will ever happen in New Haven's history." It was certainly the most ambitious.

The Church Street project covered 96 acres in the very center of New Haven's business district; the plans called for the destruction of four blocks of the most central business real estate in the city and the erection of new buildings, plus wider streets, more parking facilities, and better traffic patterns. It was, as the Redevelopment Agency said, "conceived in terms of the family car."

Eventually, the project brought to New Haven a new department store (Macy's) and a new building for an old one (Malley's); a nineteen-story hotel; the Chapel Mall, a two-level collection of small retail stores on a central court; a fourteen-story office building, and a parking garage that was bragged about more than most parking garages, inasmuch as it was designed by architect Paul Rudolph. A 320-foot-tall building to house the international headquarters of the Knights of Columbus, an old New Haven institution, was to be dedicated in 1969. Construction had started on a coliseum and convention center, and between the Connector and the train station was the site of the proposed Church Street South housing development, which contained twenty acres of land and which would provide 1,000 housing units "to serve all income groups," according to the city's plans.

Later in 1957, after the announcement of the Church Street project, Lee ran for reelection to his third term, against a Republican candidate who criticized him largely for the city's reckless spending practices (which, with the exception of Yale-baiting, was about the only theme the Republicans could develop, and one which they used in successive elections). Lee won by more than 23,000 votes, and it was safe to say that he and redevelopment had become household words in New Haven. There was talk that he would be the proper and logical man to receive the Democratic nomination for U.S. Senator. Lee put down the rumors, saying that he had unfinished business in New Haven.

The unfinished business included additional redevelopment projects, particularly those concerning three neighborhoods that surrounded downtown. The first of these to receive approval from the Board of Aldermen was Wooster Square, a 235-acre plot of land not far from the center of the city. The square and the land around it were first settled by well-to-do Yankees back when New Haven was a commercial sailing port. By 1850, according to one account, it was New Haven's most fashionable neighborhood. But the harbor decreased in importance and the city became an industrial center after the Civil War, and the immigrants came to New Haven. The Yankees, and soon the Irish, moved out to make way for the Italians. In 1890 about 5 percent of the residents of the neighborhood were Italians; by 1900, the Italians made up almost a quarter of the population, and by the end of the nineteen-sixties, they made up about 80 percent of the total neighborhood population of 7,000.

In 1959 Wooster Square was known as "Little Naples," and a generation of neglect had turned it into an industrial slum. Mayor Lee set out to rehabilitate and redevelop the area. Until 1954 federal renewal legislation provided for assistance from Washington only when an area was to be completely cleared of buildings; in 1954 the Housing Act was amended to allow federal aid for projects that included rehabilitation of existing structures as well. New Haven became the first city in the nation to utilize this provision, and it devised a plan whereby a minimum of housing in Wooster Square would be actually torn down.

The city used both carrots and sticks in its efforts at promoting rehabilitation of preservable homes in renewal project areas. The sticks were strong ones; New Haven had a tough housing code, and the will to back it up. The men whose duty it was to enforce the code were not political hacks, but people interested in serving the city. The inspectors and officials were not mired down in bureaucracy, incompetence, and bribe-taking, the way such officials often are in the larger cities. In addition, the city had the power of eminent domain—the power to condemn and take what it wanted—in renewal areas. But persuasion and flattery came in handy, too, and the city's housing and redevelopment officials were proud of what those devices produced. One of the officials, Mary S. Hommann, the director of the Redevelopment Agency's Wooster Square project (which, with its fine, old, and sometimes historic, homes, lent itself nicely to rehabilitation), explained in 1962 how the process worked:

A neighborhood rehabilitation representative first visited the homes in a block that was scheduled for a rehabilitation drive. In addition to breaking the news to the homeowner and explaining how the program worked, this representative collected information on the family, such as its size, income, and mortgage status. Later, a housing code inspector arrived for the official inspection. An architect started collecting information on the house's history, if it were available. In the case of Wooster Square, the materials of the Colonial Historical Society were utilized by the staff architect assigned to a neighborhood. "With his knowledge of the building, and of the financial ability of the owner in question," wrote Miss Hommann, "he makes recommendations for improvements that will give the property the attractive appearance essential for thorough and lasting rehabilitation."

The architect prepared color drawings of the property as it would look after rehabilitation and gave them to the owners. A homeowner, said Miss Hommann, "is *flattered* that we go to the trouble of drawing a picture of his house, *gratified* to be given a copy, and *inspired* to do good work! Very often he frames the picture and hangs it in a permanent place."

Once the owner saw the light, the city's specialist helped him plan for rehabilitation work, preparing cost estimates, helping in the selection of contractors, and checking on codes and permits. The project director also helped owners to secure loans. "Upon completion of the work," wrote Miss Hommann, "Mayor Lee, with great charm and a little speech, presents each homeowner with an official certificate of performance at a special ceremony. Later on, the owner also receives a photograph of himself receiving his certificate from the mayor."[19]

An expressway, which often guarantees little more than a first-rate urban controversy, was used in Wooster Square to the neighborhood's advantage. The planners located the path of Interstate 91, which ran from the shore-bound Connecticut Turnpike up toward Hartford, so that it would be a buffer between the rehabilitated housing and the cleared industrial slums. The cleared land became Wooster Square Industrial Park, which soon attracted more than $11 million in private investments. Merchants in other sections of the neighborhood, meanwhile, rehabilitated their own businesses, and few were forced to leave the neighborhood by the project. One of the finest pizza parlors in the East, Frank Pepe's, is still there. The city built a new headquarters for its fire department in the area, provided off-street parking, and built three new parks.

Obtaining aldermanic approval for the Wooster Square project in February of 1959, an election year, was not at all a bad move for Mayor Lee. The Church Street project was becoming bogged down, partly because a merchant was fighting it in court and partly because the financial backing for the enormous venture seemed shaky. Lee, however, did not seem shaky when he went before the aldermen in February 1959 to tell them what had happened in the past year and what he hoped would happen in the new one.

"Without question, in my mind, at least," he said, "the year 1958 was one of the most exciting in New Haven's 321 years." He was especially proud that the American Municipal League and *Look* magazine had designated New Haven an "All America City," and he was able to tell the aldermen a little more of his dreams:

> In the twelve months which have passed since last I stood before this honorable body, the face of our city has changed substantially. Massive surgery undertaken in Oak Street and in parts

---

[19] Mary S. Hommann, "Neighborhood Rehabilitation Is Working in Six Projects in New Haven; Here's How," *Journal of Housing,* Vol. 19, No. 4, May 1962.

of Church Street, our foremost projects, has begun to rid the city of its depressing slums—slums which we, not only as legislators and administrators but as thoughtful and responsible citizens, would not accept as part of normal urban living. . . .

Our goal is a slumless city—the first in the nation. In the past five years we have made substantial and significant strides towards this goal; and I am confident that, as the support and understanding of this great rebirth of our city continues to grow, we can reach this goal.

It is not too much to hope for that the City of New Haven can proudly set its target date for the elimination of all our slums—residential, commercial, industrial—within the next decade.

Still, the uncertainty of the Church Street project plagued Lee through the year. His 1959 Republican opponent, James J. Valenti, a junior high school principal, attacked the incumbent not only for his rising municipal budget but also for his handling of Church Street.

But in October 1959, just before the election, and two months ahead of schedule, the Oak Street Connector opened. Although the highway was only a few thousand feet long, and it ended abruptly once it had swept in to the center of the city from the Turnpike, it was a great convenience for motorists from outside the city who wanted to drive to work or to shop along the Green. This new convenience certainly didn't hurt Lee at the polls; he defeated Valenti by 13,984 votes, 36,694 to 22,710. But some observers, including Lee himself, thought the victory would have been greater if it had not been for the Church Street delay.[20] Lee needed something that was big, visible, beautiful and finished as proof that he was on the right track, and he very nearly didn't get it.

In the following year, 1960, the city and Lee undertook their first renewal project that involved a heavily Negro-populated

___

[20] Some years later, Lee recalled that "the Church Street project very nearly spelled my political demise." "Testimony of Richard Lee," *Hearings Before the National Commission on Urban Problems* (Washington: U.S. Government Printing Office, 1968), Vol. I, p. 116.

ghetto—the Dixwell neighborhood, which lay just to the north of Yale University. The project took on the name "University Park—Dixwell," and the New Haven Redevelopment Agency cited it (somewhat more defensively in recent years, as citizen participation has become an increasingly important issue) as an example of a project in which rehabilitation was emphasized and clearance minimized, and in which residents were "actively involved in the planning."

The city, meantime, was carrying millions of cubic yards of gravel down to its harbor and dumping it into a tidal marsh as part of its Long Wharf project. The project, 120 acres along the Turnpike, eventually attracted a regional food market terminal and modern plants housing the local giant general contractor, C. W. Blakeslee & Sons, and Sargent and Company, which had been thinking about moving out of the state. Under construction at the site by the end of the sixties were plants for Gant of New Haven, the shirt manufacturer, and the Armstrong Rubber Company.

By 1961 Richard Lee had plenty of physical evidence that redevelopment, rehabilitation, and renewal of a city was feasible—economically, socially, and politically. In the year 1960 alone, $30 million worth of public and private construction projects had been started in renewal areas, bringing the total since Lee took office to $70 millions. In 1960 500 families were relocated and 379 slum buildings demolished. Old buildings were being pushed down all over the town, landlords and homeowners were being convinced of the importance of rehabilitating the housing that was not beyond repair, traffic was moving more smoothly, the problems of Church Street were being ironed out and people could believe a little more in the nice architects' renderings they had been bombarded with, and the harbor was being turned into something other than a smelly dump. Most of all, downtown was becoming an attractive place, and it was drawing shoppers back from suburbia. Redevelopment was good for business.

People were starting to say, and to say loudly, that Richard Lee was in the process of saving New Haven. And, as more and more of it got saved, they could see a little more clearly how bad off it had been before. Lee received many accolades in those days, but one that perhaps pleased him the most came not from another politician, not from a poor slum family that had been relocated into decent housing, not from an official in Washington. It came from Yale University, the school Lee had never attended but which he so obviously admired. In June of 1961 Yale conferred an honorary master's degree upon Lee, and it told him:

"With steadfast courage, faith, and vision, you have lifted New Haven from the midden of slums and stagnation and set her on the high road to a bright and prosperous future."

Half a year later Lee ran for, and was reelected to, his fifth term. The Republican candidate, Henry H. Townshend, chose as his issues the swelling city budgets and the delays in the Church Street project. Lee won by 4,000 votes, 30,638 to 26,638.

In eight years, and largely because of the efforts of a single man, physical renewal had become a fact of life in New Haven. Residents of the once dying city seemed proud of what had happened, and what was happening, and their pride seemed to help them overcome their normal American distrust of City Hall. They bragged to visitors. The officials of other American cities, the dying and the not-so-dying, were sending delegations to New Haven by the score to find out How It Was Done. Sometimes New Haven would Show Them by scheduling a special demolition in their honor. The delegations especially wanted to know why it was that when they went to Washington to ask for redevelopment money, a lot of it already had been reserved for Richard Lee.

Lee and his assistants were happy to oblige with advice and demonstrations; after all, they had been first, and when you're first you can afford to be helpful. But at the same time, while the other mayors were wondering how to start physical renewal, Lee and his corps of talented assistants were thinking in terms of *human* renewal. As usual, they were one step ahead of everybody else.

III

Human Renewal

The appetite for progress appears insatiable.
—Mitchell Sviridoff, in 1959

BY THE BEGINNING of 1962, as Richard Lee started his fifth term in City Hall, he could look around himself and see that his dream of a reborn city was becoming a reality. The Connector was funnelling traffic into downtown, and downtown itself was being rebuilt. Those two projects, alone, once had been thought of as impossible, both politically and economically. And other projects were on the drawing boards.

Lee had succeeded in establishing urban rebirth as a viable political device. He had succeeded in remaking an archaic Democratic party machine into a mechanism that responded to his wishes, and he had been able to do this without incurring outright revolt from the party faithful and the hacks.[1] He had succeeded in making New Haven *the* city where energetic young city planners and urbanologists wanted to be.

Lee had succeeded in luring the business community into his plans—and Republican members of the business community, at that. He even was incorporating Yale University into the "parallel government" that was rebuilding New Haven. Thanks largely to

---

[1] Or perhaps it would be better to say he had achieved such power that he was able to ignore the machine when he felt like it. For a fascinating description of how Lee dealt with the machine, see Talbot's *The Mayor's Game.*

his friendship with the late Whitney Griswold, then president of Yale and the mayor's former employer, Lee in 1955 sold three high schools to Yale for $3 million. Lee needed the money to build new schools, and the university needed the land, which was adjacent to its campus. Then, in 1956, Lee enlisted Yale as a potential real estate developer. There were signs that the New Haven citizenry was still skeptical about the feasibility of renewal on the Oak Street project site, and Lee and others felt that the skepticism would be dispelled if Yale showed interest in backing an apartment complex in the area.

Much to everyone's surprise, however, when the bidding was held for the Oak Street land, Yale was outbid by a group from Boston which offered $1,150,000—far more than Lee, Yale, or the skeptics had ever imagined the bulldozed land would be worth.

But even as the bulldozers scraped away more slum housing and replaced it with highways, hotels, apartment buildings, department stores and office buildings, and as Lee and Logue thought up newer and more dramatic schemes, it became increasingly obvious that the bulldozer was not going to be enough.

Lee and those around him started talking about "human renewal"—or "people-programs," as Lee preferred to call them. As one of those who worked for Lee reflected some years later, "Utilizing the bulldozers didn't solve the problems. In fact, it just uncovered them. It uncovered human problems."

Lee himself was to recall not too long afterward: "We knew we had to develop a human renewal program which was as broad and as comprehensive as our urban renewal program." In a speech delivered in December 1962 at the annual meeting of the Norfolk, Virginia, Chamber of Commerce, the mayor provided some elaboration on the directions his thoughts and actions had been taking:

It does not take a city planner's education or a blackboard of statistics to show that our cities are in trouble. It can become quite apparent to any concerned citizen who would but take an afternoon's walk through his own city.

At first glance, he will certainly see the . . . facades of our contemporary office buildings, the concrete ribbons of our interstate highways, and the glitter and excitement of Main Street. But, let him look closer, in the shadows, down the side streets. . . .

And if he will look carefully, he will see another and even more serious dimension to the urban crisis. He will see it in most city neighborhoods, on the steps of the tenements, on the garbage-strewn streets and alleys, and on the faces of the men, the women, and the children who during their entire lives have known nothing but misery and despair.

He will see, in effect, that the haphazard growth of our cities and the years of neglect and lack of comprehensive planning have resulted not only in physical ugliness, chaos, and decay; they have also produced the terrible by-product of human waste and suffering . . .

Some of America's human problems in 1962 were not being uncovered by bulldozers at all, but by dramatic and often tragic confrontations between whites and Negroes in the South, and those who advised Lee were not unmindful of them. The advice had come as far back as 1959. In that year, when most of the Northern cities were joining in the national head-shaking over what was happening on the racial battlefields of the South, and declaring selfrighteously that life was much better up North, one of those advisors had sat down and written a memorandum on how the Movement affected New Haven and its mayor.

Mitchell Sviridoff, a young New Haven native, head of the state AFL-CIO, a Lee appointee to the Board of Education, and some-times informal advisor to the mayor on matters of labor, wrote, for 1959, a document of shocking perception. He titled it "Memo on Problems of Leadership in the Negro Community." In it, he told Mayor Lee that such leadership divided itself roughly into three categories:

The *conservatives,* wrote Sviridoff, ranged from "the apathetic, the obsequious, the compliant and the frightened" to "the highly rational but innately conformist or assimilationist personality." Once the dominant leaders in the Negro community, they now had little power:

> To rely on them today for practical assistance in coping with the potentially explosive social, economic and political problems

47

of the Negro community would be an exercise in futility. Politicians who, perhaps understandably, would prefer to wish away the unpleasant nastiness of the race problem tend to exaggerate the importance of the conservatives. They look in their direction for comfort and reassurance and sometimes even for active support. Though such politicians may get what they are looking for, the results are largely meaningless except as a sop to their own inner disturbances.

The *moderates,* he said, form a group that is "large and important" and, on the surface, "the dominant group in the community today." The educators, ministers, professionals and intellectuals who make up this group, he said,

> would appear to offer the kind of leadership with which municipal authorities could form an effective alliance for the solution of the seemingly ever-present and nagging problems of the Negro community.
> The moderates represent a leadership as acceptable to the more sophisticated white community as were the conservatives of another day. Yet they cannot be relied upon in most crises. In tough situations they seem to falter, hesitate, vacillate—and even run for cover. Why? The clue is in the significance of the third group.

Sviridoff chose to name the third group the *immoderates* or *direct actionists,* "sometimes referred to as the radical leaders in the Negro community." They ranged from responsible and objective radicals on the one hand to "extreme fanatical nationalists on the other.

> Within the group, a large centrist element swings between the two extremes—depending on the nature of the crisis and *on how the crisis is being handled by the white community.*
> Paradoxically, though in numbers the direct actionists are considerably smaller than either of the other groups, they all too frequently assume dominant leadership in the Negro community. [Italics in original.]

Sviridoff listed three reasons for this: First, the Negro community harbors "a latent bitterness and hostility of extraordinary intensity" which does not diminish as discriminatory barriers come down. "The appetite for progress appears insatiable," he said. "Is it any wonder, then, that the Negro community seems in most crises to be more responsive to the radical voice? Is it any wonder that even the term 'moderate' has come into disrepute in the community."

Second, the "direct actionists have been responsible, like it or not, for the major Negro victories."[2]

And third, wrote Sviridoff, "the ineptitude in the white community encourages dominance by radical Negro leadership." The significance of all this in terms of "political leadership at the municipal level," he concluded, could be summed up this way:

• "Irresponsible radical Negro leadership is not an accident." Sometimes it is fostered by the white community's stupidity.

• A city must understand that there is a difference between the "adjustment problems" of the Negro and those of the white minorities who "arrived" earlier. Then the city must "detect the sore spots and at least attempt to initiate positive programs and policies in consultation with a wide range of leadership from the Negro community." The alternative to this, he said, is to wait for things to explode, "with the leadership inevitably passing into the waiting hands of the 'irresponsibles.' "

• There is limited value in handing out political favors, or even appointments, to the Negro leadership. "Such tactics may even contribute to the winning over to the city administration of some important community leaders. On the other hand, they may have the effect of neutralizing the potential of these same individuals for leadership."

---

[2] It might be easy for someone reading Sviridoff's memo today to forget that it was written back in 1959, even before the sit-in movement started in Greensboro, North Carolina—at least until one discovers who Sviridoff meant by the "direct actionists." "Compare the accomplishments, for example," he wrote, "of the quiet, deliberate work of the Urban League to the militant and forceful aggressiveness of the NAACP. . . . If any of us were Negroes living with the stench of the slums always in our nostrils . . . we would not necessarily renounce the Urban League, or fail to recognize it is an important instrument for progress; but wouldn't we attribute our most meaningful progress—the truly big victories—to the NAACP?"

• Politicians who rely too heavily on "election day results and public opinion polls in connection with the problem of 'winning over' the Negro" are making a mistake. The Negro is a Democrat, and the Democratic politician will be tempted to interpret black support "as reassuring evidence that nothing more need be done in the way of genuine and positive programming." If this happens, said Sviridoff, the Negro only naturally "will continue to apply every variety of pressure; this will even include political threats, but because of the natural identification of the Negro with the Democratic Party, they will rarely work. Other types of threats, some seemingly irresponsible, too often do seem to work, however."

• Politicians, who have learned to accommodate themselves to the nationalistic pressures of earlier minority groups, tend to become self-righteous and highly moral when confronted with similar demands from Negroes. "It ought to be recognized that such pressures are part of the very scheme of things in American political life," wrote Sviridoff; "they ought therefore to be taken in stride."

• Finally, while the city administration may seek to strengthen its alliances with Negro moderates, "communications with the responsible radicals or direct actionists should not be terminated."

> True, the responsible radical may fail to show proper appreciation for progress, or even for personal favors. His behavior may even border on downright discourtesy. To cut oneself off from him completely, however, is again to invite irresponsibility. We may indeed be rejecting a valuable divining rod for real or potential community discontent, as well as cutting off a possible source of positive and constructive ideas.

Mayor Lee had had the Sviridoff memo since 1959 (there is no available record of his reply or reaction to it), and as the movement gained in scope and intensity between then and 1962 he certainly had little reason to doubt that his advisor was thinking in the right direction. Not only was the Movement showing signs of spreading from the embattled South to the selfrighteous North;

the sheer numbers of people who might make up a Northern movement—black people—were increasing. In 1950 the Negro population of New Haven was about 9,600, or 6 percent of the total. By 1960 it had reached 22,000, or almost 15 percent. It was obvious that the white exodus to the suburbs had begun; in 1950 Negroes totaled 1,327, or 1.3 percent of the population, in the other towns in New Haven's metropolitan area. By 1960 the number was up to 1,838, but the percentage was down to 1.2.

Also, the leveling of so much slum housing during the first years of the Lee administration had exposed sights, smells, and frustrations that most white, middle-class observers had neglected to observe before. As the physical renewal program progressed, the need for "people-programs" became increasingly apparent.

Thus, at a time when other medium-sized cities were just getting started with the bulldozer approach, and more than two years before Congress was to pass the Economic Opportunity Act that would provide the money to arm the generals in the war on poverty, New Haven was starting its own attack on poverty, and it was to be termed so successful that much of the federal action later would be based on New Haven's efforts.

The chief instrument of Lee's "people-programs" was an organization called Community Progress, Incorporated, and to serve as CPI's first director, Lee chose Mitchell Sviridoff.

From its beginning, in the spring of 1962, CPI's theme—one of moving from physical to human renewal—could be summarized in a preface that Mayor Lee wrote to "Opening Opportunities," one of the agency's founding and guiding documents:

> We in New Haven believe that the goal of a democratic society is the fullest possible development of the individual potentialities of all its people. In urban America, despite great material wealth, there are many obstacles to the achievement of this goal. Most visible are the blight and obsolescence of the environment of a large portion of all but the newest cities. Equally present are social, economic, and cultural obstructions which prevent people from attaining a full measure of personal fulfillment.
>
> We believe that planning and action to renew the central city

can remove some of these obstructions. Able and imaginative urban renewal programs are under way in many communities. In this respect, New Haven to date [April 1962] has outstripped other cities in the breadth of its program, the speed of execution, and the quality of the accomplishment.

As a result of physical renewal, a decent physical environment is being created for the first time in a century.

New Haven is being renewed to promote social goals. Along with the rebuilding process, basic human needs are being tackled through relocation, homemaking, education, and housing programs. The time is now at hand to expand these efforts and to put into effect a comprehensive program which goes to the root of the city's social problems. Such a program demands vision, dedication, and courage.

In calling for a new human-renewal agency, the "Opening Opportunities" report "outlines a bold and creative approach to expanding opportunities," wrote Lee:

> Its implementation will mean that the people of our city will have the chance for much greater personal achievement. The great strength of the program is its focus on self-improvement. Services are but means to ends, and the ends are the ones people select for themselves. This approach is the proper one in our democratic society.
>
> The success of this comprehensive program will depend upon the understanding, support, and cooperation of all. I call upon my fellow citizens to dedicate themselves to a great new task which will bring our total renewal program even closer to the great goal we have set before us: a slumless city with greater opportunity for all.[3]

Lee's preface to the joint report may have sounded like the busy executive's enthusiastic endorsement of something his subordinates had brought in, but actually Lee himself was one of the principal, if figurative, authors of the document. Such a proposal had been on his mind for several years.

---

[3] Preface by Mayor Richard Lee, "Opening Opportunities: New Haven's Comprehensive Program for Community Progress," City of New Haven, New Haven Board of Education, and Community Progress, Incorporated, April 1962.

In the late fifties and early sixties, as the physical renewal of New Haven had begun to take shape and, in some ways, to pay off, Lee and the Redevelopment Agency staff had started experimenting with programs that were not strictly physical. For one thing, it was obvious that something had to be done about education in New Haven. Among other problems, the city had an educational situation which almost guaranteed an increased percentage of Negroes in its schools. A large percentage of the white population was Catholic and utilized parochial schools, and another large percentage of those better-off, and more liberal, whites who called themselves New Haveners actually lived in the lily-white suburbs and sent their children to the lily-white suburban schools. Thus the "inner city," as students and practitioners of urban life were even then beginning to call it, was left with a heavily black school population. And then, as now, school boards, teaching staffs, and white voters did not show as much interest in a classroom full of black children as they did in a white or "integrated" one.

The Board of Education by 1961 had completed two surveys of educational needs, and had recommended reorganization of the schools' administrative setup and the reconstruction of more than a third of the physical plant. Lee had gone to the Ford Foundation to ask for a grant to implement these recommendations.

Also, the Community Council in New Haven had started a program of coordinated social services, called the Neighborhood Improvement Project and aimed at "multi-problem" families. Grants from the New Haven Foundation and the National Institute of Mental Health supported this project. The city, meantime, asked the Ford Foundation about the chances of getting funds to "undertake a broad program of human renewal," as one intraoffice document called it. The foundation encouraged the idea, and a team of experts in the Redevelopment Agency under Howard W. Hallman (later to become deputy director of CPI) set about composing the basic document to be used in obtaining financial and intellectual backing for the idea.[4] It was thought that one way to mount such

---

[4] Just as CPI was the forerunner of the sort of programs of human renewal that would be sponsored later by the Office of Economic Opportunity, so

a program would be through the schools, which then were in the midst of reorganization and reconstruction.

"Opening Opportunities" should be viewed as a historical document. There will be discussion later of the relevance of what New Haven did, in both physical and human renewal, and much of that discussion will be carried on in the context of what happened in the United States in the late sixties—black awareness, black power, "maximum feasible participation," Chicago and Mayor Daley, the killing of some of the nation's best and most promising leaders. It should be remembered that "Opening Opportunities" was probably at least as revolutionary a document in 1962 as the Church Street project in 1957 was a revolutionary piece of renewal. Very few people in positions of political authority, and hardly any city administration, had talked in broad terms before about "human renewal." Certainly Congress was not overly aware of the idea, although Michael Harrington's book, *The Other America: Poverty in the United States,* was being published that year. President John F. Kennedy, who was to leave to his successor the idea of a poverty program, numbered among his domestic concerns, in the spring of 1962, problems with segregation in interstate transportation in the South, with what appeared to be developing into a racial hotspot in Albany, Georgia, and with the prospect that a Negro

---

"Opening Opportunities" must have been the forerunner of what had become a standard literary device—the massive document, at first mimeographed and later Xeroxed in great quantity, and chock full of Census materials, that is used to solicit financial assistance from some funding source. These documents, often called "the Application" by those who compile them, are generally impossible to read because of their length and impossible to understand because of their reliance on bureaucratic jargon. Back in the early days, though, it was different: "Opening Opportunities" has some literary style about it. Another classic founding document was "Youth in the Ghetto: A Study of the Consequences of Powerlessness and a Blueprint for Change." Written in 1964, it set forth the basic ideas of a group, headed by Dr. Kenneth B. Clark, that was to become Haryou-Act, the Harlem antipoverty and antidelinquency agency. It was one of the few other examples of good application-writing. "Youth in the Ghetto" weighed in at 620 mimeographed pages, more than most bureaucrats and any journalists could read, but it was a compelling document—so compelling, in fact, that Dr. Clark once reported that he had seen segments of it, unattributed, turn up in other applications.

named James Meredith might attempt to enter the University of Mississippi in the fall.

The Student Nonviolent Coordinating Committee was an inter-racial organization. Students for a Democratic Society was two years old and only beginning to talk about "relevance." Daniel P. Moynihan was in Washington as a special assistant to the Secretary of Labor, and he and Nathan Glazer were talking about writing a book to be called *Beyond the Melting Pot*.

In such a context, the document that Mayor Lee, the Redevelopment Agency, and the Ford Foundation wrote might seem revolutionary indeed.

"Cities are the center of our civilization, the seat of culture, the heart of the economic system, and the leader of thought," the proposal began:

> But more and more the central cities of the metropolitan complexes are becoming places where much of the deprivation of our society is concentrated. Poverty is contrasted with wealth, and ignorance with great learning. While cities appear to offer unlimited opportunities for achievement, many city dwellers have quite limited horizons. New Haven is challenged by these problems, which constitute the contemporary urban crisis.

The report, at this point, paid the by then customary homage to what Lee had done with his bulldozers.

> As New Haven has met the need for physical improvements in a manner as yet unequalled elsewhere, so also the city intends to tackle the social problems in a comprehensive manner. The purpose of this report is to specify a series of initial programs, to indicate a workable administrative arrangement, and to outline a process for the development of future programs.

First, however, the report laid down a few basic concepts. One of them was that "opportunity will be the central theme of this comprehensive program," and that "self-improvement is a natural corollary" to opportunity. "People will be encouraged and aided to help themselves. It must be recognized, though, that encouragement alone is insufficient if inadequate resources are available and also that services alone will do no good unless people choose to use them."

Another basic fact was that "the most important manifestation of society is that social entity known as the city." And within the cities there were neighborhoods. To achieve "proper perspective," said the report, "people and their problems must be seen close-up, and this can be achieved through the concept of the neighborhood."

There were seven problem neighborhoods: State Street was close to downtown and might best be described as a business slum. The Hill, the largest of the "inner-city" neighborhoods of New Haven, had been until fairly recently a community of Italian working-class families. At the time of the 1960 Census, the Hill neighborhood, which was on the opposite side of the Connector from downtown, was overwhelmingly (86 percent) white, but it seemed in 1962 destined to attract more black and Spanish-speaking families. The trend already seemed to be toward young black and Puerto Rican families of child-bearing age, with most whites except the elderly departing for other neighborhoods.

The Dwight neighborhood was partly run-down, partly stable; it contained both poor and better-off Negroes, and elderly whites and whites connected with Yale. Wooster Square, the community which the Italians had inherited from the Yankees, was another of the seven neighborhoods. Dixwell, another, was and had been *the* black ghetto in New Haven; until after World War II it had been the only neighborhood with a substantial concentration of Negroes. In 1960 the black population of Dixwell was 72 percent. The Elm Haven low-income housing project, one of the city's original such efforts, was situated in Dixwell. Newhallville was white but had quickly changed to Negro, and it appeared to be the place where hard-working, upwardly-mobile (but not quite yet middle-income) black families were heading. Fair Haven, the seventh neighborhood of greatest physical problems, was near the Mill River, a polluted, stinking slough, and it contained Negroes and Puerto Ricans and Italians.

Together [said the report] these seven neighborhoods contain 60 per cent of the city's residents and 25 per cent of the metropolitan population. In comparison with other neighborhoods, the average income and average level of education is lowest, and the rate of juvenile delinquency[5] and per cent of population receiving public relief is highest, among the residents of these particular neighborhoods.

Although community-wide action is needed to conquer the social problems arising in these seven neighborhoods, as far as is practicable action should be carried out at the neighborhood level. This will provide a manageable administrative unit, not too distant from individual and family needs, but large enough to develop group participation. Moreover, the neighborhood schools will be the scene of many activities, and this will place programs in close proximity to the intended participants . . .

One of the most effective methods for giving neighborhoods more meaning is to create a central focus. This role will be performed by the community school. . . . The community school will become, not a monolithic structure, but truly a community institution. Through it the efforts of many will be drawn together to serve the families and the neighborhood as a whole.

The community school idea, said the report, would utilize plans already under way to build fifteen new schools in New Haven and to improve existing schools so that they could serve as "year-round public facilities, open twelve to sixteen hours a day. As a common denominator, serving all races, creeds, and classes, the schools will be a unifying force in their neighborhoods." This would be accomplished through regular educational curricula, adult education, and use of the school building as a neighborhood center.

"Opening Opportunities" set forth a list of proposed initial programs, which, the document said, should be coordinated, interrelated, and executed simultaneously. The programs would be in the areas of education, employment, leisure-time activities, community services, juvenile delinquency, housing, and services for the elderly.

---

[5] For instance: 35.3 children per 1,000 between the ages of 7 and 15 were being referred to Juvenile Court from the seven neighborhoods, while the rate for the rest of the city was 16.5 per 1,000.

57

In *education,* the authors noted that an urban school system not only must train the mind, "but it also must cope with the needs of vocational training, be a means of urbanization, educate the physically and mentally handicapped, provide stability in unstable neighborhoods, and even serve as a partial substitute for a decent home life."

To begin accomplishing this in New Haven, the document recommended that a corps of "helping teachers" be established to lead teaching teams, develop new curricula, and generally raise the level of competence of teachers in the poor neighborhoods. The reading program should be upgraded; a voluntary summer school should be established; there should be a "higher horizons" program, which was not explained in detail, but which would amount to "a concerted and consistent effort to raise the sights of students and their parents." And there would be a pre-kindergarten program for three- and four-year-olds and their mothers. This would prove to be the forerunner of Head Start.

In *employment,* the document proposed "a sustained and prodigious effort" to enlarge and strengthen the high school guidance program, which until then had concentrated on college-bound youth. A work-study program would allow high school students in the lower academic portion of their classes to work part-time and study part-time while remaining in school until the legal age of sixteen. There would be programs of technical training for high school graduates; continuation of an existing job retraining program; more emphasis on equal job opportunity, and the suggestion that a Mayor's Committee on Employment Opportunity be established.

In *leisure-time activities,* the report noted that there was a need for "greater choice" of activities for all those citizens who wanted them. The focus of leisure programs would be the community schools.

For the *elderly,* it was pointed out that both the number and the percentage of older people were increasing in New Haven. (Such information, and the political ramifications of it, were not lost on Mayor Lee, who was devoting a good deal of his time in the housing area to constructing homes for the aged. This, as one somewhat cynical but loyal supporter of the mayor pointed out, had the effect of securing votes on both ends of the age spectrum: from the aged themselves, who were thankful that a political leader had finally come along who had the sense and the decency to build housing with ramps instead of stairs, grab-bars in the bathrooms, and other thoughtful gadgets; and from the young, who were thankful that a political leader had finally come along who had the sense and the decency to relieve them of their responsibility for caring for their aged parents.)

For New Haven's elderly, "Opening Opportunities" suggested a home care program, which would utilize the services of teams to be made up of nurses, social workers, nutritionists, physical therapists, occupational therapists, housekeepers, and homemakers. There should be a program of counseling, information, and referral to help the retired and those about to retire to live independently, if they wanted to. Leisure-time activities for the elderly could be centered about the community schools. Efforts should be mounted to open up opportunities for part-time and volunteer work for the elderly.

In the area of *juvenile delinquency,* the report pointed out that the entire "human renewal" effort, with the exception of specialized projects for the elderly, "is a program for the prevention of juvenile delinquency." Specific programs, too, were needed, said the report, in order to identify and deal with the problems.

In *housing,* the founding document of CPI had to tread carefully. Housing already was supposed to be one of the most exciting features of life in New Haven. The problem was handled this way:

A decent home in a suitable environment was established as a national goal by Congress in 1949. Vast strides have been made toward achieving this goal in New Haven through urban renewal and public housing. . . .

Yet there remain several pockets of unmet need where efforts to date have been inadequate. Until solutions are found, there will not be a full measure of housing opportunity to all residents according to need.

59

The document recommended the establishment of a rent-assistance program for large, low-income families. The participants would live in privately-owned, standard housing. They would be responsible for paying as much rent as they ordinarily would pay in public housing, with the remainder coming from public funds.

Furthermore, the city should expand its participation in the federal programs which encouraged the construction of low- and moderate-income private housing by nonprofit corporations. New Haven already had completed the nation's first housing project under one of these programs. Another made available federal loans for the construction of housing for the elderly.

The report suggested that efforts be begun to turn the city's drab public housing projects into communities. One way to do this, said the document, would be to establish health clinics in the projects, since the need for such services was noncontroversial and "common to all families."

Finally, there was a need for more housing for members of minority groups. CPI, said the report, would try to break down discriminatory barriers by "education and persuasion."

Coordinated community services took up a relatively small portion of "Opening Opportunities," but it was to prove one of the more fundamental and far-reaching undertakings of Community Progress, Incorporated. The report stated that if the social problems of New Haven's "renewal and middle-ground neighborhoods" were going to be dealt with, there must be "a broad roster of community services . . . excellent in quality, sufficient in quantity, and effectively coordinated." The logical bases for such services would be the community schools.

CPI would have a "neighborhood services director" for each of the communities, a person who would "take a total approach to the social problems of the neighborhood," and who would "integrate the wide variety of services available within the neighborhood." Working under the services director in each neighborhood would be two or more "community workers," who would

work informally throughout the neighborhood, serving as a bridge between residents and service agencies. They will get to know adults and children, the elderly and the sick by visiting in homes, on the street, in stores and taverns, at ch' ches, and in jail. They will be persons to turn to in time of trouble. With the guidance of the neighborhood services director, they will know what resources are available. Above all, their presence will be tangible evidence of community concern for people and their problems.

The main qualifications of a community worker is to be empathetic with neighborhood residents, to speak their language, and to be accepted without reservation. He, therefore, might well be indigenous, and he need not have professional education. He will receive training and daily supervision from the neighborhood services director, whom he in turn will serve as eyes, ears, hands, and heart.

The community workers also could spend some of their time developing "a favorable attitude toward the importance of education, especially among parents."

In addition to the neighborhood services director and his community workers, specialized services would be necessary "if substantial progress is to be made in solving the complex social problems." One such specialty that was needed, according to the authors, was a neighborhood-based program of legal services.

Although the Supreme Court ruling in the *Miranda* and other such cases, a revolutionary recognition of the rights of the accused, was four years off, "Opening Opportunities" recommended that lawyers' services be made available, through the community schools, to "provide legal advice on simple matters, and . . . make referrals on more complex cases. Supplementing this service would be a fund to aid persons, where necessary, in paying fees and bail and to grant financial assistance to families of prisoners and those released who have not yet found employment or who are participating in the retraining program."

There also would be community participation, although the concept in 1962 had not yet attained the importance it soon would enjoy. Said the document:

> While many of the neighborhood problems can be solved only through the intervention of governmental and voluntary agencies, there are tasks which can be performed only by the residents

61

themselves, working through their own organizations. Residents have a perception of their problems which may differ from that of professional workers, who are often from a different background. Moreover, neighborhood organizations fulfill an important role by encouraging fellow residents to support neighborhood improvement activities and in voicing their views to elective officials.

We have a considerable body of experience of this through citizen participation in urban renewal. In each of the five neighborhoods where renewal is in execution or where housing rehabilitation is under way, there is an active neighborhood organization. Without this support renewal could not succeed.

Neighborhood organizations, said the report, could help plan and support the programs for the community schools and for dealing with the problems of juvenile delinquency.

To execute a program that could only be called, in 1962 and even today, ambitious, "Opening Opportunities" suggested the organization of a staff for CPI, whose main function at the beginning would be to formulate programs. The staff would be assisted by the creation of a "community seminar," which would include representatives of public and voluntary agencies, state and federal officials, local and state lawmakers, political party leaders, "university scholars and other community leaders." No specific mention was made in 1962 of involving the poor, or their *bona fide* "representatives," in the planning.

A research division would be established, with the help of Yale University. Finally, Community Progress, Incorporated, itself, would be organized as a nonprofit corporation. "Opening Opportunities" explained who would run CPI. Once again, there was no mention of the poor themselves:

> [CPI] will be governed by a board of directors consisting of persons appointed by the Mayor of New Haven, the Board of Education, Redevelopment Agency, Citizens Action Commission, United Fund, Community Council, and Yale University. The board of directors will be the policy-making body. The board will select an executive director who will select other staff and administer the operations of the organization.

Appended to the blue-bound "Opening Opportunities" report were copies of letters to Mayor Lee from various community leaders, expressing their endorsement of the CPI proposals and pledging their support. The Community Council of Greater New Haven, Incorporated, said it was all for the idea. Kingman Brewster, Jr., Yale's provost (and later to become its president), wrote that the proposed program would mutually benefit the city and the school. Vincent J. Sirabella, the president of the Greater New Haven Central Labor Council, promised his support, reminded the mayor of the role played by labor in overcoming "bias in employment by encouraging qualified young people to join our unions," and suggested that a labor staff man be hired full-time by the program.

John Dempsey, the Governor of Connecticut, said he would help. So did the Citizens Action Commission, the United Fund of Greater New Haven, the president of the Board of Education, and the New Haven Foundation. There were no letters from the National Association for the Advancement of Colored People, which at that time was thought (by whites, at least) to be a militant organization; or from Fred Harris, a 25-year-old black man whose father worked for the hospital run by Yale, and who was beginning to sense that something was wrong in New Haven; or from Willie Counsel, another black man, who in 1962 was 21 years old, who had arrived two years before from Tuskegee, Alabama, and who already had become dissatisfied with the reluctance of the existing Negro and civil rights organizations to address themselves to what he called "the real grass roots of the *problem*."

But perhaps 1962 was too early to start talking and wondering about people like Fred Harris and Willie Counsel, too early to start thinking about the involvement of the poor in the formulation of the programs of "human renewal" that presumably would serve them. In 1962 Richard Lee was *the* civil rights leader in New Haven, Connecticut, and a major reason for that was that no one else challenged him in a credentials dispute.

Only at election time did someone seriously question his stewardship, and then the questioning was done, ordinarily, by a Republican candidate who merely reflected his party's near-zero understanding of what was going on in New Haven in the twentieth century, much less the nineteen-sixties. Certainly no concerted questioning was undertaken by the organizations that, at that time, were believed (by whites and Negroes) to represent the poor, or the black, or the alienated.

And the poor, the black, and the alienated voted along with the rich, the white, and the involved in returning Richard Lee to office over and over again. For a politician, no better proof of stewardship and of acceptance could exist.

IV

The Prelude

*. . . it is clear that what we have struggled and
sacrificed for has been or soon will be attained.*
—Mayor Lee, in 1964

THINGS WERE looking good for Mayor Lee and his city. The
notion of physical renewal had become firmly fixed in the minds
of the citizens, and its tangible reality was fast becoming fixed in
their eyes. Only a few Republicans and the always conservative,
frequently reactionary *New Haven Register* questioned, after 1962,
whether urban renewal was economically feasible. Nobody questioned whether it was politically feasible.

Despite the fact that his hometown newspaper did not know,
or would not admit, that he was important, Lee had the satisfaction
of knowing that others did know. By the time Community
Progress, Incorporated, was getting tooled up, Lee had become
in great demand as a speech-maker and as an expert witness. In
one piece of testimony, delivered to a House subcommittee that
was considering the establishment of a federal department to deal
with urban problems, Lee remarked that he had testified a dozen
times before Congress, either as a representative of the United
States Conference of Mayors or as the chairman of the American
Municipal Association's advisory committee on urban renewal.

A month after that, Lee was a guest speaker at a national
housing conference. He brushed aside the notion that he was

speaking as the mayor of the Model City: "I appear in a simple role: a mayor trying to overcome seemingly insurmountable obstacles in making our city a better place in which to live today, and an even better place tomorrow."

But his fellows did not think Lee's role was quite so modest. They elected him president of the Conference of Mayors that year.

CPI, meantime, was starting to spend a $2.5-million grant from the Ford Foundation, the first of its sort in the nation. (Ford would supply another $2.5 million in 1965.) Soon two other renewal programs were begun—the Dwight and Fair Haven projects. In 1963 Lee ran for his sixth term, once more against Henry Townshend, whom he had defeated two years before by 4,000 votes, and won this time by 11,345 votes, 33,150 to 21,805. This time the Church Street project was much further along, and it undoubtedly helped Lee recover from the close election of two years before. The Newhallville project was started late in 1963.

By early 1964 Lee was fairly bursting with pride. In his state of the city message to the aldermen in February, he said:

> In 1954, we set out to transform the face of New Haven—to build on the foundations of a proud and historic New England city the structures and the facilities of a modern American city.
>
> As I look at the accomplishment of 1963, I can report to you with both pride and humility that the success of this transformation is now assured . . . and it is clear that what we have struggled and sacrificed for has been or soon will be attained.

The reevaluation, said Lee, would include implementation of better and broader efforts in the areas of employment, civil rights, mass transit, code enforcement, pollution abatement, additional redevelopment, and education.

In the election of 1965, Lee was challenged by Joseph Einhorn, the leader of a citizens' group called the Better Education Committee, which was opposed to a school bussing plan that had been started in New Haven in 1964. The Better Education Committee, according to one account, was "composed exclusively of Republican political figures."[1] Einhorn promised to "free the people of New Haven from the vicious stronghold of the City Hall political machine," to bring an end to "turning over our city to outsiders, consultants, advisers, goldbrickers, and the like," and to end all appropriations for "forced, involuntary bussing."[2]

New Haven apparently was not ready for that sort of backlash, however, and Lee received another giant mandate in 1965, a margin of 16,293 votes, 33,392 to 17,099, and he carried into office with him all 33 Democratic aldermanic candidates.

By 1966 and 1967 the renewal projects were in high gear, and New Haven was having little difficulty getting federal support for its ideas—so little difficulty that after John Lindsay became mayor of New York City and started referring to his burden as "Fun City," observers of the New Haven scene replied that their town was named "Fund City." Even snarls in the traffic, hardly congested by big-city standards but bad enough to irritate New Haveners, had been smoothed out, thanks to a system of stop-and-go lights that rewarded drivers who used the streets the city wanted them to use, and punished those who insisted on using the clogged thoroughfares.[3]

Not only was New Haven putting new buildings on land that once had harbored slums and decaying businesses; the new buildings—after that aesthetically dry run on Oak Street, at least—were being designed by renowned architects. One of the city's proudest examples of its romance with architecture was the 1,380-car parking garage situated in the Church Street project. The garage was designed by Paul Rudolph, the former chairman of Yale's department of architecture. Rudolph was responsible, too, for the Art and Architecture Building at Yale, and he also designed a public housing project for the elderly. The firm of Skidmore Owings and Merrill designed, among other things, the Conte elementary school in Wooster Square. Yale, in the mean-

---

[1] William Lee Miller, *op. cit.,* p. 134.
[2] *Ibid.,* p. 244.
[3] The system, and its creator, William R. McGrath, are described in Talbot, *op. cit.,* pp. 110–15.

time, undertook some daring architecture of its own in a program that, in the words of its alumni magazine, "has contributed greatly, in its way, to New Haven's new look."

One of the more startling of Yale's constructions was its Ingalls Rink, a skating rink designed by Eero Saarinen and thought by some residents to be a thing of great beauty, by others to be a replica of a decomposing whale. Saarinen also designed the Stiles and Morse Colleges at Yale (on the land where the three old city high schools had stood). Philip Johnson was responsible for the Rockefeller Virus Laboratory and the Kline Science Building. The latter structure was known by some citizens as the "Tootsie Roll Building" because of its shape and color.

As the projects progressed, and as the war on poverty was declared nationally, and as race became accepted more and more as a real issue in the North (ordinarily its acceptance followed a riot), the distinction in New Haven between physical and human renewal became less easy to detect. No longer did physical renewal mean only tearing down the homes of slum-dwellers and replacing them with luxury apartment buildings and ugly offices. A typical urban renewal project, by now, had several human renewal components.

And the city was starting to brag that its comprehensive approach was taking the citizens' desires and needs into consideration—that there was citizen and neighborhood participation in the redevelopment projects. But there were limits to the degree of participation (severe limits, as some critics were beginning to charge); Melvin Adams, the city's development administrator, overseer of the Redevelopment Agency, and Mayor Lee's right-hand man in matters of city-rebirth, responded this way to the question, "Is neighborhood participation possible in a redevelopment program?"

> Yes, but not by going to people with a map of the area and asking, "What do you want here?" It can be possible by talking to and meeting with people in the neighborhoods. We can get ideas, try to put them in a plan, take the plan back to the neighborhood and ask the people what they think. We should hammer

it out with them. But, whatever citizen participation we get will never be but a small percentage of the total population. Citizen participation is valuable only if it continues even *after* the redevelopment program is over. People must continue their concern, and if we help maintain their concern, this might be our greatest contribution.[4]

Early on, back when CPI was getting organized, there was a great deal of talk around New Haven about jobs. Unemployment was seen as a major problem, one that called for the best efforts of the human renewal specialists. Gradually, however, emphasis in New Haven—judging from what was discussed publicly—seemed to shift from employment to housing. By 1966 it was estimated that one-third of the city's land area was involved in some sort of renewal. Within that area, about 3,000 new housing units had been built, were in the process of being built, or were on the drawing boards. A total of 8,200 buildings had been rehabilitated, a thousand of them in Wooster Square. The city estimated that $250 million had been invested in redevelopment since the start; the Department of Housing and Urban Development had spent $75 million on New Haven.

One of the distinctive features of housing renewal in New Haven has been mentioned before: the city's heavy emphasis on rehabilitation. Another was the city's reluctance to indulge in continued construction of traditional public housing. Early in his career as mayor, Lee had toyed with the expansion of a project called Elm Haven, the city's largest public housing project, and he had not liked the results. A modern-day visitor to New Haven who wishes to inspect the city's housing, and who receives the official Redevelopment Agency tour, is shown public housing, but he is shown it as an after-thought, almost as a historical oddity. Public housing is in the past in New Haven.

In the place of more public housing, Lee and his planners substituted what has come to be known as "scatterization"—the

---

[4] New Haven Redevelopment Agency, "New Haven's Approach to Neighborhood Improvement," undated (but published in 1968).

69

dispersal throughout the city of those in need of housing assistance, rather than the concentration of them in one or more ghettoes. This was no easy trick; voters have a way of rejecting proposals that *sound* like public housing as well as those that actually are public housing. And, since black and poor people were among those to be scattered, and since it was reasonable to assume that the residents of the host neighborhoods were as discriminatory and bigoted as anyone else in privileged positions, scatterization would be a tricky maneuver.

Once again, Lee's political acumen and the manageable size of his city made it possible for him to proceed with his plans. He separated his housing program into three categories, and thus minimized the risk: There would be housing for the elderly (politically, as has been mentioned before, this had a high chance of success); there would be housing for the poor who had jobs, and there would be housing for those who were the welfare poor.

The scatterization plan apparently met most of its objectives. A map of government-assisted housing in New Haven as of May 1968, published by the Redevelopment Agency with the help of the Department of Housing and Urban Development, showed no long lines of high-rise ghettoes of the sort that Richard Daley had built in Chicago, no clusters of ugly public-housing towers of the sort that various mayors of New York City had erected. In New Haven the federally-assisted housing was scattered all over the city—so scattered, in fact, that students of social planning and change had difficulty obtaining precise socio-economic information about the residents from the standard census tract data.

For the *elderly,* by the spring of 1968 New Haven had completed 403 units of publicly-assisted, low-income housing; another 30 were being built, and 480 were in the planning stages. As of that date, no privately-funded, but federally-assisted, moderate income housing had been constructed for the elderly, but 217 units were being planned.

One housing project for the low-income elderly was Winslow-Celentano Park, a six-story reinforced concrete building of modern design in the Wooster Square neighborhood. There were 32 one-bedroom apartments and an equal number of efficiency units. Each had such refinements for the elderly as out-of-reach heat sources, emergency communication systems which the residents could use to call for assistance, showers with seats and grab-rails, and large balconies. Best of all, the project was not set off by itself, so its residents did not get the feeling that they had been sent off to a rest home. From the balconies they could overlook the harbor and New Haven's changing skyline.

For the *working poor,* the Lee administration sought out co-operative housing, but most of what was available was what was termed "221 (d) 3" housing, for the section, paragraph, and line of the National Housing Act. Such housing was built by private organizations, which received artificially low interest rates on loans in return for agreeing to certain obligations. They promised to build housing for moderate-income families (the families' allowable income was fixed, and tenants paid no more than 25 percent of their income for housing); profits, too, were limited.

The intent of Section 221 (d) 3 was to provide cooperative middle-income housing,[5] and this would have the effect of slowing the exodus of middle-class families from the cities to the suburbs, but New Haven turned the provision into housing for low-income families, as well, by subsidizing the fees. Low-income applicants were required only to make the required downpayment of $325 and to pay a portion of the carrying charges. The New Haven Housing Authority, using federal funds, paid the rest. The result was that the low-income families paid fees comparable to the rents they would have paid in public housing.

Since the $325 downpayment might be a burden for many of the working poor, the city arranged with a local foundation to establish a revolving loan fund which provided interest-free downpayment loans for low- and moderate-income families. In addition,

---

[5] For New Haven, as of the spring of 1968, the annual income ceiling limitations for families of "moderate" means, as set by the Federal Housing Authority, were $6,900, gross, for a family of two; $8,100 for three and four, and $9,300 for five or six. At the same time the FHA defined "low income" as $3,500, net, for a family of two, and so on, in $500 increments for each additional family member.

the non-profit corporation which was set up to administer the fund guaranteed payment of carrying charges for families who could afford them, but who failed to meet federal requirements.

In early 1968 the first group of low-income tenants in the nation to occupy the formerly all-middle-income 221 (d) 3 housing started moving into Ethan Gardens, a cooperative not far from Yale. A total of eight poor families was scattered throughout the 28-unit project. "Neither they nor their apartments are specially identified in any way," said the Redevelopment Agency. The program was developed by the city in cooperation with federal officials, who watched its outcome carefully. Once again New Haven provided an example for the nation; the Department of Housing and Urban Development used the program as the basis for national guidelines for low-income co-ops.

And, as nine other 221 (d) 3 projects were being constructed in 1968, the city announced that "nearly 200" units in them had been reserved for low-income tenants. Said the Redevelopment Agency: "Thus every family, regardless of its income, will be able to live in cooperative housing which previously was primarily within the means of only moderate-income families."[6]

For the *welfare poor,* those at whom much of the rhetoric but little of the action of the war on poverty had been aimed, New Haven had, or devised, a variety of housing programs. As of April 1968 the city had seven public housing projects with a total of 1,626 units. The projects were standard and dreary examples of

---

[6] New Haven Redevelopment Agency, "What's Happening in Housing in New Haven," April 1968. As the program was picked up elsewhere, it became less possible to claim that "every family, regardless of its income," really could expect an equal chance to move into subsidized moderate-income housing. In New York State, the officials of a program called "Capital Grant Low-Rent Assistance," which subsidized the rentals and carrying charges of low-income families who wanted to live in restricted-profit, middle-income apartments and cooperatives, made much the same claim. But a survey in 1968 and 1969 showed that only the cream of the poor—those who might reasonably be expected to overcome enough of their problems *anyway* so they could move into middle-class life—were actually populating the program. These "poor" included, in one middle-income project in Brooklyn, a law student and his family whose only poverty was academic. They had a car, a baby grand piano, and a maid.

the forties approach to public housing: Farnum Court, with 300 units; Quinnipiac Terrace, with 248, and Elm Haven, with 487 units.

There obviously was a need for more public housing; many of New Haven's poor could hardly hope to negotiate a $325 down-payment on a cooperative, even if the money were loaned to them on an interest-free basis. The drawbacks of continued construction of high-rise ghettoes were many, though. For one thing, it was thought to be economically impossible to construct that sort of housing, within standard budgets, and have it turn out to be anything other than an architectural monstrosity—and New Haven was becoming more sophisticated about its architecture. For another, it was a strategic mistake to go on concentrating the poor, and the black, and the poor black, in tall, easily-defended brick castles at a time when poor blacks were arming themselves and participating in riots in other cities, riots that seemed destined to sweep across all the nation.

In addition to recognizing the difficulties inherent in traditional public housing, New Haven had been faced, since Oak Street, with the problem of finding decent housing for the poor who were being displaced by renewal. Relatively early in the game, in 1962, the city hit on a scheme of renting apartments in private housing and then subletting them to low-income families. This plan was called the Rent Certificate, or Leased Housing, program.

The Housing Authority contracted with a landlord for an apartment "in an existing dwelling in any neighborhood," signed a lease that would run up to ten years, and rented the apartment to a low-income family for 23.08 percent of its gross income— the same amount the family would have paid in traditional public housing. The Housing Authority, using federal funds, made up the difference to the landlord.

Before an apartment could be included in the program, it had to be brought up to housing code standards and the landlord had to agree to take proper care of the unit; if he did not, the Housing Authority had the power to withhold the rent. There were other provisions, though, that made the landlord feel he was enjoying freedom of choice: "Private owners," said the city, "take part voluntarily in the program and have the right to select tenants from applicants meeting Housing Authority requirements."[7]

By early 1968 the city had placed 210 (or 150—the city's claims were conflicting) low-income families, including the elderly, in leased housing around the city, and negotiations were under way with landlords for more. The plan had proved to be a perfect example of scatterization; those families had stopped being visible "problems" for the City of New Haven.

Another tool the city used to provide shelter for the welfare poor was called "turnkey" housing. In this plan, a private developer was encourage to construct low-income housing. When he completed it, the city purchased the housing from him (the builder "turned the key over to the city") and rented it to low-income families. The scheme had several advantages; since the land was being developed and the housing built by private enterprise, and not by bureaucrats, there was less red tape. Processing and construction times were shorter, and costs were lower. Also, better-off residents of neighborhoods destined to receive such low-income housing were not as likely to become scared or agitated as they would have been if a traditional public housing project were begun nearby.

The city experimented with, and rejected on the grounds that it was "unworkable," a plan of direct rent subsidies for the poor and a few other programs. By and large, the effort at providing housing for the welfare poor was confined to existing public housing, rent certificates, and the turnkey program, with heavy emphasis on housing code enforcement and rehabilitation. The last two efforts were particularly important in view of the fact that the city was deeply engaged in renewal projects and was constantly faced with the problems of relocating families whose housing had been torn down. No city could have built enough housing to take care of all those relocated families, and so New Haven had to rely to a great extent on finding and utilizing existing hous-

[7] Ibid.

ing that was standard and finding substandard housing and forcing its owners to bring it up to acceptable levels.

Rehabilitation in perhaps its "nicest" sense in New Haven—the inducement of homeowners in Wooster Square to restore their fine old homes, with flattery and full-color architects' renditions—has been discussed in Chapter II. The city used other devices in neighborhoods less historic. A program was begun whereby private, non-profit sponsoring organizations were given the authority, the financial help, and a title (community housing development corporation), and sent out to rehabilitate housing. One of them, Community Housing, Incorporated, was formed by the New Haven Council of Churches, the Roman Catholic Archdiocese of Hartford, and the Jewish Community Council. Another was run by the Dixwell Avenue Congregational Church, which had long expressed interest in upgrading the city's housing.

By 1968 Mayor Lee was able to claim that private homeowners had rehabilitated 9,000 dwelling units, "about $17 million worth of housing, and we're ready to go back to the same houses again and to others."[8] A good deal of this rehabilitation had been accomplished through the voluntary efforts of the homeowners, but New Haven's housing code helped, too.

The code was administered through the Division of Neighborhood Improvement. DNI was a creature of the Redevelopment Agency, and as such it was responsible for enforcing housing standards in dwelling units that were under urban renewal planning—approximately half the units in the city.

The division had a lot going for it: a large corps of inspectors (more than all other Connecticut cities combined), a housing code that was considered one of the most modern in the nation, and a relatively great degree of coordination. As a "last resort," the inspectors would utilize a state law, passed in 1965, to take a piece of property away from a stubborn landlord and use the rents to repair it or remove the violations.

The $17 million worth of rehabilitated housing cited by Mayor

---

[8] New Haven Redevelopment Agency, "New Haven's Approach to Neighborhood Improvement," *op. cit.*

Lee did not include another $2.8 million which a special group of property-owners, the absentee owners of large quantities of slum properties, spent on rehabilitation between 1959 and 1968. In 1959 the city mounted an effort called the "large operator program" in which all the holdings of these landlords were systematically, and almost simultaneously, inspected. Elliott A. Segal, then the director of the Division of Neighborhood Improvement, reported in 1968 that before the program was started "a large number of complaints in the inner city came from properties that were owned by a few landlords—or by corporations whose principals, it was found, turned out to be the same individuals or groups of individuals. For example, a study of complaint patterns indicated that owners in the Slum Landlord Program accounted for twenty percent of a year's complaints, although the housing involved accounted for less than two percent of the housing stock. And so, in 1959, a program began where seven landlords were chosen and all of their properties were systematically inspected. Simultaneously, orders were issued on all the landlords' holdings regardless of the area where the properties were located."

Segal then explained how the system worked: The slum landlord was given so many orders that it was unlikely he could comply with them within the time limit. Landlords then had three recourses. They could try to ignore the orders, they could tell DNI that they were not able to do the work in the time allotted, or they could start rehabilitation. Depending on the landlord's reactions, the division then pursued several courses. If a landlord appeared to be willing to work, DNI made services available to him—blueprints, specifications, help in obtaining contractors, help in getting mortgages. If a landlord resisted, he was summoned to a quasi-legal administrative summons session, where inspectors produced photographs of violations and other information of an evidential nature. Usually consent agreements resulted from these meetings. But if a landlord continued to resist, he was arrested and prosecuted.

In the course of identifying and dealing with slum landlords, said Segal, DNI encountered various stalling tactics, and the city had to devise ways of coping with them. Someone familiar with the tactics of slumlords in larger cities, such as New York, and the apparent inability of the authorities there to change the system by a scintilla, might conclude that DNI in New Haven had worked some sort of miracle. Segal cautioned against such an attitude:

> Slums cannot be eliminated. They are a public health problem in the same sense as polio and venereal disease. They can at best be controlled—but with strong preventive measures. New tools and new approaches must be found. The focus must be toward improving the housing conditions of the poor slum-dweller. Too many obstacles operate to perpetuate the status quo, which means continued bad housing.[9]

What *may* have been an item of almost miraculous proportions was the way in which New Haven managed to carry out its housing and other programs with a minimum of overt controversy, anger, and public outcry from anyone except the biennial Republican candidate for mayor and the annual counter-state-of-the-city address by George J. Montano, the Republican Town Chairman. (A 1967 example of the latter: "Nineteen-sixty-six was the first year in the history of New Haven that our city government was entrusted completely to one political party, the Democratic Party. By the end of 1966, the evils of one-party government began to manifest itself through acts of arrogance, secrecy, and self-interest." Montano did not elaborate on these charges other than to accuse the mayor of not having enough press conferences.)

In the matter of slumlords, for example, New Haven was able to frighten, threaten, and in some cases arrest and jail and keep in jail violators who presumably had some financial and political power of their own, and yet Richard Lee remained in office. Similarly, the city was able to avoid major controversies over its approach to relocation, although the mere mention of the subject in some other cities was enough to bring about debilitating

---

[9] Elliott A. Segal, "A Slum Landlord Program—An Essential Ingredient in a Housing Code Enforcement Program," *American Journal of Public Health,* Vol. 58, No. 3, March 1968.

acrimony. In 1964 Martin Anderson, then a student in industrial management at the Massachusetts Institute of Technology, had written a book, *The Federal Bulldozer,* that had caused a small storm and contributed a phrase to the vocabulary. Anderson had denounced urban renewal in America generally, said private enterprise was doing the job much better, and (in a 1965 paper summarizing his findings) projected that by 1972 renewal would result in the "forcible displacement" of four million Americans from their homes.[10] Herbert J. Gans, a Columbia University sociologist who had little truck with Anderson's ideas (Gans had called him an "ultraconservative economist and often irresponsible polemicist"), in the same year issued another denunciation of the national program:

> It has cleared slums to make room for many luxury-housing and a few middle-income projects, and it has also provided inexpensive land for the expansion of colleges, hospitals, libraries, shopping centers, and other such institutions located in slum areas.
> . . . a 1961 study of renewal projects in 41 cities showed that 60 per cent of the dispossessed tenants were merely relocated in other slums; and in big cities, the proportion was even higher. . . . Renewal sometimes even created new slums by pushing relocatees into areas and buildings which then became overcrowded and deteriorated rapidly. This has principally been the case with Negroes who, both for economic and racial reasons, have been forced to double up in other ghettoes. Indeed, because almost two-thirds of the cleared slum units have been occupied by Negroes, the urban renewal program has often been characterized as Negro clearance, and in too many cities, this has been its intent.[11]

New Haven felt that such criticisms might apply to other cities, but not to itself. (It was obvious to any visitor entering by the city's "front door," however, that the first chunk of renewal, Oak

---

10 Martin Anderson, "Fiasco of Urban Renewal," *Harvard Business Review,* Vol. 43, No. 1, January–February, 1965, reprinted in James Q. Wilson, editor, *Urban Renewal: The Record and the Controversy* (Cambridge: MIT Press, 1967), pp. 491–508, as "The Federal Bulldozer."
11 Herbert J. Gans, "The Failure of Urban Renewal," *Commentary,* April 1965, reprinted in James Q. Wilson, editor, *op. cit.,* pp. 537–57.

Street, was not a very sophisticated example of planning—the construction of a drab $15-million telephone company building that quickly took on the patina of a faded and abandoned Holiday Inn, an expressway that zipped along to an abrupt dead end, and a cluster of high-rise luxury apartment buildings, the sight of which must have nauseated the former tenants of the slum where Richard Lee had once vomited, if any of them were around in New Haven when the project was finished.)

In New Haven, according to a redevelopment official in 1967, "relocation has been made a housing opportunity." Furthermore, said Mrs. Kathryn Feidelson of the Redevelopment Agency, since CPI came into existence in 1962 relocation had not only been a housing opportunity but an opportunity for human renewal.

Of 5,615 families and individuals relocated up to the fall of 1966, she wrote, 4,034 families had moved into private rental units. (Included in that figure were 898 families who had moved out of New Haven.) Eight hundred and thirty-four families or individuals had purchased homes, and 747 had gone into public housing.

Renewal did not mean "Negro removal" in New Haven, wrote Mrs. Feidelson. Of the families relocated up to 1966, 60 percent were white. And "the bulk of the attention has been directed toward developing middle- and low-income housing," she added.

To do all this, the relocation officials in New Haven relied on staff members with separate and specialized functions. And CPI and other agencies helped. It was work such as this—and most of this amounts simply to sensitivity on the part of the city—that gave New Haven the reputation of being a "good" redevelopment city, and that helped some of the critics to forget momentarily about the Oak Street fiasco. The way relocation was carried out in New Haven, there was reason to believe that it had become, as Mrs. Feidelson put it in her description of what such a program should be, "an opportunity in the broadest sense, a chance to upgrade not only a family's housing but also its mode of life."[12]

---

[12] Kathryn Feidelson, "A Total Approach to Family Relocation," *Journal of Housing*, No. 3, April 1967.

By 1965 not only was CPI established as an institution in New Haven, and as a permanent portion of Mayor Lee's "parallel government," but also some of the programs that CPI had first talked about were being used as prototypes in the national war on poverty. The pre-kindergarten effort and New Haven's concentration on schools as community centers were largely responsible for the national Project Head Start program. Neighborhood legal assistance programs were being started all over the nation, although it took them a long time to get going because of the resistance of established bar groups. An adult literacy program provided much of the foundation for the national program called adult basic education.

The human renewal agency was being run by people who acted and talked as if they knew what they were doing; they were like a second generation of Logue's young men in the Redevelopment Agency. Although the field they had created might theoretically be mistaken for an extension of the old welfare-social service-community chest-type work, the CPI people had none of that sanctimonious, overly paternalistic, social-worker attitude. Rather they were suave, self-assured young men with attaché cases, airplane tickets to Washington, tiny tape recorders, and impressively multi-buttoned telephones. Just as the programs they were developing were to become national prototypes, these young men were to become the prototypes of the professional poverty hustler.

Like the programs and the people who were to follow them, these young men devoted a good portion of their time and interest to research. One of the reasons that new human renewal programs were needed was that the old ones had not worked adequately, and research was needed to find out why. In addition, a new academic generation of researchers—sociologists, psychologists and psychiatrists, political scientists and others who thought they fit into the general category of "behavioral scientist"—had sprung up, engaged in considerable self-examination on the question of whether it was relevant to what was happening in contemporary America, and was starting to populate the human renewal scene. Research, and researchers, suddenly became valuable. Hardly any grant, whether it was from private or public sources, went out to a "demonstration program" such as those in which New Haven was engaged without a necessary "research component."

One such piece of research undertaken by CPI in the spring and summer of 1966 was called the "Inner City Survey,"[13] and it was designed to find out what people in the "inner city" wanted and to enable CPI staffers to identify those who wanted it. The survey also sought to measure the effectiveness of CPI, which had been in existence for about four years. At the time of the survey, five of the neighborhoods under study had these population characteristics:

Neighborhood	Population (Approximate)	White	Negro	Puerto Rican
The Hill	23,000	49.9%	42.5	7.6
Dwight	8,000	48.0	50.1	1.9
Dixwell	6,000	10.5	85.1	4.4
Newhallville	10,000	24.2	74.5	1.3
Fair Haven	14,000	59.1	35.5	5.4

The other findings included these:

• Of those surveyed, half of the heads of white households were born in New Haven and about 5 percent were born in the South; only 13 percent of the Negro heads of household were born in New Haven, while 74 percent were born in the South. Nine out of ten of the Puerto Ricans surveyed were born in Puerto Rico. Almost one-quarter of the whites were born in Europe or Asia.

• "With minor exceptions," the white population in the inner city was composed of "the elderly and the childless. The overwhelming majority of the inner city population increase has come within the Negro and Puerto Rican groups. Of these two groups, the Puerto Rican population is increasing proportionately faster than the Negro." The survey estimated that the 1966 black population of New Haven was between 33,000 and 35,000, an in-

---

[13] Alan Mallach *et al.*, "CPI Manpower Division Inner City Survey, Final Report," Community Progress, Incorporated, undated.

crease of 11,000 to 13,000 since 1960; the Puerto Rican population was estimated to be 4,000, an increase of 3,000 over the 1960 Census.

• While the unemployment rate in New Haven in 1966 was low (3 percent), largely because of its concentration on war industries, "The persistence of higher rates of unemployment in the inner city makes it clear that this propensity has had only a tangential effect on the labor market position of inner city residents. . . . It is clear that the Puerto Rican population is concentrated in the worst jobs, jobs with no future, and jobs presenting little opportunity to earn a decent living."

• Almost a third of the inner-city whites owned their homes (and, it could be speculated, a major reason they were still in the inner city was that they were homeowners); about 16 percent of the Negroes owned their homes, along with 7 percent of the Puerto Ricans. Black home ownership was highest (one-third) in Newhallville, lowest (6 percent) in Fair Haven, and it stood at about 11 percent in Dixwell, the Hill, and Dwight.

The mean monthly rent and/or carrying charges for whites in the inner city was $84.18. For Negroes it was $99.06, and for Puerto Ricans, $96.93.

About 13 percent of the whites were found to be living in overcrowded conditions (defined as less than one room for each person in a family); for Negroes and Puerto Ricans, it was around 25 percent.

• One out of every three inner-city residents was receiving some form of public financial assistance, either social security or aid for families with dependent children (ADC); one out of every eight was receiving ADC. CPI estimated that 25 to 30 percent of the inner-city population could be defined as impoverished by Office of Economic Opportunity standards.

• The surveyors asked residents what services they most needed. ". . . with the exception of the public housing projects," the finding was, "aspects of housing and recreation dominate all expressed needs of inner-city residents."

Several of the questions asked by the CPI interviewers had to do with the respondents' familiarity with, and opinions of, Community Progress, Incorporated. They asked: "Have you ever heard of Community Progress, Incorporated?" and "How effective do you think CPI programs and services are?" Yet the report did not provide a detailed breakdown of the respondents' replies, and the information that *was* presented was confusing, leading readers to wonder if CPI's batting average in the inner-city was not rather low.

By January 1968 CPI reported that the city's "willingness to undertake a major human-resources program, to meet the complex and difficult problems facing the inner city, had attracted some $18 million in private, federal, and state funds to New Haven in the past five and a half years." In a summary of its programs then in existence, the agency added:

> These funds have made possible for the deprived and disadvantaged people of the inner city a great number of opportunities which were never before available. They have meant a chance for the economically disfranchised to train for good jobs and to obtain social and health services for themselves and their families. This has resulted in $1,737,694 in private funds for the improvement of and strengthening of the New Haven school system.
>
> Had CPI not brought these funds to New Haven, these services would have to have been paid for out of the pockets of the taxpayers.[14] Without CPI, the impact on the taxpayers for urgently-needed inner-city programs would have been much heavier. Under ordinary circumstances they would have had to pay taxes for the services which CPI was able to provide with private funds.
>
> In addition to its highly successful efforts to obtain private and other non-city funds directly, CPI has played a crucial role in helping develop the understanding necessary to secure enactment of state and federal appropriations for education and for many other community-action programs.[15]

---

[14] If a note of defensiveness is detected here, it is because CPI's summary was published in response to a thorough attack on the agency, made not long before, by Congressman Robert N. Giaimo of Connecticut. Representative Giaimo's feelings about CPI will be discussed later.

[15] Community Progress Incorporated, "Summary of Programs," January 1968.

The funds which CPI received for itself were fairly large, by middle- and late-sixties standards. In fiscal year 1966 to 1967, the agency received $5,033,000 from the federal government, $271,000 from the state, $272,000 from the city and other local sources, and $555,000 from private sources, including foundations. The staff totaled more than 300 persons.

During that fiscal year, the largest single portion of CPI's budget (28 percent) went for *manpower* programs, or those designed to relieve unemployment and to upgrade the skills of those already employed. "Racial discrimination, poor educational preparation, unfamiliarity with an industrial economy (especially with migrants from the rural South and Puerto Rico), and poor work histories make many inner-city residents virtually unemployable," said the agency.[16]

To cope with the problems of those who were coming to be

---

16 Here was a theme that was to become established in New Haven among those who sought to explain the city's troubles: The assumption that a lot of the problems of Northern urban life could be explained by the phrase, "migrants from the rural South." The phrase seemed to assume that it was well-known that migrants from the rural South were uneducable, unemployable, and somewhat wild on Saturday nights. The McCone Commission, which investigated the Watts, California, riot of 1965, blamed much of the trouble on such people. The conclusion about Watts seemed, to someone familiar with the riots, just another dodge on the part of politically-appointed surveyors who wanted to shift the blame. J. Edgar Hoover and his Federal Bureau of Investigation had engaged in the same sort of unscientific sociology with the Eastern riots of 1964, when they concluded that the trouble was "a senseless attack on all constituted authority without purpose or object," and quoted "responsible people" as identifying the rioters as "school dropouts," "young punks," "common hoodlums," and "drunken kids." Two sociologists at the University of California, Raymond J. Murphy and James M. Watson, conducted a more comprehensive survey of the Watts riot, however, and knocked down both the "Southern migrant" theory and the "young punks" excuse. In their paper, "The Structure of Discontent: The Relationship Between Social Structure, Grievance, and Support for the Los Angeles Riots," Murphy and Watson found no significant relationship between the rioters' places of origin and their level of discontent. Furthermore, they found that there was no basis for white optimism that middle-class blacks would exert a moderating influence on future racial struggles. "If our analysis is correct," they wrote, "the problems of urban life for the Negro, even in the palm-lined spaciousness of Los Angeles, have grown acute and a significant number of Negroes, successful or unsuccessful, are emotionally prepared for violence as a strategy or solution to end the problems of segregation, exploitation, and subordination."

called the "hard-core unemployed" (and who also had been the hard-core neglected, as far as other agencies and governmental efforts had been concerned), CPI designed, and by the end of the sixties was operating, a variety of programs that were a far cry from the traditional and largely ineffective state employment service-type job placement programs. The flagships of the CPI manpower effort were the neighborhood employment centers which served the seven low-income neighborhoods. "A neighborhood employment center," said CPI in a report, "differs markedly from traditional agencies because its aims are different. CPI focuses on making the unskilled applicant better qualified through special programs such as basic education, work-experience, counseling, and other social services. The centers actively recruit applicants and develop jobs for them if available jobs are not suitable."

The social services were provided through a battery of aptitude and ability tests and vocational counseling, with special attention given to those applicants who were designated as "unemployable." Between October 1963 and July 1967, CPI said, almost 13,000 persons had applied for help at the centers, and around 6,500 had been placed in "training and/or employment."

In addition to the neighborhood centers, CPI sponsored or assisted such other manpower programs as the Neighborhood Youth Corps out-of-school program, which trained dropouts who were unemployed because they lacked skills. Two Residential Youth Centers were established to house Neighborhood Youth Corps trainees who had troubles at home. A program of adult work training, which started in 1966, dealt with "older and hard-core workers who are disadvantaged economically, educationally, physically, or emotionally."

CPI was the overseer of an on-the-job training program, in connection with about 300 local firms, which aimed applicants toward such jobs as secretary, machine operator, apprentice electrician, cook, telephone operator, and electronics technician. By 1968 CPI estimated that more than 80 percent of the trainees in that program went into the apprenticed trades. "CPI's role [in] putting applicants in apprenticed trades is a major breakthrough for minority group members," said the agency.

The Elm Haven Vocational Rehabilitation Unit was operated as part of the low-income housing project's Concerted Services Program. It offered the more or less standard job placement services, but coordinated them with medical, psychological, and psychiatric examinations and treatment; aptitude testing; counseling; entrance into federal and local job-training programs; referrals to schools and colleges and financial assistance toward tuition and transportation, and referral to other agencies.

The high school work-training program sought to keep potential dropouts in school by helping them earn money at such after-school jobs as stock clerk, tutorial aide, laboratory aide, and library aide. And, as rioting in Northern cities became an annual summertime event, CPI joined other urban areas in setting up enlarged summer programs to keep people, especially young people, busy and making a little money. More than 1,000 young people obtained part- or full-time employment in the summer of 1967, said CPI, which estimated that all of the programs for which it provided funds had served a total of 6,000 people. In 1967 the agency spent about $200,000 on summer programs.

Thirteen percent of CPI's budget in fiscal 1966 to 1967 was spent on *community services,* that element of the agency's program which Mayor Lee had referred to in 1962 when he wrote, in "Opening Opportunities," that "Services are but means to ends, and the ends are the ones people select for themselves."

In order to facilitate such selection of ends, CPI established six neighborhood offices as "the base from which CPI neighborhood action operates." These offices, said the agency, formed a "vital link between residents and services and opportunity programs." Their staffs recruited in the neighborhoods for service programs and, according to CPI, helped "residents form their own organizations to act on neighborhood problems, and help existing neighborhood organizations."

Resident participation[17] was said to constitute a large part of

---

[17] The term was used interchangeably in New Haven with "citizen participation." It could be considered identical with the phrase "maximum feasible participation," which had its origins in the federal Economic Opportunity

CPI's community services effort. Residents of the poor areas were expected to make known, through the neighborhood offices, their desires for and opinions of the sort of programs they wanted. It was in this area that New Haven—and every other city—encountered the most difficulties. Somewhat defensively, CPI commented in 1968: "Resident participation in the actual operation of programs has become more and more meaningful in the CPI scheme of things and will continue to do so."[18]

In actuality, CPI had not exactly thought up the idea of "more and more meaningful" resident participation all on its own. In early 1966 the Office of Economic Opportunity had sent out directives to the recipients of its funds, reminding them of the phrase, "maximum feasible participation," which by then was becoming a rather embarrassing piece of language, as mayor after mayor recoiled in horror at the idea of anything short of the total feasible participation of City Hall.

CPI had responded by enlarging its board to include seven new members, one from each of the poor neighborhoods. (The original board, it will be recalled, consisted of persons appointed by the mayor, the Board of Education, the Redevelopment Agency, the Citizens Action Commission, the United Fund, the Community Council, and Yale.) A Residents' Advisory Committee, which had the power only to advise and be consulted, was made up of three members from each of the neighborhoods.

Despite the reluctance of CPI (or any other antipoverty agency that was a creature of the Establishment) to wholeheartedly com-

Act of 1964. Title II of that act, which concerned itself with "Urban and Rural Community Action Programs," stated that community resources would be marshalled into an attack on poverty, and that the attack would develop services "of sufficient scope and size to give promise of progress toward elimination of poverty." The programs to be started under Title II, said the act, would be "developed, conducted, and administered with the maximum feasible participation of residents of the areas and members of the groups served." The story of the controversy that followed the introduction of "maximum feasible participation" into the language of the war on poverty is the story of America's failure to win the war. The particular meaning of "maximum feasible participation" for New Haven will be discussed at length later.
18 Community Progress, Incorporated, "Summary of Programs," *op. cit.*

mit itself to all-out resident participation, there were some neighborhood groups, and neighborhood people, who expected participation to happen and who tried to get their ideas before the agency.

In the late spring and early summer of 1967, one such group in New Haven was at work on specific programs for improving the Hill community. Fred Harris, the president of the Hill Parents Association, along with a bright young Negro couple, Richard and Joan Thornell, represented the sort of leadership that Mitchell Sviridoff had defined back in 1959, in his memo to Mayor Lee, as "immoderate," "direct actionist," or "responsible radical" leadership. It was that sort of leadership, Sviridoff had said, with whom communication should be maintained.

In June 1967 the Hill leaders talked over their proposals with Peter Almond, the young white man who was the representative of CPI on the Hill. Almond was impressed with the ideas, and he thought the city and CPI should provide funds for them. Above all, Almond thought, as Sviridoff had thought years before, communications should be kept up.

But communications with Fred Harris, Richard and Joan Thornell, and the Hill Parents Association were not kept up, as we shall see later.

The remainder of CPI's programs, while perhaps not as exciting and innovative as multi-purpose employment centers and neighborhood community action offices, nevertheless were important components of the nation's prototype human renewal agency. The Office of Economic Opportunity asked CPI in 1965 to set up a Community Action Institute for the purpose of training antipoverty warriors in the New England states. During 1967 the institute, under the direction of a young man named Frank Logue (a brother of Edward Logue), attracted more than 4,000 persons to various seminars and conferences, including meetings for policemen, public officials, community action personnel, agency staffers, and nonprofessionals. Nine percent of the CPI budget in fiscal 1966 to 1967 went to the institute.

Thirty-nine percent of CPI's budget went for delegated programs, which included such items as neighborhood centers in the library system, the Boy Scouts, and various education programs. Head Start, of course, had been begun in New Haven as an experiment by the agency and the Board of Education in 1963. And the community school program, which occupied so much of the attention of the authors of "Opening Opportunities," had turned into a permanent portion of New Haven's efforts at human renewal.

On August 27, 1962, not long after "Opening Opportunities" had been released, the Board of Education adopted a policy statement that declared that community schools would be established to serve not only as centers of education, but also as centers of neighborhood activities, community services, and "community life." The community school, said the board, would be "an institution assisting citizens in the study and solution of neighborhood problems."

Visitors to the city were invariably shown the Harry A. Conte School, situated in Wooster Square, which had opened in September 1962, on a day-and-night, twelve-months-a-year schedule. There were regular classes for kindergarten through the eighth grade, and there were a senior citizen center, library, gymnasium, pool, teenage lounge, health facility, and a courtyard, all of which were available for community use. If lack of unfavorable publicity, public outcry, strikes, and riot and disorder were any measure, the community school idea, as exemplified by the Conte school, was a success.

CPI was one of the conduits through which funds were provided to operate the program of the Legal Assistance Association. The contribution of the association was the establishment of neighborhood offices "where anyone with a legal problem can get help," as CPI put it. Seven months after local offices were opened in the Newhallville-Dixwell and Hill-Dwight neighborhoods in 1965, a total of 625 people had received service, about half of them in civil matters, half in criminal matters.

About 10 percent of CPI's budget went for administrative costs, and about 1 percent went for research.[19]

---

[19] One percent of more than $6 million may be considered a tiny sum by many, but for behavioral scientists, those who do the research and who

The agency was proud of itself, and it was especially proud of its reputation and position as a prototype for the war on poverty. Many of those who were to administer the war from Washington, or who were to direct it from high positions in other, larger cities, got their start in New Haven. "Proof of the high caliber of CPI personnel, past and present," wrote the agency, "is the large number who have moved on to much higher-paying positions in the Northeast and elsewhere in the nation. CPI has been one of the nation's most important training grounds for leaders in antipoverty and urban-improvement programs."

CPI, the city, its mayor, and the Redevelopment Agency all seemed happy. They kept reminding visitors that the bulldozer had only unearthed the human problems, and that the initial attacks on those human problems had served only to emphasize their magnitude and complexity, but there were those who were calling New Haven a Model City, and who had been calling it a Model City for some years, and the city did not discourage such acclaim.

Willard Wirtz, the Secretary of Labor, said that New Haven was "the greatest success story in the history of the world."[20] Robert C. Weaver, the secretary of housing and urban development, commented in a manner only slightly less all-encompassing: "I think New Haven is coming closest to our dream of a slumless city."[21] And President Lyndon Johnson sent Lee one of the pens he had used to sign the act establishing the Department of Housing and Urban Development, with the note: "You deserve a lion's share of the credit for efforts leading to the new department which will advance the progress of our cities."

Another way of putting it might have been to say that Lee and the members of his "parallel government," by finding a cause and hitching themselves to it (after having experienced the political tragedy of losing two campaigns with no cause); by seeking out the

have long envied the vast sums spent on research for the "hard," or physical, sciences, it is a lot.
[20] Quoted in "An Old Industrial City Wages Dramatic War on Poverty," *Trenton* (New Jersey) *Sunday Times Advertiser,* July 12, 1964.
[21] Robert Cormier, *op. cit.*

best possible talent and hiring it; by determining where the financial aid could come from and then getting it, by the bushel basketful; by sensing, long before other cities had sensed it, that if physical renewal were to work it must be accompanied by equal efforts at human renewal; by doing all this with a measure of sensitivity and fairness; and doing it in a decaying, unattractive New England town—Lee and his government had shown, or were about to show, that one of the more difficult aspects of democracy could and would work, and that a man who stood for all this could continue getting himself reelected to office.

Then, in August of 1967, as the city's Democrats were about to assemble to endorse Richard Lee as their candidate for an eighth term, New Haven had its riot.

Since 1964 in Harlem, cities all over the nation had been having their black summertime rebellions, and most of the mayors of cities that had not yet blown up had long since learned that it would be stupid to say, as some of them had said before, that "It can't happen here." Richard Lee had not said that. But neither had he really expected violence. "I seriously thought that something like this wouldn't happen here," he was quoted as saying at the time, "although I never would leave the city during the summer."[22]

The riot, which many New Haveners still refer to as a "disturbance" because its toll in injuries and property damage was so relatively low, started on a Saturday evening, August 19, 1967, and by all accounts the act that touched it off was the shooting of a Puerto Rican by a white merchant in the Hill section. Violence spread from the Hill to three other poor neighborhoods—Newhallville, Fair Haven, and Dixwell. Lee declared a state of emergency, which lasted until the following Thursday.

On the day that Lee lifted the curfew, the city's Democrats gathered again to nominate him for mayor. As Lee accepted the nomination and began the campaign (which he was to win, despite the fact that ill health cut his public appearances down to almost nothing), he said:

---

[22] "New Haven: Model City?" *Progressive Architecture,* January 1968.

As your mayor, but also as your Democratic candidate for re-election, I am sure there is no need to tell this convention how distressed and anguished I am . . .

The events of the past five days have saddened all of the people in this city, regardless of neighborhood, race, or ethnic origin. As mayor, in these same five days, I have done little else than involve myself in attempts to bring reason out of chaos, normalcy out of disorder, and peace out of violence.

What can I say? It has been the most agonizing experience in my fourteen years as mayor—indeed, the most agonizing experience in my life. This city has long enjoyed a reputation for peace and stability. Then, in a few days, a small number of lawless individuals—many of them young people without regard or concern for what has been done in the past decade—these few people, whether wittingly or not, have disrupted and temporarily hindered the strides forward we are and have been making in the areas of social opportunity.

The cities of America are in crisis, and New Haven is among those cities. If the people of New Haven did not realize this before, the events of the last few days must certainly make them realize it now. Urban America, 1967, involves New Haven as it never has before.

We seek answers to age-old problems, but, tragically, they have not all been found, not nearly. In New Haven we have been at those problems for more than a decade. But in a decade we have been trying to solve things which have been wrong with urban America for a century or more.

We seek total commitment from all levels of the city and its people, but tragically this has not been accomplished either. That is my challenge and that is the job to which I have, and will, with your help, continue to give all my strength and all of my heart and all of my soul, not only in the remaining months of my term, but for as long as I am mayor of our city . . .

I have no political speech in my soul tonight, nor even a comment, however jesting or wry, about my opposition. I intend to tell you simply and straightforwardly that I am your candidate for mayor. I accept the nomination for mayor, but I accept it with a heart filled with sadness, not bitterness. I accept it weary and tired, but not discouraged or dejected—indeed, I accept it with continued faith, and with confidence and with optimism . . .

My job is to work with all people. My job—God help me and all mayors who believe in the things in which I believe—is at once the most awesome, depressing, the most exciting and most challenging, the most satisfying and the most demanding job in domestic America today.

Have I failed? Who can tell? . . .

The answer, of course, was that Richard Lee *had* failed, and that New Haven had failed, just as the failure of every other city in the nation had manifested itself, or was about to manifest itself, in the most dramatic of terms. The real question was whether any lessons could be learned from the failures. If any *could* be learned, then perhaps New Haven, and the cities, could be saved. If New Haven and its mayor could not learn anything from all that had happened, then perhaps there was adequate reason to believe that New Haven, and cities in general, or maybe even democracy, could or even should not be saved. One thing was certain in the summer of 1967: New Haven had indeed become a model city.

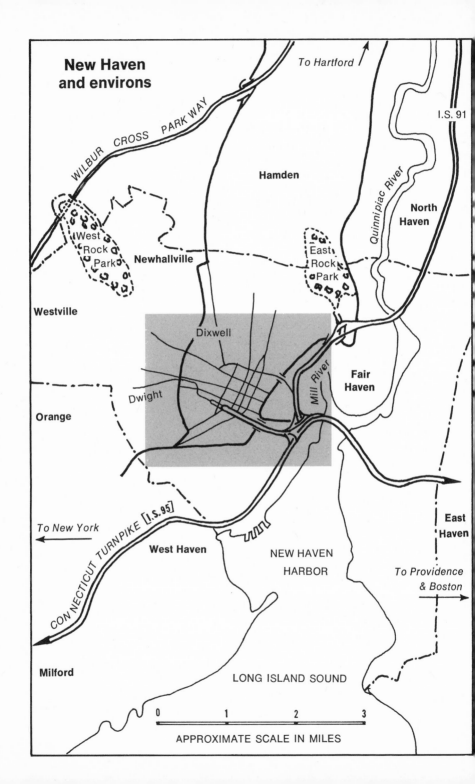

New Haven and environs

WILBUR CROSS PARK WAY

To Hartford

I.S. 91

Hamden

Quinnipiac River

North Haven

West Rock Park

Newhallville

East Rock Park

Westville

Dixwell

Mill River

Fair Haven

Dwight

Orange

To New York

CONNECTICUT TURNPIKE [I.S. 95]

West Haven

NEW HAVEN HARBOR

East Haven

To Providence & Boston

Milford

LONG ISLAND SOUND

0   1   2   3
APPROXIMATE SCALE IN MILES

Detail of downtown New Haven

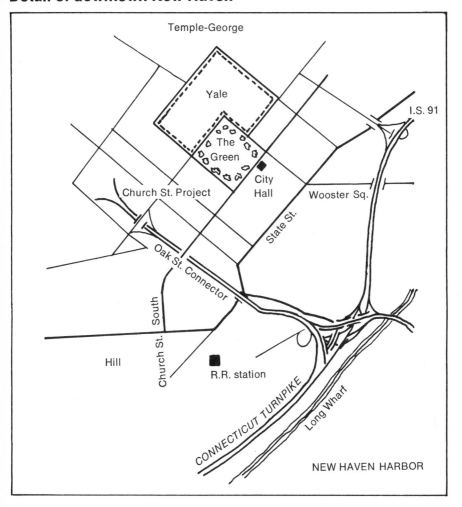

Temple-George

Yale

The Green

City Hall

Church St. Project

Wooster Sq.

I.S. 91

State St.

Oak St. Connector

South

Church St.

Hill

R.R. station

CONNECTICUT TURNPIKE

Long Wharf

NEW HAVEN HARBOR

Mayor Richard C. Lee.

A corner of the New Haven Green, the geographical and traditional center of the city. Yale University rises beyond the United Church.

Much of downtown was like this before the Church Street Project was begun.

[ALL PHOTOGRAPHS NOT OTHERWISE CREDITED WERE TAKEN BY THE AUTHOR.]

Church Street, before and after.

A house in the Dixwell Project area, before and after rehabilitation.

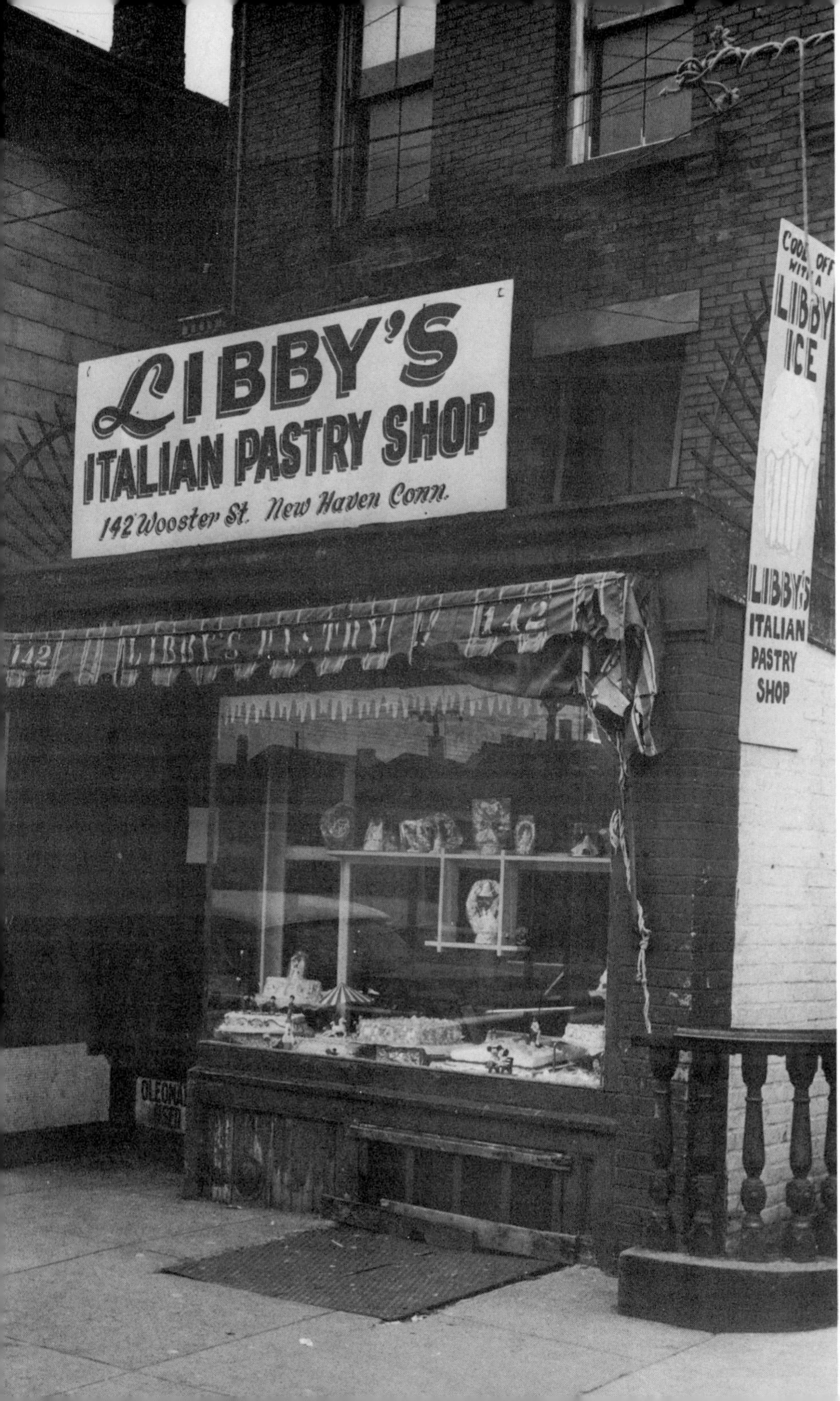

NEW HAVEN REDEVELOPMENT AGENCY•CHARLES R. SCHULZE

Wooster Square: Lee's urban renewal program was the first in the nation that rehabilitated, rather than destroyed, a deteriorating neighborhood. Not only were homes preserved; so were some of the locally famous businesses, such as Libby's Italian Pastry Shop.

The new New Haven architecture: The Knights of Columbus building, designed by Kevin Roche, John Dinkeloo and Associates, guards one of the entrances to downtown. The structure, essentially four tall cylinders covered with brown tile and connected by glass walls, houses the national headquarters of the fraternal organization.

The architectural key to the Church Street complex is a parking garage, designed by Paul Rudolph.

Yale University still has its residential colleges and arched entranceways, but it has been unable to resist some change. Now there are coeds living in the dormitories and posters stuck to the arches.

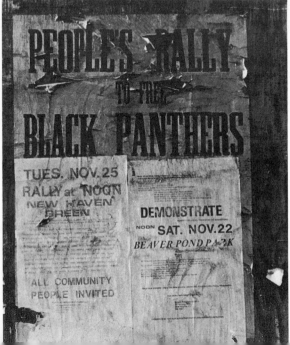

Posters in the Hill, mounted on post-riot architecture: plywood windows.

Fred Harris, standing in front of a vacant lot in the Hill neighborhood, the last slum area to receive New Haven's attention. Hill people who believed in citizen participation, led by Harris and his Hill Parents Association, built a small park in the lot one summer. Now it is shielded from the street and from the people by cyclone fencing.

Young men of the Hill.

V

The Model City

Someone said that the Agency was insulting the intelligence of the public by picking and choosing the questions they wanted to answer. He said . . . that they should be prosecuted as criminals . . .

Someone requested that each of the members put in their resignations . . . He said he would call for a federal investigation.

Kathryn Tilson of Hamden said that the Agency had money from State, Federal and local sources, about $250 million since 1954. She asked if the members knew how many buildings of low income housing they had constructed. She asked if they knew there were only twelve units of low income housing built since 1954. She asked if they knew how many they had demolished—between 5–6,000. She asked if they were trying to run the poor out of New Haven.

Reverend Gilmore asked for a correction on the figures.

There were more outbursts.

—From the minutes of the December 31, 1968, meeting of the New Haven Redevelopment Agency

IN NEW HAVEN, as in other urban centers that had been struck with violence, the riot seemed to change everything. It is unlikely that it *really* changed anything at all; the riot in New Haven, like the riots elsewhere, seemed more to be the outward manifestation of a violence and decay that had been going on all along, but that had been ignored or unnoticed by the majority community. It was, as far as the majority was concerned, beneath the surface. In New Haven, though, to an extent greater than in other cities, what was on the surface had been rehabilitated, and paved, and reconstructed, and repainted, with promises and reports of success. The riot merely burned off the paint; it helped to open a Pandora's box that was bound to open anyway. No one should have been surprised that it happened, but there were some whites who *were* taken by surprise, just as there is traditionally a certain portion of the citizenry that does not know the Vice President's name.

According to contemporary standards, the riot in New Haven was not an exceptionally destructive one. The National Advisory Commission on Civil Disorders, which was established by President Johnson to look into the 1967 summer of violence in America, in which more than 150 cities reported racial disorders, chose New Haven as one of 23 cities for its survey.[1] The commission, whose investigations dealt with the major riots of that summer in Detroit and Newark as well as with less destructive outbreaks in other cities, rated the disturbances on a scale of "major," "serious," and "minor." New Haven's riot was found to be "serious."

According to the official compilation, no one was killed in New Haven, and only three persons were injured in the emergency period. (The city has said that not a shot was fired by the police;

---

[1] The National Advisory Commission on Civil Disorders, *Report* to the President (Washington: U.S. Government Printing Office, 1968). Some of the commission's chief findings, it will be recalled, were that "The urban disorders of the summer of 1967 were not caused by, nor were they the consequence of, any organized plan or 'conspiracy'"; that the disorders "involved Negroes acting against local symbols of white American society, authority, and property in Negro neighborhoods—rather than against white persons" and that the police were prime among those symbols; and that "White racism is essentially responsible for the explosive mixture which has been accumulating in our cities since the end of World War II."

some residents of the black community have disputed this.) The commonly-agreed-upon spark that started New Haven's riot was the non-fatal shooting, by the white proprietor of a lunchroom in the Hill section, of a Puerto Rican citizen. It was alleged that the Puerto Rican had threatened the white man with a knife. The Puerto Rican was later charged with aggravated assault, and the white man was charged with assault with intent to kill.

A chart drawn up by the National Advisory Commission showed that the violence in New Haven started with the throwing of rocks and bottles at passing automobiles in the Hill section, and was followed by some breakage of windows and looting, then fires, then a gradual tapering off of violence. This final period was characterized by sporadic looting and some fires. The commission said that the property damage in New Haven, and in other cities with similar patterns, "appears to have been, at least in part, the result of deliberate attacks on white-owned businesses characterized in the Negro community as unfair or disrespectful toward Negroes." Later on, the policemen and firemen who were sent to the scene became targets of verbal and physical abuse, and their equipment was damaged.

The trouble spread from the Hill to Newhallville, Fair Haven, and Dixwell. Later on there was some looting in Wooster Square and even the predominantly white Westville neighborhood. White vigilante groups visited the scenes of the rioting, offering to help put down the rebels; in some cases they were broken up or their members arrested by the police. Many of the arrests of both whites and Negroes were made on the basis of curfew violations.

In addition to the city police, under the command of Chief Francis V. McManus, the state police came to the riot, and a National Guard unit, which had been in summer encampment not far away, was mobilized and brought to the edge of the city.

Mayor Lee, who spent much of the time during the riot in an emergency control center downtown, went on the radio and called the violence "the work of a small number of people." By Sunday, according to one account, he was saying: "There are no outside influences involved in the ferment; what happened here is part of urban America, 1967. It can happen regardless of the city or state, anywhere in the nation." On Tuesday, he was quoted as saying that the incidents "were not racially motivated; they are wanton acts of violence and disregard for the law."[2]

Later, more than a year after the violence, Mayor Lee reflected on it: "I think that it's safe to say that the disturbance, to put it mildly, put me in an unhappy frame of mind. Many people had counseled me, especially Negro leaders, that no matter what I did or what I tried to do, I had to be prepared, because they felt it was only a matter of time until we had these major disturbances.

"But I firmly believed that we had a chance of escaping that, and of course they were right and I was wrong.

"I don't know whether *any* city can avoid major violence, through the dedication of a mayor or through the leadership of the community itself beyond the political power structure. Some of these things are just signs of our times. A few years ago, it was fashionable to sit in. Then it became fashionable to demonstrate. Then it became fashionable to picket. Then it became fashionable to riot. Now, I think riots have reached the turning point and they'll go on to something else."

Another major figure in the riot was Fred Harris, the young president of the Hill Parents Association, the predominantly black organization on the Hill which had been trying to obtain city money to fund community action programs. Harris walked the streets, putting his reputation as a black leader on the line by asking the rioters to cool down, and trying to convince the police that the situation might improve if they withdrew a bit. But, he

---

[2] Quoted in *Progressive Architecture, op. cit.* The *Progressive Architecture* article offered a thorough examination of what its editors considered the causes of the riot, along with a moment-by-moment account of it, all generally unfavorable to Mayor Lee and what it called the city's paternalistic approach to its problems. The article aroused some furor among New Haven citizens. One of them, architect Gilbert Switzer, wrote to *P/A* and accused the publication of distorting the facts and resorting to innuendo and other devices in order to convey "the impression of a ruthless Mayor who has spent fourteen years destroying neighborhoods, tearing down landmarks, and generally setting the city up for a bloody holocaust which he then crushed with brute force." Switzer's letter was not published.

said, he was slugged with a rifle butt and shot at; later he reported being sprayed with Mace (the chemical agent which in 1967 was only beginning to meet with the widespread approval of police departments) after he had carried a crippled woman from a burning building. He was quoted as saying: "I've had it helping the police. I'm losing my own guys in helping, and then the cops go after me. You can't do nothing. They deserve whatever's going to happen. There's no talking or reasoning with them."[3]

Still, Harris continued trying to put down, rather than encourage, the rioting. He asked the city to send a hundred brooms and a couple of sanitation trucks to the Hill; the idea was that the nonrioters, who were still in the vast majority, would help clean up the broken glass. The city sent the trucks loaded with the brooms, but police would not let them in.

Later, when the Hill Parents Association asked Yale University to provide rooms in its dormitories for Hill families made temporarily homeless by the riot, Yale refused.

After the riot, some aspects of New Haven life seemed to be returning to normal. For one thing, Mayor Lee was running for reelection, and the campaign provided some distraction for the citizens. Even those who were not prepared to be distracted, on the grounds that Lee would win, as usual, found some excitement: The mayor was almost totally incapable of campaigning. The reason, he said, was a vocal-cord problem brought on by exhaustion during the riot.

"I went through the campaign without making any speeches," Lee said later. "My staff worked like hell. My brother and my sister and my wife and my daughter were all out campaigning and —ask my mother; she was out, a tiny little old lady who's tottering, 86 years old then and made of steel. She's great. She's about as shaky on her feet as the Eiffel Tower, but she's got to play her role, as I have to play my role. I think basically we're all actors. We won by 62 per cent."

---

[3] *Ibid.*

Lee won by less than 10,000 votes, one of his lowest pluralities. Factors in the outcome included, certainly, the riot and Lee's health, and some observers saw also the reflection of a deepening split between Lee and the Democratic Town Chairman, Arthur T. Barbieri, the man who under ordinary circumstances could be depended on to get out the vote of the party faithful.

Lee, however, said he was pleased by the result. "We made a survey," he said, "that showed 89 per cent of the blacks in the survey approved of the way we handled the summer disturbances; 88 per cent approved of my record generally, and 84 per cent voted for me. Now what do you want? I don't think Pope John could do better than that."

The campaign may have taken some New Haveners' minds off the events of the previous August, but still there were some subtle changes in the white community.

For one thing, people's language seemed changed. Before long, everybody was agreeing with City Hall that the five nights of violence should be called a "disturbance." The lawyers who gathered in Lindy's luncheonette on Church Street, near the courts and City Hall, were calling it a "disturbance," too. Not a shot had been fired, everybody said. White radicals, some of whom claimed that shots *had* been fired, but who could not prove it, called it a "riot," perhaps with some satisfaction, and some black militants termed it a "rebellion."

The language changed in other ways, too. No longer was it wise to say that "relocation is a housing opportunity" or to talk about the prospect of a "slumless city." One had to qualify such remarks now. Mayor Lee had been saying, for some time, when someone asked him about the Model City, that "If New Haven is regarded as a Model City, God help urban America." Now he said it even more frequently and defensively. And those who had not listened very closely when he said it before found themselves saying it, now, for there was a riot to explain now.

The tone was that, sure, New Haven had been given more opportunities and more money than other cities, and that it had started long before other cities, and that it had been blessed with a liberal, dynamic, Democratic mayor, one it had had the good sense to reelect seven times, and that the riot only showed how deep and complex the problems were, and that good and decent men would continue to work hard to eradicate the causes of the problems. As *The New York Times* put it in an editorial during the riot:

> To a bitter minority of New Haveners, their city is still no model. But their lawless actions do not mean the city's efforts have been a failure, much less that it is pointless to extend them.
>
> What the disorders do demonstrate is that even thirteen years of continuing commitment is not enough to eradicate all the roots of frustration in the ghetto. This is no new discovery for Mayor Lee. . . .
>
> New Haven's mayor has made it plain that he has no intention of giving up. He did not hesitate to employ all the armed force he considered essential to restore peace to his anguished community—a necessary first step in any riot—but he is also keeping his sights on the deeper causes of unrest. He told reporters yesterday: "We will review what has been done and what needs to be done at the base roots."
>
> New Haven and its Mayor are still a model for the nation.[4]

The business of keeping one's sights set on the deeper causes of unrest meant that, since the riot, a lot of statistics and facts became more meaningful. Before, only one statistic seemed to be quoted with any regularity—the amount of money the federal government had invested in the city's renewal efforts. Now some New Haveners started to wonder where all that money had gone, and whether it had done any good.

Some of the more dramatic statistics concerned population. New Haven was becoming blacker. The suburbs around it were growing, but they were remaining quite white. By 1967, when a special census was held, there were 108,116 whites left in New Haven, along with 33,636 nonwhites, or 31 percent. ("Nonwhites" were defined here as including Negroes, Spanish-speaking persons, and Orientals.) An examination of the census tracts used in that survey shows that there was considerable residential segregation in

---

[4] "Upset in New Haven," *The New York Times,* August 22, 1967.

the city. In the neighborhood that saw the most violence during the summer of 1967, the Hill, the black population was still considerably less than the white population, but it appeared to be growing rapidly. Census tracts comprising the Hill reflected a good deal of residential segregation.[5]

It was not difficult to see where the whites were going. The 1967 survey showed these population statistics for New Haven's suburbs, as compared with the 1960 population.[6]

Suburb	1960 Total Population	1967 White	Nonwhite
Branford	16,610	18,976	234
East Haven	21,388	25,144	110
North Haven	15,935	21,092	314
Hamden	41,056	45,650	1,402
Woodbridge	5,182	6,595	108
Orange	8,547	12,719	72
West Haven	43,002	47,815	2,143
Guilford	7,913	10,373	127
North Branford	—	10,222	28
Bethany	2,384	3,041	77

In 1968 a group of researchers engaged in projecting the city's needs for the next fifteen years determined that the New Haven metropolitan area would grow from its current population of 347,000 to at least 420,000 by 1980 and thus would feel many of the "big city" problems which New Haven first felt at the turn of the century, including higher tax rates, the deterioration of older buildings, overcrowding, a critical shortage of open space, a great strain on the educational system, and the mixture of incompatible land uses.[7]

---

[5] U.S. Department of Commerce, Bureau of the Census, "Distribution of White and Non-White Population by City, Town, and Census Tracts in New Haven S.M.S.A.," April 5, 1967. In some cases the census tract boundaries (which enclose geographical units, arbitrarily chosen for census-taking purposes) do not follow exactly the popularly-accepted neighborhood boundaries.

[6] *Ibid.* and "City Population Levels at 139,000," *New Haven Register,* April 7, 1969.

[7] New Haven Redevelopment Agency, City Plan Commission, and the Citizens Action Commission, "CRP: New Haven Community Renewal Program," April 1968.

What the researchers did not say quite so clearly was that it was very likely that the population of the city itself would become less white and more black. The Negro population was in 1967 younger and more likely to have children (almost half of the non-whites were under the age of twenty), and the only group of white citizens likely to remain constant in size over the years was the elderly. Also, because of housing discrimination in the sub-urbs, it was unlikely that any of the city's swelling nonwhite population was going to "escape" to less crowded land, regardless of how financially successful they might become.

Housing in general became a loaded set of statistics. Before, a lot of the people who liked to call New Haven a Model City meant, when they called it that, the new, exciting buildings that were going up to house merchants and office workers and the in-habitants of luxury apartments—buildings that were being designed by renowned architects and that were pleasing, sometimes even exciting, to the eye. But there were also 3,800 families in New Haven who lived in substandard housing and 23,500 individuals living in overcrowded housing.[8] And the projection was for more housing problems in the future: By 1980, according to the city's own statistics, New Haven would need 400 or 500 additional units of housing for the elderly; there would be 625 to 700 large, low-income families needing space; 2,000 families would have to be relocated. It looked as if New Haven, with all its talk of housing opportunity and bold new programs, still had been unable to deal with the problems of housing its poor citizens. In this respect, the city was not very different from most other urban areas—Atlanta and Philadelphia, Pittsburgh and Boston, they all seemed inclined to equate the construction of a stadium or a luxury apartment building or a new "civic center" with housing for the poor, even when they built no housing for the poor.

There was considerable confusion over how much housing actually had been built in the years before 1968—and of that which had been built, how much of it had been rented or sold

---

[8] Community Progress, Incorporated, "Summary of Programs," *op. cit.*

to low-income families. The allegation quoted at the beginning of this chapter—that only a dozen units of low-income housing had been constructed since 1954—was typical of this confusion.

The critics (and these included vocal spokesmen for the black community, along with a growing group of white liberals and radicals) seemed to feel that City Hall had hatched a plot against "the people," and that urban renewal, in New Haven and elsewhere, had been used as a dodge to make rich merchants and land-speculators richer at the expense of poor, black, and powerless people. In the case of New Haven, it did not hurt the critics' case at all that Mayor Lee's first project, the Oak Street Connector, had resulted, tangibly and quite visibly to everyone who drove down it, in the erection of some tasteless and expensive architecture. Nor did the critics fail to point out that Lee's most ambitious project, the Church Street effort, had resulted in a hotel that charged $15 to $22 a day for a double room, and that the ground-floor centerpiece of the project, the Chapel Mall, had turned out to be little more than a collection of hosiery shops, candy stores of the sort that sell only one brand, and small, relatively expensive specialty shops, arranged around an indoor fountain that was situated partly under an escalator, and frequented by teen-agers to the extent that special policemen had to be hired to keep them from loitering.

Even statistics showing that renewal was an economically feasible venture, which might be exciting news to chambers of commerce and mayors, were interpreted by the critics as only confirming their suspicion that the poor were being fleeced for the benefit of the rich. From 1954 to 1963, retail sales in New Haven decreased by 6 percent while they increased by 28 percent in the whole metropolitan area. Once downtown renewal became a fact, the trend was reversed. Between January 1963 and January 1968 retail sales in the city increased by 41 percent.[9] Some might interpret such a dramatic increase as boding well for the city and all its citizens; the critics—or some of them—chose to see it as further evidence of heartless, insensitive exploitation. Sales were

[9] New Haven Redevelopment Agency, City Plan Commission, and the Citizens Action Commission, *op. cit.*

going up, they said, because highways, parking lots, and stores were being built on land where poor people once lived.

The critics also were skeptical of the quality of the work being done by the Division of Neighborhood Improvement (the housing code enforcement agency), and over the fate of the families who had been forced to move out of the way of renewal projects. It was clearly the suspicion of some citizens that perfectly good, if old, housing had been wantonly destroyed and its low-income inhabitants turned out to make room for expressways, department stores, a hotel, and an aesthetically pleasing (to some) parking lot. Particularly vexing for the critics of the city's housing efforts was the fact that the Redevelopment Agency kept referring to "low and moderate income housing" in the same sentence—never specifying how much of the total was low-income, and how much was moderate-income. Such critical groups as the Coalition of Concerned Citizens, a largely white group, suspected that this was the agency's way of covering up its failure to build or find low-income housing and evidence of its eagerness to build units suitable only for middle-income families.

The coalition, at that New Year's Eve meeting with the agency at which there were "more outbursts," bore down on the agency and, in particular, on the city's development administrator, Melvin Adams. He was "evasive and unresponsive" in matters of code enforcement, the coalition told members of the Redevelopment Agency; in addition, "it would be useful if you directed Mr. Adams to stop lumping 'low' and 'moderate-income' housing together in his propaganda."

In response to such criticism, the Redevelopment Agency and the rest of the city officialdom became unusually defensive. It had been a common charge among critics of the Lee administration that all their complaints were ignored; their telephone calls unreturned and their requests for hearings forgotten. Now, however, the city seemed to become a little more responsive to those whom it previously had considered "cranks," "crackpots," and "left-wingers."[10]

---

[10] City officials sometimes used these terms in private conversations to describe those of their critics whose motives they doubted or failed to

The Redevelopment Agency turned out a report[11] that showed statistically that the city's greatest housing need, as of the time of the coalition's criticism, was for units for the elderly. Another major need, said the agency, was for housing for low-income families of six or more persons.

As for relocation and demolition, the agency replied with the latest statistics. Since urban renewal began, it said, 6,970 families and individuals had moved because of renewal, highway acquisition, and housing code enforcement. This is what happened to them:

• About 70 percent were relocated to private rental housing. Of the 70 percent, about 57 percent were white.

• About 15 percent were relocated to public housing. Almost 80 percent of those were Negroes.

• About 15 percent purchased homes. Some 80 percent of those were white.

Since 1954, said the agency, about 6,000 dwelling units had been demolished because of urban renewal or highway construction. "Less than half of these were low-income units, occupied by families, elderly couples, and individuals—who in many cases were paying high monthly rents."

And, said the city, there was a good reason for lumping "low-" and "moderate-income" housing together in the statistics. Any time the agency spoke of building or acquiring "low-income" housing, there was "strong neighborhood antagonism":

> Consistent public opposition to every specific low-income development proposed by the Housing Authority—no matter what neighborhood the project is planned for—has been largely responsible for the limited construction of new family public housing. In the past twelve years, the Housing Authority and the Redevelopment Agency have encountered strong neighborhood opposition to plans for low-income housing in every area of the city; whether a low-income area, a middle-income area or an upper-income area, whether it's a racially-mixed neighborhood, a

---

understand. Critics who were obviously motivated by partisan politics were just "playing the political game," but nonpolitical social reformers were "crackpots."

[11] New Haven Redevelopment Agency, "Housing Report," February 20, 1969.

predominantly black neighborhood or a predominantly white neighborhood.

Furthermore, there was virtually no vacant land in New Haven on which new housing could be built. As Mayor Lee commented in 1967: "Less than 2 percent of the land in New Haven is undeveloped. Most of that 2 percent is marsh land which should be maintained as open spaces. The only way that we are going to renew our city . . . is to do exactly what we are doing—which some people fail to understand or accept—which is to tear down and rebuild or restore."[12]

New Haven's practice of putting low- and middle-income families together in cooperative housing, however—and therefore making it impossible to distinguish between poor and non-poor residents—served to overcome some of the public objection to low-income housing and some of the problem of land area. It "meets with neighborhood approval in almost all cases," said the Redevelopment Agency. "We feel basically this is a better solution because it takes away the stigma that public housing can place on the family, does not result in the building of new ghettoes and does not concentrate large numbers of low-income families in one area."

New Haven was not alone in finding it difficult to build (the critics would say "in its reluctance to build") housing for low-income families. The National Commission on Urban Problems, created by President Johnson in January 1967, to determine how an adequate supply of low-income housing could be provided, conducted hearings all over the nation in that year and found that the housing was not being built. The former executive director of the commission, Howard E. Shuman, wrote in *The Washington Monthly* for July 1969 of the inter-governmental frictions and disputes that surrounded the commission's work—most notably the pressures exerted on it by the Department of Housing and Urban Development to become "HUD's handmaiden and apolo-

---

12 *Hearings Before the National Commission on Urban Problems, op. cit.,* p. 118.

gist" and to help suppress HUD's awful record of meeting the nation's housing needs.

Shuman noted that the commission had found, among other things, that: The Housing Act of 1949 had authorized 800,-000 units of public housing to be built in six years, but that only two-thirds of that had been built in nearly two decades; in 1967 30,000 public housing units were being built each year, and more than half of them were small apartments for the elderly ("virtually no housing was being built in the ghettoes of the United States for the poor families—particularly poor Negro families—who needed it most"); urban renewal had destroyed 400,000 units of low-income housing, but the program would build only one-twentieth of that number of units on the land thus bulldozed; in all, 2 million units of housing had been destroyed by renewal, highways, demolition for public housing, code enforcement, and the like, but "only a million units of subsidized housing had been created" and the commission's projections showed that "this pattern would continue."

Shuman spoke specifically of the commission's New Haven hearing of May 1967: "In New Haven," he wrote, "HUD's showcase for urban renewal, we sensed great local hostility to the program. Over $800 per capita had been spent—the highest rate in the country—but the community was seething and later erupted in a riot. Unknown to us until the end of our day of hearings there, the New Haven police had been stationed inside and outside the hall in case our hearings got out of hand. We prevented that by welcoming the views of unscheduled as well as scheduled witnesses. In fact, the 'walk-in' witnesses talked with a fire and an eloquence which the others did not match."[13]

---

[13] The transcript of the commission's hearings in New Haven show that the "welcome" of which Shuman wrote was not exactly unrestrained. After Mayor Lee had testified at length, Fred Harris, one of the unscheduled guests, rose to interject:

You people have listened to the Mayor. How about listening to us? If this is supposed to be a public hearing, you should allow the people that are involved in all this redevelopment area to speak their opinion, seeing that we are the ones that have to go through all this

Furthermore, the difficulties over housing came to the surface at a time when New Haven, like all other cities, had less reason than ever before to hope for continued assistance from Washington. The days of "Fund City" were quite clearly drawing to a close. President Johnson was obviously disenchanted with the war on poverty he had declared such a short time before. The war in Vietnam, of course, did not help. Johnson had promised that there would be both guns and butter, but the butter soon turned to margarine and then it melted away altogether.

The disenchantment soon spread to the generals and lieutenants in Washington's social revolution, many of whom left the government as quickly as possible and headed for jobs in other wars. Some went to New Jersey, which was distinguishing itself in its attempts to mount its own statewide antipoverty strategy; some hired out as consultants, selling their expertise to cities and or-

---

redevelopment, all these urban programs. If you are having a public hearing, how can you not let the poor people stand up and voice their opinions as to what is happening to their lives?

[Coleman Woodbury, a commission member]: I hope very much that we can have an opportunity for you.

[Harris]: You hope?

[Woodbury]: One of the witnesses has to catch a train shortly after noon.

[Harris]: How are you people helping us when you listen to people like that, that decide what happens to our lives, and we are never given a chance to speak up and say what we think should help our neighborhoods?

[Woodbury]: What I am saying is that we will try to give you a chance to speak.

[Harris]: You will try? Our lives are involved. Our wives and children are involved in all this, and you are going to try? What is trying, man?

[Woodbury]: Do you want us not to try?

[Harris]: We want you to give us a chance to talk, and let some of these people talk that go through this stuff. You have got the man presenting a big whitewash up here, and you are not letting the people that go through this stuff voice their opinion.

[Woodbury] We will proceed with our next two people.

[Harris]: It's a lot of jive—a public hearing, man. We have to go through this. We have to live through this.

[Woodbury]: We will proceed with the scheduled program . . .

Later, Harris and other representatives of the opposition were allowed to speak.

ganizations that needed to know how to file a proper application for funds; some went to work for private agencies. The river of money from Washington seemed to dry up. It was to get even drier under the Nixon Administration, which turned out not only disenchanted with some of the imaginative antipoverty programs, but also downright uninterested.

Other statistics that were being seen in a new light were concerned with employment. New Haven and Connecticut, with their various war-related industries, were enjoying unusual prosperity, and the unemployment rate was believed to be low.[14] But it was not low for everybody; for whites, the official unemployment rate shortly after the "disturbance" was 3.9 percent, while for Negroes it was 7.7 percent and for Puerto Ricans it was 7.6 percent[15] The official rate was challenged, however. JeRoyd W. Greene, Jr., the president of Operation Breakthrough in New Haven, an organization which sought to improve employment opportunities for the "hard-core" unemployed, said in 1968 that a "conservative" estimate would be between 12 and 15 percent of the total city population.

In the area of education, New Haven had become accustomed to feeling a certain amount of pride. Its school administrators were professionals, and they were believed to be relatively successful at attracting bright, energetic teachers to the city system. The teacher-pupil ratio was down (to 1 to 21 in 1967, from 1 to 26

---

[14] Sixty-nine of the nation's 500 largest industrial corporations had plants in Connecticut, and 30 of the 500 had plants in the New Haven area. Among those in and around New Haven were United Aircraft, U.S. Steel, Swift, Monsanto, Textron, Uniroyal, Consolidated Foods, B. F. Goodrich, Olin Mathieson, American Machine & Foundry, Stanley Works, and Western Electric. An executive of one of the largest firms in New Haven, the Winchester-Western firearms plant, a division of Olin Mathieson Chemical Corporation, estimated that about 15,000 Connecticut citizens were employed by the firearms industry, at an annual payroll of more than $100 million. About 800 of those employed in the military ammunition section of the industry were in New Haven. ("State's Gun Industry Employs 15,000, Has Annual Payroll Over $100 Million," *The New Haven Register,* June 2, 1969.)
[15] Community Progress, Incorporated, "Summary of Programs," *op. cit.*

five years before), and this was no easy feat for an urban school system.

Still, there were troublesome statistics. The National Education Association surveyed the system in 1967 and found that the students' reading achievement levels ranged from one month below grade level in the second grade to fourteen months below in the eighth grade. The New Haven Board of Education did its own survey, which it released in May 1968, and which showed that 43 percent of the students in the city read one to two years below level, and 4 percent were three years below grade level. The New Haven Commission on Equal Opportunities, which presented those statistics in a study it did of education, commented: "Reading is the key to the entire learning process. This renders the above facts staggering, if not criminal . . . we consider this an intolerable practice demanding immediate remedy."[16]

There were other disquieting statistics:

The turnover of students in the city's schools, almost always a sign of social upheaval of some sort, was high, ranging from 20 to 40 percent of the student bodies.

Vandalism and violence contributed statistics of their own. In the first five months of the 1968 to 1969 school year, the city spent $40,000 replacing broken windows in school buildings. But such vandalism seemed minor compared with the real violence that occurred in 1967 and 1968.

The first such outbreak occurred in December 1967 at Hillhouse High. According to some reports, it started when a Negro girl decided not to stand during the recital of the Pledge of Allegiance. A white boy behind her punched her in the back. Black students, angered when they found out that the white boy had not been expelled for his actions, squared off against white students in the school cafeteria, and before long there was a melee, with the arrival of police, the use of Mace, arrests, and injuries.

In early 1968 there were similar incidents at Hillhouse again,

---

[16] New Haven Commission on Equal Opportunities, "A Report on Racial Discrimination and Tensions in the New Haven Public Schools," undated (but published in 1969).

and at Lee High School, a new school designed by the architectural firm of Kevin Roche–John Dinkeloo and Associates and named after the mayor. (The building had been cited by *Fortune* magazine in 1966 as "one of the best ten buildings of an era.") Police were assigned to the schools on a temporary basis. A few weeks later, there was violence at the Sheridan Middle School.

The Commission on Equal Opportunities conducted an investigation of the school violence, and it concluded, in a comment that was directed at academic institutions in general, that:

> Students are revolting against the enormity of the schools and classrooms in a giant system which renders them insignificant and powerless as individuals. They are protesting against a philosophical approach which rewards "giving the teacher the answer he wants" rather than one which fosters creativity. Students are rebelling against the mediocrity which pervades educational institutions everywhere.
>
> Administrators who are chosen on the basis of political influence rather than competence or expertise frequently design and administer policies which are both irrelevant and unjust to the student body. They perpetuate an out-dated establishment rule which sorely needs to be re-evaluated periodically and subsequently implemented and up-dated in order to be pertinent to its stated goals of producing an educated citizenry. Students object with keen perceptiveness to instructors whose own limitations allow them to continue in their posts without adequate classroom preparation, demanding little except attendance of their pupils, and, accordingly, achieving negligible educational results. Vague in their pedagogical presentations, they are often stern and authoritarian regarding classroom behavior and in their disciplinary methods.

The specific troubles in New Haven, said the commission, grew out of "long smoldering discontent involving high school principals, faculty and students. . . . Increasing racial tensions and consequent police actions have served to exacerbate this situation."

On the basis of testimony from 65 persons, the commission came up with the following conclusions:

- Although the sort of evidence that might stand up in court was lacking, the "weight and color" of the testimony indicated that "racial prejudice does exist among teachers and administrators in the New Haven school system."

• The inability of the students to read was appalling.

• Guidance counseling was geared to the youth who was headed for college, the " 'success-oriented' middle-class youngster," and not to "most Black and Hispanos students."

• One of the commission's prime recommendations was that there be more community participation in the running of the schools:

> One of the most powerful issues we face in urban education today—to which New Haven is no exception—is the basic position of powerlessness from which Black and Hispanos parents operate. It is our thesis that for them to become truly involved in the educational system they must have a powerful voice in its decisions and directions.
>
> We recommend that some form of significant community participation be incorporated into the structure of the New Haven public school system, demonstrating that parents and professional educators are partners in public education.
>
> We must also call attention to the fact that the present Board of Education which serves a predominantly non-White population itself remains conspicuously White, and with no Hispanos representation. We believe that an increase of Black representatives and the addition of Hispanos to the Board of Education is essential.[17]

Those few statistics and facts about the problems of education might seem minuscule, compared to those faced by students and their parents in cities such as New York, where the system of public education was almost completely broken down. But to New Haveners, and the residents of many other American cities, the unresolved issues of school desegregation, teacher quality, and community participation were large ones indeed. During the late sixties much of the wrath of people caught up in New Haven's urban crisis was turned on their school system.

[17] *Ibid.*

And there were other statistics:

• It cost more to run the city. With the affluent whites leaving, the city needed to spend more on social services, but the old taxes would not bring in enough. In 1969 Mayor Lee asked for, and the Board of Aldermen approved, a budget of almost $53 million, which was more than $6 million higher than the budget of the previous year.

But the tax base was shrinking. Worried researchers discovered that one-third of all New Haven property—about $278 million worth—was tax-exempt (and one-third of *that* was owned by Yale). If taxes were paid on that property, the city would get an extra $17 million a year.

In the meantime, the cost of running a city was increasing rapidly, in New Haven as elsewhere. The welfare caseload went up, as did the reported crime rate.[18] The birth rate fell, but the rate of illegitimate births doubled between 1962 and 1967. At the same time, it was discovered that the median weight for white infants born in New Haven was 3,240 grams, while for nonwhite infants it was 3,082 grams.

• Although there was a feeling of general prosperity, due in part to Connecticut's and New Haven's cashing in on the industries of war, it was possible to determine that the prosperity was limited. In other words, the rich were getting richer and the poor were very likely to continue in their poverty. Connecticut's per-capita personal income in 1967 was $3,865, the highest in the nation. The median family income in the New Haven metropolitan area in 1959 had been $6,620; for the city itself it had been $5,864, and for nonwhites in the city it had been $4,205. Researchers projected that the city median would rise to $8,260 by 1980, but they added this grim comment:

". . . this 40 per cent overall increase in real income masks the continuing discrepancies between income groups, Thus, while 35

---

[18] The Federal Bureau of Investigation (whose statistics are questioned by some critics) reported a 124 percent increase in crimes against persons in New Haven during the year 1968, along with a 58 percent increase in crimes against property.

per cent of the population will be earning more than $10,000 per year (compared with 15 per cent in 1959), 24 per cent of New Haven families will be earning less than $5,000 (compared with 38 per cent in 1959)."[19]

• Pollution was not a problem of the big cities alone. In New Haven, 360 manufacturing plants contributed industrial waste to the air, making it frequently as gray and poisonous-looking as New York City's sky. One hundred and one firms dumped 32,200,000 gallons of waste every day into the sewers, the rivers, or the New Haven harbor, most of it untreated or inadequately treated. "Pollution within the inner harbor," said a report, ". . . has reached levels which have made it necessary to prohibit swimming and the taking of shellfish for human consumption." In eleven years, the city had spent $20 million on the war against pollution, "the most dramatic and significant effort of its kind ever undertaken in Connecticut," but that had only been able to make a small dent in the problem.[20]

• New Haven's police department was slow in becoming a professional organization. The police, armed with a series of absurd laws that could be used repressively (such as "Found Intoxicated," "Lascivious Carriage," "Being in Manifest Danger of Falling into Habits of Vice," and the old standby, the "Breach of Peace" holding charge, which was used without a great deal of discrimination), their little black spray cans of Mace, and a department leadership that exhibited little interest in individual rights, were jumpy and unpredictable and very dangerous in any but the most routine situations.

They became particularly nervous when in the presence of large crowds of people whom they did not understand. Such crowds included Negroes. (Until 1968 not one of New Haven's 31 nonwhite policemen, out of a total of 446, had been allowed to rise above the rank of patrolman.) Neither did the police seem to understand young people, regardless of their race.

---

[19] New Haven Redevelopment Agency, City Plan Commission, and the Citizens Action Commission, *op. cit.*
[20] *Ibid.*

Crowds of the sort that bothered the police tended to gather in New Haven at the Arena, a large, old coliseum that was used for sporting events, concerts, and exhibitions. In December 1965 the police got out of hand and attacked a crowd during a concert there by the popular black singer, James Brown, and charges of police brutality resulted. The New Haven Commission on Equal Opportunities, in a report on the incident, declared that the police had used "poor judgment" and "excessive force."

In another incident involving the Arena, the police showed their dislike for, and misunderstanding of, a group of whites who bothered the police because they were young and liberated-looking —that is, they wore modern clothes, some of them had long hair, and they failed to exhibit what the police seemed to consider the proper degree of respect for authority—namely, total.

The occasion was also a musical concert, this time by a white acid-rock group, the Doors. Before the performance the police sprayed Mace in the face of the group's lead singer when they found him in a dressing room talking (he said) or necking (some of the police said) with a girl.[21]

The concert went on as scheduled, although a little late. Policemen ringed the stage and the coliseum. They did nothing when the singer, Jim Morrison, who was noted for his lusty lyrics and singing techniques, writhed sensuously and screamed a few incoherent phrases that could be identified as obscenities only by someone who had studied the lyrics seriously. Later on, however, when the singer started to tell, in song, about the incident backstage with the Mace, the police moved in, arrested him, and caused a near-panic among the spectators, many of whom they shoved, intimidated, and arrested. The singer was charged with giving an indecent performance. It was the police who were indecent that night.

---

[21] Later, some policemen, in referring to the incident, seemed to justify their actions on the grounds that the singer was not just talking at all, but kissing and hugging the girl. Left unsettled was the question of whether the police had a right to painfully immobilize a young man for kissing and hugging a young woman in the privacy of his dressing room.

Among the particular targets of the police that evening, as in subsequent demonstrations of police rioting such as Chicago at the time of the Democratic Convention of 1968, were members of the press. A group of journalists working on a magazine story about rock music was there, and some of the reporters were arrested. What appeared to be overtures were soon received from the city, as the cases approached trial, that indicated that if the reporters and photographer pleaded guilty a small fine would be imposed and the whole thing forgotten. The reporters decided to fight the allegations, which included the Breach of Peace charge and another, resisting arrest, that seemed to come into play the moment a suspect says "But officer . . ." There were repeated postponements in the trial at the request of the city (the reporters, who had to come from New York for each session, felt the postponements were attempts to discourage them from fighting any longer), and while waiting for their cases to come up the visitors had a chance to observe some of New Haven's justice.

The courtroom where minor offenses were tried was destined for demolition; a new government complex would be built before long, as one of the last stages of Mayor Lee's renewal program. For the time being, court was being held in a large, airy, cube-shaped room that had a balcony and a distinct look, feel, and smell of deterioration.

The judge sat behind the bench, looking mostly down at the papers before him. There was a flaccid American flag at one side. The ceiling was ornate, in a New England way; there were simple wooden mouldings where, in a region less given to emphasizing architectural simplicity, there would have been elaborate plaster carvings. The courtroom, an observer might conclude, could have been handsome, even as it approached demolition, except for the indiscriminate way in which fluorescent fixtures had been hung from the ceiling. The room looked very much like country courtrooms in the Deep South where so much degenerate justice has been handed out. All that was needed to complete the scene was a slowly-revolving wooden-bladed ceiling fan and a cuspidor by the judge's bench.

As court started, a bailiff conducted a parade of shuffling, hat-holding, embarrassed-looking men from a side door that led to the city jail. Most of the men, like most of the spectators, were black. The men hardly ever looked straight at their wives and children and brothers and uncles who sat in the audience; sometimes they stole quick glances.

"Found intoxicated," said a court officer.

"Guilty, ten days," replied the judge, rarely looking up.

Occasionally, when a defendant made a short statement on his own (usually a promise not to do it again), the judge would vary his reply: "Guilty, ten days, execution suspended." And the prisoner would look around, not quite certain what "execution suspended" meant, and the bailiff would hustle him off to another group, the prisoners who would be released. Most of the men, however, returned to the jail a few seconds after they entered the courtroom.

Finally, after a number of postponements, including one in which the witness for the police failed to show because, he said, he had laryngitis, the trial of the journalists took place. One of them, a photographer, had gone to Vietnam on an assignment and thus had forfeited his bail. The other two were found not guilty. During the relatively brief trial, witnesses for both sides were sequestered in the hall outside the courtroom. At one point a youth walked up the stairs and started to enter the courtroom, but he was stopped, for no apparent reason, by a bailiff. The officer told the boy to leave. The boy wagged a finger at the bailiff and started to say: "You know, if you were a regular guy . . ."

He was interrupted by an arm around his neck. A detective, waiting to testify in the Arena case, and wearing civilian clothes, collared the boy, said "You're under arrest," and rushed the frightened, surprised, and unresisting youth down the stairs to the jail, dragging him part of the way. Later the detective returned and said the youth would be charged with "Abusing a police officer." He thought a minute, and then added: "And probably 'found intoxicated.' "

The National Advisory Commission on Civil Disorders had

both negative and positive things to say about the conduct of the New Haven police during and before the August 1967 "disturbance." Said the commission:

> In several of the cities [studied], police-community relations units had been established within the police department. . . . Only those in Detroit, New Haven, and Tucson had been in existence for more than two years prior to the disorder. . . . Four police departments [one of them New Haven's] had specialized complaint bureaus with the department. . . . In eight of the cities surveyed, municipal administrators took some action to strengthen police-community relations. . . . In New Haven, the police department opened a store-front office in the disturbance area where citizens could make complaints or seek assistance. The office was also designed to serve as a cooling-off center to avoid the need for a trip to the central station house in minor matters such as domestic quarrels.[22]

But the commission also noted that some Negroes in New Haven felt the city's police review board was "worthless," and it commented further on allegations of police brutality. Violence in the cities studied, said the commission, "was generated by an increasingly disturbed social atmosphere, in which typically not one, but a series of incidents occurred over a period of weeks or months prior to the outbreak of disorders."

About 40 percent of the "prior incidents" involved "allegedly abusive or discriminatory police actions," said the commission, and these prior incidents were found to be present in New Haven's case. "Negro demonstrations, rallies, or protest meetings" were another source of "prior incidents," and these, too, occurred in New Haven.

Also, said the riot commission, the residents of the ghetto were not limited to feeling that they were the particular targets of police abuse. "The strength of ghetto feelings about hostile police conduct," it said, referring to the nation's ghettoes as a whole, "may even be exceeded by the conviction that ghetto neighborhoods are

---

[22] The National Advisory Commission on Civil Disorders, *op. cit.*

not given adequate police protection." Then the commission quoted
from the report of a community group in New Haven:

> The problems of the adequacy of current police protection
> ranked with "police misconduct" as the most serious sore points
> in police-community relations. . . . When calls for help are
> registered, it is all too frequent that police respond too slowly or
> not at all. . . . When they do come, [they] arrive with many more
> men and cars than are necessary, . . . brandishing guns and add-
> ing to the confusion.[23]

The report of the riot commission bore down heavily on the
point that the institutions of government at all levels—and not
just at the level of the police department—had failed to come to
grips with the problems of the cities. First, said the commission,
speaking of urban America generally, there was a "widening gulf
in communications between local government and the residents of
the erupting ghettoes of the city." Second, "Many city governments are poorly organized to respond effectively to the needs of
ghetto residents, even when those needs are made known to appropriate public officials. . . . In most of the riot cities surveyed
. . . we found little or no meaningful coordination among city
agencies, either in responding to the needs of ghetto residents on
an ongoing basis or in planning to head off disturbances."

Finally, and most importantly, said the commission, "ghetto
residents increasingly believe that they are excluded from the
decision-making process which affects their lives and their community." There was no "neighborhood participation," no "maximum feasible participation." And in issuing this finding, the
commission had a special comment for New Haven:

"In part, this is the lesson of Detroit and New Haven, where
well-intentioned programs designed to respond to the needs of
ghetto residents were not worked out and implemented sufficiently
in cooperation with the intended beneficiaries."

---

[23] Hill-Dwight Citizens Commission on Police Community Relations, "In
Search of Fair and Adequate Law Enforcement," June 1967, quoted in
Ibid.

Such a finding, directed at a city that had prided itself on its "people-programs" and its "community participation," might have surprised some New Haveners. Since 1954 they had been hearing that citizens were actively involved in the plotting of the destiny of their city; that was when Mayor Lee had created the Citizens Action Commission. In 1965, when the question of resident participation became a national issue, thanks to those three little words, "maximum feasible participation," New Haven had moved quickly to establish a Residents' Advisory Committee to inject community thinking into the policy and planning levels at Community Progress, Incorporated.

There had been attacks on the Lee administration before, of course. *The New Haven Register,* which advocated a return to the old values and old morals (and, apparently, to old journalism, judging from its brand of news coverage, its editorials, and its selection of columnists), frequently took issue with anything that sounded like the expenditure of public money. Congressman Robert N. Giaimo, of North Haven, New Haven's representative in Washington since 1958, had attacked early in 1968 the operations of CPI:

> As one who supported the legislation which created the OEO and [community action programs], I certainly did not expect a miracle to result from the implementation and operation of the programs, but I did expect that the infusion of $18 million into a city of only 140,000 would have made substantial impact upon the problems of unemployment and education. Instead I found a great deal of waste: high administrative costs, exorbitant salaries and fringe benefits, and questionable funding practices. . . .
>
> I am concerned about the crisis in our City of New Haven. I am concerned about the plight of the unemployed Negro. I want to do something effective to remedy this situation. Most important of all, I am concerned over the growing disregard for law and order. . . .
>
> We are told that in New Haven, the so-called model city, conditions are worse than ever. The rate of unemployment among Negroes is higher than before; the quality of education in our city schools has definitely deteriorated; there is a serious shortage of adequate low-cost housing for low-income or unemployed

families: there is a serious lack of communications with inner-city neighborhood residents, and there is increasing disregard for law and order. In the light of these deplorable conditions, what has CPI done to remedy these situations? My own impression, verified by investigation, is that CPI has made very little impact.[24]

Congressman Giaimo listed what he found to be CPI's faults:

• Salaries, wages, and fringe benefits for employees accounted for 50 percent of CPI's expenses. More than $90,000 was spent on travel and $60,000 on telephone costs. ". . . the money we are appropriating is not getting to the poor in the form of action programs," he said.

• CPI's "administrative superstructure," which he likened to an inverted pyramid, "has created a great deal of hostility in the black community."

• CPI had used its propaganda machine to create "the image that it is achieving monumental results." The agency had distorted the statistics showing the success of its programs. Persons enrolled in the manpower program were counted twice—once when they entered a training program and again when they were placed in jobs.

• CPI's publicity was successful from one standpoint—in propelling Mitchell Sviridoff, its former director, "to a $50,000 job at the Ford Foundation."

Such criticism may have delighted some skeptics and critics in New Haven, but it also was of limited significance. Congressman Giaimo had been a critic of CPI and the Lee administration for some time; he was a political figure, and political figures are likely to sound off in the *Congressional Record;* and he was a member of the House of Representatives, which is not known for its penny-pinching nature when it comes to such matters as fringe benefits, travel and telephone expenses.

What *did* surprise some New Haveners was an event which occurred in the spring of 1968, almost simultaneously with the

---

[24] Hon. Robert N. Giaimo of Connecticut, "Investigation Into the Operations of Community Progress, Inc.," *Congressional Record,* January 18, 1968.

publication of the riot commission report. This condemnation of the city's efforts came from the Ford Foundation, the very father of CPI and its "people-programs." There was not enough resident participation in New Haven, said the foundation.

Actually, the Ford investigation of CPI was carried out in June 1967, shortly before the riot, but it did not come to the attention of the public until March 1968, when *The New Haven Register,* in one of those rare bursts of resourceful journalism that it seemed to save for stories which embarrassed the Lee administration, published a good-sized chunk of it in an eight-column-wide story across the top of Page One. The news story, and an accompanying editorial, made the point that the Ford Foundation study had been kept "under wraps" and never released to the general public. *The Register* obtained a copy of the 41-page mimeographed document without official sanction from the foundation.[25]

The foundation later denied that the report was any sort of a secret document. It was more in the nature of a memorandum to be circulated among offices, said Mitchell Sviridoff, the ex-CPI leader who had become vice president of the foundation. In an interview, Sviridoff commented: "The report wasn't suppressed because it was an internal document. Those things are done, really, as discussion documents, so that the foundation has something—a jump-off point—for discussion, and they usually are deliberately provocative. . . . They are not evaluations in depth. They tend to be very superficial." He said, however, that he thought "much of what it said was accurate."

The authors of the evaluation noted that they had started their

---

[25] The editorial, entitled "Ford And CPI Sit On A Report," seemed more outraged over the unavailability of the document than anything it said. "It is typical of the Ford Foundation's own cool isolation and of CPI's ingrained arrogance," said *The Register,* "that nary a hint of these officially-stated deficiencies was offered to the community for evaluation in the community's own terms. Instead it has been—once again—a case of big-brother at the Foundation and big-brother at CPI getting together in confidential terms to hush-up any notion of waste or weakness and to settle things quietly between themselves. The point of all this is a simple one: Ford Foundation officials are willing to pour millions of their easy-come, easy-go dollars into New Haven but they are not really willing to share decisions within the community."

work with "high expectations." For one thing, Ford had put a lot of money into the agency—$5 per capita since CPI started. The report also said:

> One finds in the small city of New Haven many contrasts. Indeed, some are so unexpected as to be almost unbelievable. Here is an urban setting which for a decade has served as the focal point for pioneering efforts to redevelop and revitalize blighted areas. Downtown glistens and some neighborhoods have been handsomely rehabilitated. In 1962 New Haven's leadership began a social development effort which has been hailed by the national press and attracted visitors from all parts of the world. A multi-million-dollar manpower training and job placement system operated which has helped place thousands into jobs. An aura of success surrounds the city—especially when viewed from afar.
>
> Up close, one sees the attractive new integrated town houses in the Dixwell neighborhood, but also the Hill neighborhood pocked with dilapidated housing where many of the Dixwell relocatees have crowded in. There are the organized residents of public housing in West Rock successfully negotiating improved services from the Housing Authority, while on oppressive Grand Avenue in Fair Haven poor Negroes gather in a tiny storefront to make primitive plans for desperately needed social services, as if the glowing ten years of community renewal had never touched them.
>
> One meets intelligent young Negro dropouts who have made it into prosperous career lines through the manpower network; but files in the neighborhood employment centers are bulging with cards of hard-core unemployed the network has never been able to help.
>
> Visitors are badgered by small groups of residents who complain because so much is decided for their neighborhoods without their involvement.
>
> New Haven is a complex of contradictions and paradoxes. To make an accurate appraisal of its social development effort is difficult. Evidence can be found to support any hypothesis, positive or negative.

The survey team said it had encountered many groups of "neighborhood people" who complained that CPI and Mayor Lee retained all the power, rarely consulting with the citizens. A group of mothers from the Dixwell and Newhallville neighborhoods

charged that CPI "has made no significant impact on the fundamental problems of employment, housing, and education in their
community," said the report, "because residents are not consulted
and do not participate meaningfully in program development and
implementation." The Residents Advisory Committee, said the
investigators, "is considered a 'rubber stamp' by these mothers
because allegedly elected representatives are not allowed enough
time to bring proposed programs back to the community for consideration, discussion, and amendment."

The report continued:

> . . . the review team found some disparity between image and
> activities. CPI has achieved much and created a number of serv-
> ices and approaches now part of the national antipoverty pro-
> gram. But the momentum of innovation does not seem to have
> been sustained, and the indispensable tools of research and resi-
> dent participation seem to have been insufficiently employed. . . .

Specifically, the researchers found that New Haven had fallen
victim to the thing that Mayor Lee had created, out of necessity,
early in his career at City Hall: the "executive-centered coalition"
or "order," as Professor Dahl called it. Said the Ford survey team:

> It was assumed that power-plus planning, without the ingredi-
> ent of "community participation," would lead to success—an
> assumption more valid five years ago than today.
> During its early and formative years, CPI's strategy aimed at
> producing results through carefully controlled services delivered
> to neighborhood people. In a time when urban people are de-
> manding more of a voice in the decisions that control their lives,
> this strategy has inevitably given rise to severe pressures inside
> and outside the organization. . . .
> Social action has been discouraged; it would pose threats to
> the coalition. Neighborhood organizations have been encouraged,
> but largely as conduits, antennae, and supporters, rather than
> as social action organizations.
> This old strategy produced tangible gains but resulted in con-
> flict.

Among the conflicts that resulted, said the team, were controversies over "maximum feasible participation." CPI had re-

sponded by enlarging its board and establishing the Residents Advisory Committee.

These changes provided the beginning of a structure for participation, but the new RAC and neighborhood councils were delegated no formal powers, and they gained none through their own efforts. The control strategy remained largely unchanged. Pressures have continued to build up.

It would seem advisable that the CPI Board of Directors, with the RAC, develop a more contemporary and aggressive strategy to meet new opportunities, in order to broaden resident participation in the decision-making of the organization.

Such a recommendation—that New Haven, the pioneer city, the city that had started being reborn long before other cities had caught on to the fact that they were dying, "develop a more contemporary and aggressive strategy" in resident participation—must have hurt some of the people at CPI and at City Hall. Yet, said the survey team, such a revised strategy was needed if the city was to avoid its continued "piecemeal reaction to crises."

The investigators came up with these additional specific findings, among others:

• CPI should develop a mechanism for disbursing funds to neighborhood organizations that will not result in co-option of the organizations' leaders. "As the few independent, critical groups in the city are given CPI grants," asked the team, "what will happen to their independence? Dependence upon any single source of funds—such as CPI—and preoccupation with details of operating a service program may sap the militancy of a neighborhood organization and divert it from a vital function as a CPI critic."

• CPI's manpower program—which accounted for the largest single portion of the agency's budget and which was distinguished by the neighborhood centers—was slowing down as it finished skimming the cream of the unemployed and approached the infinitely more difficult task of finding jobs for the "hard-core" unemployed.[26] CPI's "admitted failure to establish a continuing

---

[26] In many, if not most, of the other cities of the nation in the summer of 1967, the business of finding jobs for the "hard-core" unemployed had not even been considered.

working relationship with large employers for job development purposes," said the team from Ford, "suggests dim prospects for helping many hard-core workers. . . ."

· In education, the investigators took a look at the community schools. The community schools, "Opening Opportunities" had stated back in 1962, would be the "central focus," a "community institution" through which neighborhoods would be given "more meaning." Said the investigators:

> . . . the review team questions whether or not these facilities are only handsome buildings offering ordinary recreational, health, and education services. The team was unimpressed with the newness of the community schools and their routine operation. . . . This much-touted and expensive program appeared to be merely a morning-to-night offering of voluntary services.

· In human relations, the Ford investigators found that CPI was not doing enough; its manpower and educational programs were "only scratching the surface. Here again," said the team,

> there is reason for involving more neighborhood people of all races in decision-making and bringing them into program development. . . . The review team heard accusations by critics of the CPI program that the organization has attempted to co-opt civil rights leadership by offering jobs to the most powerful voices. Furthermore, CPI seems to have done a minimum toward promoting a racially-mixed central professional staff.

· There was praise for one of CPI's projects, its legal services program, which was operated by the New Haven Legal Assistance Association. The program, "a unique and true experiment in providing aid for the poor," should be made permanent, said the team.

· CPI's research and evaluation unit, which was not involved in the day-to-day, actual running of programs, was found wanting: It was staffed by people who were well-trained but "somewhat removed from the day-to-day problems of the neighborhood. . . . CPI should serve not only as a laboratory for scholars and intellectuals who are primarily interested in fundamental research. Research should be action-oriented to be effective."

• The Community Progress, Incorporated, staff was found to be "impressive" and of "high caliber," but there was a great deal of turnover. In addition, some staffers from the central office "rarely visit the neighborhoods." This, said the team, "suggests among other things that they may prefer CPI's more familiar method of 'giving' services rather than working out solutions to problems with the people."

The upshot of the Ford investigators' findings, as could be seen from their specific remarks, was that there was not enough resident participation, neighborhood participation, citizen participation, or maximum feasible participation in New Haven. The researchers said:

> Members of the review team are keenly aware from their experiences with a variety of social development projects in recent years that the problem of the city cannot be solved without the involvement of the people, including the residents of the "middle-ground neighborhoods." Unless the people are involved as decision-makers, the projects are nothing but souped-up versions of the welfare game which has had limited success in the past and has fallen into disrepute. . . .
>
> [The team's] analysis points to one conclusion. CPI seems to be cast in the mold of doing for rather than with people, and is having a most difficult time breaking out of this mold. . . . The "executive coalition" strategy has resulted in limited, elitist resident participation at the neighborhood level as at the city-wide level. Needed is machinery for large-scale participation, whether it be block clubs, neighborhood conferences, or some totally new form.
>
> Within a developing national climate of open urban democracy, no city can successfully keep to a control strategy in social development programming. The more CPI attempts to deliver without indigenous participation in planning and execution the more it is likely to fail. No amount of technical expertise and public relations can make the control approach work.[27]

---

[27] "Report," to John R. Coleman, program officer in charge, office of social development, the Ford Foundation, from "Consultant Review Team," August 1967.

The reaction of CPI to this criticism from the foundation that had created it was one of hurt, and barely suppressed anger. There were "factual errors" in the Ford document; the review team had gotten some of its information from members of a group (not named, but presumably the Hill Parents Association) who did not really represent the neighborhood; and Ford should have known that CPI, at the time of the investigation, was trying to determine better ways to guarantee neighborhood participation in its decisions and policies. "There should have been no doubt on the Team's part of CPI's genuine concern about expanded neighborhood participation before, during, and after the Team's visit to New Haven," said CPI in a memorandum on the subject.

But all that was suddenly beside the point. It made little difference that in the summer of 1967—a few days before the riot, as it turned out—Community Progress, Incorporated, was thinking about broadening the participation of citizens in its programs.

New Haven was supposed to be several steps ahead of every other city in the nation. It had been many steps ahead with physical renewal. It was ahead in the matter of demolishing homes, demolishing downtown, then rebuilding. It was ahead of all the others when it was a question of plotting the move from physical renewal to human renewal. New Haven was ahead on Head Start; it was ahead on employment; it was ahead on legal services. It was ahead on a lot of things. But it was not ahead on the most vital single issue of the social revolution, the issue that made all the other statistics not quite so important: the participation by the citizens in the decisions affecting their futures.

By the summer of 1967 New Haven was no longer unique. *Every* city of any size and importance was dealing with the issue of citizen participation by the summer of 1967—not necessarily dealing successfully with it, but dealing with it nevertheless. Of all the cities which should have been a step ahead in devising workable plans of community involvement, New Haven was the first. But there was very little citizen involvement in New Haven. The Model City had become tragically typical.

VI
The Citizens Participate

New Haven's just as bad as Mississippi. *In fact, I think it's worse, because of the psychological effect it has on black people. It destroys their minds, you know . . .*

—Comment, in 1968, by Fred Harris, black; president, Hill Parents Association; unsuccessful candidate for the Connecticut House of Representatives; under indictment on a narcotics charge; not long before released from jail after serving 30 days for demonstrating.

About CPI, in 1966: They *would call meetings, at which* their *programs were discussed. There was never, at least at any meeting I ever attended, any opening where the citizen's word would have any kind of direct and obvious impact . . . And that is where CPI and the city and the mayor all failed, as far as I'm concerned.*

—Peter Almond, white; former representative of CPI in the Hill

IT IS, of course, almost impossible to properly define "citizen participation" or any of its synonyms.

The terms have been tentatively defined and redefined almost continually, ever since they first came into use, and what they meant in 1964 is not at all what they meant in 1969. What they meant in New Haven is not what they meant in Jackson, Mississippi. What they meant after January 20, 1969, when Richard Nixon became President, is not what they meant on January 19. What they meant to Lyndon Johnson on January 19 is not what they meant to him a year before.

Among the various and conflicting definitions of the concept, there was what might be called the "emotional definition," with its variations. Widely used by public speakers and writers, it went something like this: Citizen participation is the ability (power, right) of people (citizens, Negroes, dissidents, neighborhoods, Mexican-Americans, communities) to decide (participate in, help decide, direct, control) their own destinies (futures, self-help programs, neighborhoods).

The emotional definition is probably the one that comes closest to describing the feelings of the under-people, along with those of the professors, social workers, and others who try often to serve as their spokesmen, when they talk about citizen participation. And the politicians used it too. Mayor Lee, asked in 1968 what he had found to be important in urban affairs, replied that it was citizen participation, which he defined as people's plotting "their own destiny."

Of course, no people on the face of the earth, with perhaps the exception of a few kings and queens and hermits, have the power to control their own destinies, or even to plan them. It is an exquisite goal to work toward, but as yet no member of a society has attained it.

There was, in addition to the emotional definition, the War on Poverty definition, which was not a single definition at all, but rather a chronology of definitions proceeding out of the use of the words, "maximum feasible participation," in the Economic Opportunity Act of 1964. To a lot of observers, "maximum feasible participation" meant pretty much the same thing as the emotional definition; in practical terms it meant that community action programs set up under Title II of the act would be planned and implemented not just by professors and bureaucrats, but also by the poor.

Some interpreted the words as meaning that the poor would have total control (or, at least, a majority of the votes) in such planning and implementation. Others thought it meant the poor and the not-so-poor would work in equality and harmony; some thought it meant the poor would achieve their maximum participation by *advising* the professors and bureaucrats, by telling the professionals what they thought of the programs, often after the proposals had gone off to Washington and when there was little chance of revising them. Among the group that defined the words in this way must be included most of the mayors and other elected officials of the nation.

One fairly common variation on the definition seemed to be held especially by those who were professionally involved in antipoverty efforts, and by political jurisdictions, such as New York City, that enjoyed a reputation for liberal social involvement. It was a feeling that citizen participation was fine, but that there were limits to it, and the limits were imposed by the citizens' lack of technical competence to deal with complicated problems. This might be called the paternalistic attitude, or definition, since it often was issued by people who sincerely felt they were sympathetic to the plight of the poor but who frequently demonstrated, in their words and actions, that their attitude toward the poor was like the attitude of a parent toward a child.

The attitude of Community Progress, Incorporated, seemed to reflect the paternalistic attitude. Reuben A. Holden, the secretary of Yale University, was an original incorporator of CPI, and for a time was the chairman of its board. When he was asked, in 1968, for his definition of, and feelings on, citizen participation, he replied this way:

"I don't think it's any longer an issue, because everybody accepts it. It's a normal thing now. When we first got started, all of these outfits around the country hadn't really thought of that kind of participation because agencies had never worked that way before. But now they do, and they realize that it's a good thing to do, and they certainly do it in name, and where possible in actual functioning.

"The truth of it is, of course, that a lot of the neighborhood participation at that level is not very active and not that interested. They're interested in the *concept* of it, but when it comes down to the capacity to do it, or the time to do it, or the interest really to follow through with the detail, it's lacking. . . ."

"You can't count on this participation in the neighborhood to be complete. It's going to be spasmodic. It's going to be interested and aggressive at times, and quite indifferent at other times. So you need some stable elements.

"I believe in the idea of representation, but I don't believe they can be left fully responsible, because they just don't have that background or interest or competence to do it all."

The paternalistic argument may seem, to some, a sound one. It is probably true that few "neighborhood people" possess the skill—or, more importantly, the patience—to negotiate the massive piles of paperwork that go into an application for a federal antipoverty grant. But, of course, there is no reason why the massive piles of paperwork cannot be made less massive. And it could be argued that those *with* the skills and professional training haven't been very successful, either. And, too, the fact remains that the neighborhood people have never been allowed to try.

Among the brighter, more sensitive mayors of the nation—those who have been called the "new breed" mayors, those who took advantage of the interest of the Kennedy and Johnson Administrations in urban problems—citizen participation came to mean a further variation on the paternalistic definition: a form of participation that brought the poor and the black into decision-making, but that left the final responsibility in the hands of the chief municipal executive. It meant participation of the same sort, they said, that had been enjoyed for years by the more affluent segments of society. Those mayors' approaches to the question of participation will be discussed in a later chapter.

Of course, some mayors and others in authoritative positions interpreted the words along even more conservative lines. Maximum feasible participation, they argued, meant only that the professionals would decide, and that the nonprofessionals would advise, but also that the poor would not even be directly represented among the powerless advisors. Rather, they would select (or, more likely, have selected for them) their *representatives* to sit in with the professionals. And the representatives of the poor usually turned out to include a priest, a minister, and a rabbi (representatives of a field that had been extremely laggard and short-sighted in matters of civil rights, race relations, and poverty); an educator (part of one of the systems that most needed change, and that most resisted it); a social worker (part of another system that had been engaged in perpetuating the plight of the poor, through the consistent denial to the poor of any opportunity to accumulate dignity), and a representative of organized labor (a system that not only resisted change and perpetuated the problems of the poor, but that often actively worked to make the problems of the black poor even worse).

As of the end of the decade, six years after the three little words had become part of the nation's vocabulary, they still had not been defined properly. One man who was on hand for the creation of the Economic Opportunity Act, Daniel P. Moynihan, wrote a book about the phrase[1] in which he argued that the authors' intent was nothing nearly so exciting as the emotional definition, and not even as exciting as most of the other definitions, either.

It was Moynihan's recollection that the phrase got into the act simply because members of the task force writing the legislation for President Johnson were concerned about Negroes in the South. In those programs under Title I such as the Job Corps and the Neighborhood Youth Corps, the federal government retained tight control and could insure that Southern Negroes would not be the victims of discrimination. "But what of community action," wrote Moynihan, "where local option would decide how to spend the new federal money?"

> Inasmuch as the local white power structure would control the allocation of community action money, how could it be ensured that impoverished Negroes would get something like a

---

[1] Daniel P. Moynihan, *Maximum Feasible Misunderstanding: Community Action in the War on Poverty* (New York: The Free Press, 1969).

proportionate share? The task force . . . came up with the equally obvious answer: Provide for it in the legislation. . . . [An early] White House draft had provided for "appropriate representation of and participation by the key governmental agencies, community and neighborhood groups, and key professional and other organizations in the area. . . ." But the one thing it did *not* provide for was the poor, especially the Southern Negro poor who, whatever else their qualities, certainly were not organized.[2] A simple idea occurred to someone present: Why not include language that would require the poor to participate, much as it was provided that other entities should do so?

Moynihan added that his recollection and available records of the task force's meetings indicated that the inclusion of the phrase

was intended to do no more than ensure that persons excluded from the political process in the South and elsewhere would nevertheless participate in the *benefits* of the community action programs of the new legislation. It was taken as a matter beneath notice that such programs would be dominated by the local political structure.[3]

Congress apparently did not learn its lesson about using such loaded phrases as "maximum feasible participation." Two years after the passage of the Economic Opportunity Act, and at a time

---

[2] Of course, the Southern Negro poor *were* organized, and organized far better than the Northern Negro poor were in 1964, or would be in the following several years.

[3] Moynihan, *op. cit.*, pp. 86–87. Moynihan's own feelings about citizen participation were clear: "It may be that the poor are never 'ready' to assume power in an advanced society," he wrote: "the exercise of power in an effective manner is an ability acquired through apprenticeship and seasoning. Thrust on an individual or a group, the results are often painful to observe, and when what in fact is conveyed is not power, but a kind of playacting at power, the results can be absurd." (*Ibid.*, pp. 136–37.) It should be pointed out that at the time Moynihan wrote his book, he was a scholar—the director of the Joint Center for Urban Studies of the Massachusetts Institute of Technology and Harvard University. Later—at about the time the book was published—he was appointed, as what some called the Token Democrat, to the Nixon Administration, as the executive secretary of the new President's Council on Urban Affairs. Moynihan's views in *Maximum Feasible Misunderstanding,* therefore, did not reflect his friendship with and stewardship in the Nixon Administration. It was possible, however, that his appointment to the Administration reflected his feelings as expressed in *Maximum Feasible Misunderstanding.*

when the m.f.p. thunderstorm was breaking in city halls all across the country, Congress passed the Demonstration Cities and Metropolitan Development Act of 1966, the Model Cities program. The program's purpose, according to its author, Lyndon Johnson, was "To build not just housing units, but neighborhoods, not just to construct schools, but to educate children, not just to raise income, but to create beauty and end the poisoning of our environment."

Right there in Title I, it said that cities would be eligible for participation only if they established comprehensive demonstration programs that promised a number of things: to "make a substantial impact on the physical and social problems and to remove or arrest blight and decay in entire sections or neighborhoods"; to make "marked progress" in alleviating "social and educational disadvantages, ill health, underemployment, and enforced idleness"; and to insure "widespread citizen participation in the program."

In a set of guidelines published in 1967, the Department of Housing and Urban Development further spelled out what was meant by "widespread citizen participation." There would be "constructive involvement of citizens in the Model Neighborhood and the city as a whole in planning and carrying out the program," said HUD, and "the development of means of introducing the views of area residents in policy making and the provision of opportunities to area residents to participate actively in planning and carrying out the program."

In New Haven and in some other cities, HUD allocated funds for demonstration programs that appeared to be heavy on the side of citizen participation—that seemed to follow the guidelines. But times change, and so do the definitions of federal intent. The Nixon Administration quickly assured those interested in the definition of "widespread citizen participation" that it no longer meant, if it ever did,[4] citizen control over citizen destinies. Robert

---

[4] Given President Johnson's obvious displeasure with the way the war on poverty was turning out (it had become, as Moynihan pointed out, a war of the Democratic poor against the nation's Democratic mayors), it was

H. Baida, the deputy assistant secretary for Model Cities, said in a speech in the summer of 1969 that there was a distinct difference between participation and control, and that the new administration was well aware of that difference:

> While the line dividing the two is not always well defined, the message of the administration is clear: The Model Cities program is not to be controlled by citizen groups. Control and responsibility rests with local government. Unfortunately, this administration inherited a philosophy in many areas of the country dedicated toward extensive citizen control.

"Citizen participation," then, like beauty, has been in the eye of the beholder since its first mention. It may at first have meant some sort of protection for the poor and allegedly defenseless Negroes of the South. Whatever its meaning, and regardless of who its beholders were, the fact is that a lot of people were turned on by the idea. The lunch-counter sit-ins in the South in the early sixties were the beginning of a distinct phase of the movement for civil rights and, as it turned out, for black togetherness. It was necessary for those sit-ins—relatively harmless, really—to take place before their organizers could learn that the freedom to sit at a lunch-counter was negligible unless the person sitting there had a decent job which allowed him the further freedom of buying his lunch. So it was with the words "citizen participation." It was not until the issue came up that people started demanding it. And

---

not too difficult to imagine that the Model Cities program represented a retreat from the "unconditional" war on poverty that the President had promised. Commented one Democratic mayor, who had been accustomed to getting handsome antipoverty grants from Washington, but who was dismayed at what had happened after the disenchantment had set in: "Model Cities is baloney. The Johnson administration, in its last two years, has engaged in delaying tactics and postponing tactics, and I have become an increasingly frustrated man, because I know what's going on, and *I'm* a loyal Democrat. The thing of it is that in order to pay for the war in Vietnam, increasingly the war on poverty and the war to rebuild our cities have been cut back. And so they develop Model Cities, and what is that? All they give you is planning money and now they're even cutting *that* back. The whole Model Cities program was a farce. It was designed to stretch out the buck and get a greater bang for fewer cents."

once they started demanding it, there was no stopping them, although few mayors, urban experts, or elected officials on the national level recognized this.

Citizen participation in New Haven once meant the Citizens Action Commission. Later on, it meant pleas from poor people, demands from poor people, and perhaps it even meant the riot of August 1967. But before the riot, citizens of New Haven had asked for participation in the planning of their own destinies, and their requests had been denied.

The city's action in frustrating those who made the requests—and not the riot—may have been the turning point, the moment at which New Haven ceased being a Model City and started being just a typical city. New Haven, the leader, did no better than other cities—places like New York City, Rochester, Chicago, Philadelphia, Birmingham, Los Angeles—when it came time to recognize that a denial of citizen participation would mean certain disaster. One by one, the cities of America refused to allow more than token participation, and one by one they fell.

It was not surprising that the citizens who made the demands in New Haven came from the Hill neighborhood, which had been a dumping ground for persons relocated—sometimes more than once—from the other urban renewal areas, and a neighborhood which had seen little renewal or rehabilitation of its own. And it was not surprising that one of the names that came up, again, was Fred Harris.

Mayor Lee had been advised before about people like Fred Harris. Mitchell Sviridoff, in that 1959 memorandum, had told Lee that the "responsible radical may fail to show proper appreciation for progress," and his "behavior may even border on downright discourtesy." But, Sviridoff had added, communications must be maintained with the responsible radical.

Fred Harris fit the description of a "responsible radical" almost perfectly. He was a leader, and a good one, with an appreciation of, and communication with, people on the street, and he had a facility for failing to show proper appreciation for what others called progress and, sometimes, for being downright discourteous. Such attributes should not have been surprising or disgusting to the white leaders of New Haven—especially those, like the mayor, who were familiar with the Irish Catholic politics of New England —but they were. The white Establishment failed to recognize Harris' leadership; at first it ignored him, his organization, and their requests and demands, despite the fact that the Hill Parents Association was obviously one of the few truly grass-roots groups in New Haven. And in the end, according to some interpretations, the whites deliberately had Fred Harris and several of his associates arrested and jailed in an exhibition of the Establishment's desire to forbid dissent, even reasonable dissent.

Fred Harris was born in September 1937 in New Haven. Like Mayor Lee, he was born in a cold-water flat. He remembered that it was a big thrill to be able to move into a public housing project, because in the project there was running hot water. His father was a waiter at the Yale Faculty Club, and when Fred was old enough he worked at Yale, too, where he was impressed with the clothing and carriage of the white students. "I got the idea that the essence of cool was wearing a three-button suit and a rep tie," said Harris one time, "and it took me a long time to undo that." In 1969 he was wearing colorful clothing of African origin.

Harris grew up, married, became a father, and lived in the Hill. He developed a definition of "citizen participation," the emotional definition: "People should be allowed to determine their own destiny." Harris readily agreed that few people are allowed such luxury. But it was necessary to work toward such a lofty goal, he said: "I think you have to take that position, because if you want to change things, I don't think you can compromise. You have to work for the ultimate goal, or work to overshoot the target, because most of the time you're going to get half of what you ask for, or a quarter, or you might get lucky and get three-quarters.

"But it's very necessary for people to determine their own destiny if this country is really honestly concerned about dealing with the issues and the problems. And if people don't determine their own destiny, then they cannot be productive and cannot contribute anything to the city or the state or the country. And the danger of controlling one's own destiny means that you might just eradicate welfare. You just might eradicate bad schools. You just might have a whole lot of people that can meet the impossible, or the almost impossible, qualifications that are generally put on ghettoized people in order to get, for instance, jobs. And the man realizes that. He realizes it very clearly."

At first, Fred Harris could have been called an integrationist. Throughout his youth, because of his father's job at Yale, he had been exposed not only to whites, but to whites who thought of themselves as far above prejudice and intolerance. He thought— erroneously, he said later—that there might be enough decent whites in and around New Haven who could be aroused to help their Negro brethren. So in 1966, at the age of 29, Fred Harris ran for a seat in the Connecticut General Assembly. He ran as an independent candidate in the 106th Assembly District, a district that was curiously gerrymandered to include a small portion of the Hill, the railroad station and other slum buildings near the Harbor, and Wooster Square. His Democratic opponent was Anthony N. Ciarlone, and the Republican was Paul Capra.

The New Haven Register practically ignored Harris' candidacy, but in a roundup of candidates' feelings on issues the newspaper did manage to ask Harris the same questions it asked the other contenders. Harris said he was opposed to a sales tax; that money should be raised from "those with money to spare" such as businesses—especially those "making so much money from the New Haven Redevelopment Agency"; large real estate holders, especially slumlords; and the well-to-do. If elected, he said, he would attempt to keep government from "running over the people, especially the poor." He wanted industry to bear the cost of cleaning up the Mill River, which ran through the district, on the grounds that industry had polluted it. Other issues raised by the other candidates included state aid to deaf mutes, automobile driving courses for foreigners, and state aid for private schools (which the Democratic candidate was for). Ciarlone won the election with 1,584 votes; Capra was second with 857, and Harris came in last with 119.

Some time later, Harris discussed the campaign. "It was impossible to win," he said, "but I was naïve enough to think that if white people knew the problems in the Hill, and also middle-class blacks, they would get involved and help us. That was the only ground I ran on. But that failed, and it really opened my eyes at how people really are and how this city is.

"But running also provided me a platform to speak from, and get to the ears of the people, and that was the real reason why I ran. I wasn't really interested in being a state assemblyman."

Sharing the platform with Harris was his organization, the Hill Parents Association, which had been formed not long before around the issue of the quality of public education, and which was expanding its goals.[5] The HPA had its origins in a predominantly white organization called the Hill Neighborhood Union that had been established by the Yale students Harris had once envied. Eventually the Union was absorbed by neighborhood blacks. "Then it was taken over by the Hill Parents Association," said Harris, "which was a group of people who had got together around a school issue and gathered people together. Then they were victorious in getting rid of the principal at the school, getting the school cleaned up, getting new books, getting the school painted and getting the floors washed and waxed and things like that." The organization's scope enlarged to take in protests over the welfare system. A march was held on the state welfare offices in Hartford; the police broke it up, and Harris went to jail for 30 days on a breach of peace conviction.

Although the HPA had changed in leadership from white to

---

[5] By 1967 the HPA was describing itself (in a legal action seeking to restrain the city from harassing it) as "a non-stock corporation organized under the laws of Connecticut, its purposes being to eliminate prejudice and discrimination, to defend and exercise human and civil rights, to combat community deterioration, and in accomplishing these ends to work toward the solution of problems of discrimination, sub-standard housing, unemployment, inadequate schools and related problems of poverty and racism, in the area of New Haven known as 'The Hill,' and in other ghetto areas of New Haven."

black, Harris never engaged in the sort of anti-white racism that some other black leaders have found necessary as an initial organizing tool. Mike Avery, a white Yale law student at the time, and an HPA worker, marveled at Harris' ability to maintain alliances with his white friends while he was asserting his black leadership of the organization.

"All I'd done before," said Avery, "was the *noblesse oblige* type of Yale student activity—tutoring and so on. There were three or four of us in that kind of program who decided that what we'd been doing all along was a kind of baby-sitting at best, and not worth too much, and we decided to move over to the Hill and start working for Fred and the HPA.

"HPA has a thing going, I think, and Fred and HPA have a very sophisticated way of relating to white people who want to help. I think the white people who are involved in HPA are sensitive to the kind of role they should be playing, and that HPA, on the other hand, has the attitude that they need some of the skills that some of the white students have, and they utilize their skills in a way that's very constructive. And now HPA has a history: It's an organization that's run by black people, and by black people from the community, and the question of white students' taking it over or running things is not a real question. It just doesn't happen."

It was essential that HPA's first and major function be to organize New Haven blacks. All around the nation in the late sixties, black community organizations were trying to do this, but in New Haven the task was perhaps a little more difficult. For years the black leadership, as it had emerged, had been quickly co-opted by the white leadership. A Negro who broke the surface and was obviously skilled, or articulate, or both, had little difficulty getting a job in CPI or the Redevelopment Agency, where his value as a potential dissenter, of course, would be quickly wiped out.

Harris, commenting on this, noted that in the latter part of the decade Negroes in New Haven were "together," but they were not organized. "New Haven is such a conservative town," he said.

"the only thing here was the NAACP and CORE, and CORE has sort of petered out; it had a lot of white people in it. And this kept away a lot of blacks. After HPA got started, this was a new kind of thing: It was the first real militant *black* organization that was saying the things that black people really wanted to say. Whites were working with us, and trying to help in any way they could help, but it was under *our* leadership, which was a completely different type of thing from what CORE and NAACP had been. The whites who had been involved with them were sort of leading the thing. Now, HPA has set the tone in this city; HPA is the ones who are really making the black people move."

Some of the motion came during Fred Harris' 1966 assembly campaign, and the result, according to many knowledgeable observers, was that the city became intensely aware of HPA's presence and started considering it, and Harris, as threats to what they considered the public good. An overture was made to Harris from a black politician whom Harris considered a stooge of Lee; would he like to run for something as a Democrat? Harris refused. "We were really shaking them up with the campaign," recalled Harris. "This was a very unusual campaign to most people in the city, except for the neighborhood people, who had never been involved in campaigns before. We ran it just like the day-to-day workings of HPA—going into people's homes, talking about the problems, and addressing ourselves to the problems. And trying to eliminate the individual problems of the people who had them, which was most of the people. A lot of the problems did get solved—problems like people not knowing how to deal with the Redevelopment Agency and landlords and things like that. At least we made some temporary change for the people, and they recognized that. And I think it sort of formulated a *base,* because most of those people who were involved in the campaign are still active today in some form or another, or if they're called upon they'll be active."

Among the agencies which were shook up by the Harris campaign and the emergence of the Hill Parents Association was Community Progress, Incorporated, the organization that was supposed to be the community action agency in the Hill and elsewhere.

Peter Almond, a young white man, was one of CPI's bright young employees at that time. He surprised some of his superiors in September 1966 by asking to be sent to one of the neighborhoods, rather than to an assignment in the central office. "I sought the opportunity," he recalled, "to get out of the mainstream of the antipoverty agency administration and go find out what was on the other end of all those programs that I wrote up and negotiated with federal and foundation officials over."

The CPI coordinator on the Hill, a black man named Charles Simmons, welcomed Almond, who later was to succeed him. "I was sort of moving against the stream," said Almond, describing his departure to the Hill. "The normal flow, if you're making progress in an institution like the poverty program, was to go from the neighborhood office to the central office, to a bigger and better title with a bigger and better office, and so on—all the trappings of any other institution." What fascinated Almond was the prospect of learning to serve, as "Opening Opportunities" had described it back in 1962, as a "bridge between residents and service agencies," as an advocate for the neighborhood, as a person whose presence would be "tangible evidence of community concern for people and their problems."

Almond arrived in the Hill at about the time the Harris campaign was getting under way. "I was fascinated by the fact," he said, "that CPI was so closely identified with the opposition. That is, even though they didn't come out and support the two party candidates against Harris, it was quite clear that they were involved in a real resistance to the radical community organizers" who worked with Harris and the HPA. "I had this kind of morally outraged response that this was simply wrong for this agency, which was supposed to be dealing with the community, supporting community organization work as well as providing basic social services, to be taking a side one way or the other.

"I guess I would have argued—or I hope I would have argued—that we should not have supported Harris either, in his campaign. But we should have kept ourselves open to the new movement that really represented what was going on in the Hill, in what was going on in the kind of awakening parts of the black Hill. So this was a fascinating introduction for me. I don't think that I would have been as intensely aware of the militants' activity and the essential irresponsibility of the city officials and the anti-poverty agency officials—my superiors, I guess—in their resistance to Harris and to the Hill Parents Association, had it not been for that campaign.

"They were resistant to Harris essentially because he was a troublemaker; because he defied the system which operated more effectively in the Hill than anyplace else: a system of highly centralized, effective neighborhood operation, which consolidated a number of community organizations which promoted service activities like the Boy Scouts."

When Almond arrived in the Hill office, he found it an example of what he called the "Bureau of the Budget concept of the war on poverty. That is, a good central bureaucracy, like CPI had, supports a strong neighborhood program where you have firm leadership, clear direction, rather innocuous community organization work going on—you know, civic groups that don't go any further than you want them to—and the CPI neighborhood officials relate to the CPI *downtown* officials, who, in turn, relate to City Hall."

Few CPI downtown officials, said Almond, were talking about citizen participation in any way similar to the way in which the neighborhood people were discussing the concept. "What was so disappointing to me," he said, "was that most of the directives regarding citizen participation were restrictive: They would say that one had gone too *far* in one project or another."

There were several CPI staffers, said Almond, who were "really quite committed to the concept of community participation and who worked at it full time." But "what was fascinating, of course, was the CPI central office and neighborhood office dilemma on the question of community participation. They were asking 'How do you get people involved?' 'How do you get people to come to a meeting you've called?'

"It was a question of How do you get *them* interested in what *you* are trying to do? *They* would call meetings, at which *their* programs were discussed. There was never, at least at any meeting I ever attended, any opening where the citizen's word would have any kind of direct and obvious impact. And that's just impact; I'm not talking about where the antipoverty official listens to the neighborhood group that has come up with *its* program, which is obviously the other side of the fence. And that is where CPI and the city and the mayor all failed, as far as I'm concerned; failed in the sense that they simply could not tolerate, or understand, or accept the implications and the fact that a neighborhood group could devise and plan and opt to run its own program."

If Fred Harris had been white, and Irish, or perhaps Italian, in New Haven, there is a possibility that the executive-centered coalition down at City Hall and at CPI might have seen its way clear to making some sort of an accommodation with him and with his organization. After all, the Hill Parents Association was emerging as a group with some political strength, and Harris had some of the characteristics of a potential political leader. The assembly campaign, carried out as it was in a gerrymandered district, was really not much proof one way or the other of his real potential. But Fred Harris had two strikes against him: He was black, and he was young. In New Haven, the people who run things are "protective" of the young to the point of repression. And when the young speak up in New Haven, they are put down and silenced as quickly as blacks in the South in the early sixties. Harris had another strike: He had been accused of using heroin. This was later to become an important factor in the city's relations with Fred Harris.

The white leadership of the city may have harbored secret ideas that HPA, Fred Harris, his activist wife, Rose, and others, such as Ron Johnson and Willie Counsel, were something other than troublemakers—that perhaps they could help bring about the city's salvation. If so, this feeling did not come through in the leadership's conversations, both public and private. A black man, who held an important city position, and who might be said to reflect a social-work approach to urban problems, had this to say when asked for his position of HPA's demands for community control of neighborhood programs:

"When you are one of them and you know damn good and well that they represent a very small minority, you know how to react to it. Most of them are not parents in the true sense of the word, and their following is very, very small."

Melvin J. Adams, the city's development administrator, looked upon the criticism voiced by HPA as the somewhat misguided rantings of a group whose expectations had been raised:

"I think part of their problem is a realization that although there's a lot wrong with New Haven, there's also a lot right. And I think for their purposes, they'd be happier if there were less right, because then the confrontation would have more meaning. Part of the increase in criticism, I think, is a reflection of the fact that we have been doing a pretty good job. People in Bridgeport or Waterbury don't make these charges, don't get involved, and those cities have done virtually nothing. In the process of raising opportunities, we raise expectations. People feel that things can change and therefore they can play a greater role in changing them, faster."

For another high city official, Dennis Rezendes, the deputy mayor in charge of administration, Fred Harris was "a mixed-up man."

"He's torn inside," said Rezendes. "He faces the many problems that a young Negro in this city, or throughout the country, faces. He's torn. I think he's let emotions get the better part of him, the better part of his judgment. I don't think he knows himself where he's going. And in the process he doesn't become helpful to himself or—to use his word—to his fellow 'black men.' You cannot, in my opinion, continue to achieve a goal or objective by using the sledgehammer approach. If you're going to have a society that's going to live at peace with itself, there has to be some rational dialogue.

"Their basic argument is valid. It's absolutely right. And I think, through the dialogue process, they can win over the vast majority of white America. And I think they were at this point, and ready to accomplish it, until they went off the deep end. They get the argument hands down. So use it! You can use all kinds of techniques, through the political process and otherwise, and they can be beneficial and help expedite things.

"But you can go to the extreme end and lose white America if you're not careful."

By the spring of 1967 a crisis was developing in New Haven that was evident to many of her citizens and that should have been evident to City Hall, the Redevelopment Agency, and CPI.

The crisis was, quite plainly, the Hill neighborhood. The Hill had benefited little from the imaginative rehabilitation work in Wooster Square (although, thanks to the gerrymandered 106th District, it shared a state legislator with the Italians and the WASPs who lived in the elegant town houses). Many of the other programs touched the Hill not at all or, if they did touch the neighborhood, they were quickly found inadequate. The beneficiaries (as the city would put it) and the victims (as the critics would say) of relocation in other neighborhoods piled into the Hill. On one side, Yale University and its medical center expanded slowly but surely and ominously, adding another bit of insecurity to the lives of those who lived there.

The Hill yielded some relevant statistics of its own in 1967:

· Fifteen percent of the city's total housing was there. But the neighborhood accounted for more than 20 percent of the city's substandard housing.

· Three of the neighborhood's schools were built in the nineteenth century, one of them in 1883. The neighborhood library and the firehouse were considered obsolete and substandard. The sewer system was termed "a hazard to health."

· The infant mortality rate in the Hill was 35.5 per 1,000 live births, the highest in the city. The rate of immature live births was 13 per 1,000, compared to 9.3 per 1,000 in the rest of the city. The accidental death rate was 69.2 in the Hill; for the city as a whole it was 39. The tuberculosis rate was 59.6 per 100,000; in the rest of the city it was 44.8. In 1966 in New Haven there were 42 cases of lead poisoning, which usually is caused by children's ingesting fragments of peeling lead-based paint; 13 of the cases came from the Hill.

• The neighborhood's population represented about 15 percent of the total city population, but close to a quarter of all juvenile court referrals in the city came from there. About 2.5 percent of the population of the area covered by the New Haven State Jail was in the Hill, but 12 percent of the jail's inmates came from the neighborhood.

• Of the city's 20 parks, which contained a total of 1,862 acres of land, only one was in the Hill, and it contained seven acres.

• In the four-year period ending in 1966, the number of Aid to Dependent Children cases rose by 60 percent in the neighborhood.

• It appeared that the unemployment rate in the Hill was more than double that for the city as a whole.[6]

It should not have been surprising that the Hill was the neighborhood that gave birth to the Hill Parents Association and to the leadership of Fred Harris. But the white portion of the city refused to recognize this; it especially refused to recognize or appreciate the potential in Fred Harris. The great majority of the whites did not understand him, and they made little effort to understand him.

At any rate, in the late spring and early summer of 1967, Fred Harris, Ronald Johnson and others of HPA went to Community Progress, Incorporated, with an idea. The Parents Association wanted to operate three programs in the Hill during the summer: a day camp and educational program; a recreation and playground project, and a venture called Operation Breakthrough, which had as its aim the development of jobs for the "hard-core" unemployed.

---

[6] "Ideas for the Hill Model Neighborhood Program," April 1967; authors not listed, but the document is a compilation of facts and proposals by various city agencies.

Hill Parents Association wanted approximately $37,000 from CPI to operate the programs.

Fred Harris said he thought the proposals stood a good chance of being funded, although, he added, "We had presented proposals to them before, which they had always turned down."

It was clear that CPI was suspicious and, perhaps, even fearful of the proposals. Not only had HPA spent three or four months drawing up the plans on its own, without playing the usual Bureau of the Budget game with the CPI central office staff; it wanted a far greater degree of control over the summer programs than CPI had ever allowed before.

"We presented it to CPI," recalled Harris, "and they said they'd look at it. And when they finally made up their minds, they said they'd give us $6,000, which wasn't enough to begin to cover any of the programs. And then the people in the community showed their disapproval, and CPI did come up with about $33,000."

The "disapproval" shown by the residents consisted of violence, practiced by citizens on CPI storefront offices. The antipoverty organization came up, finally, with $32,120 to fund the HPA programs, but not until the situation had reached the point of crisis.

Harris said later he felt CPI had been wary of dealing with the group from the Hill because "we were a political threat to them. And there was a riot potential there; that bothered them, too. And there was a potential, once they agreed to do this type of thing, that *other* communities would be asking to handle their own money and design their own programs. Because up until that point, CPI had been designing the programs for the community, which nine out of ten times turned out to be failures because they weren't designing the programs around the wishes of the community.

"They designed them around what *they* felt were the needs of the community. Or they designed the programs around the kinds of things that would be easy to be funded and where the city would come off looking good. You know, all these things contributed to New Haven getting more money per capita than any other city in the country."

A semi-official record of the crisis was kept that summer by

Richard Belford, a white attorney who, at that time, was the head of Mayor Lee's Commission on Equal Opportunities (and who shortly was to fall from official favor). Belford had a habit, as some lawyers do, of making notes to himself on what happens around him, and of making the notes while events are still fresh in his mind. While he was the executive director of the CEO, he was a prodigious narrative-writer and memo-compiler.

As early as December 1966, Belford said, he had started discussions with Mayor Lee's director of administration, Dennis Rezendes, on the subject of the city's approach to race relations. "A few of us at the commission," recalled Belford, "were very concerned about the possibility of riots and violence the following summer—1967. We were also concerned, in a very related way, with the fact that people living in the slum areas don't have much of a say, much of a determination, much control over their own destiny."

Belford wrote a memorandum to Rezendes, in which he emphasized the importance of citizen participation. He also noted that "one probable inevitable result" of increased participation would be a greater political awareness on the part of the affected citizens. " 'For better or worse,' " he said, reading from his copy of the memo, " 'political action may take a form which is antagonistic to the existing political structure of the city, but it is suggested that this may be inevitable during the transitional period in achieving political sophistication.' "

Belford said he heard nothing of his proposals for almost five months. Then, in May, he learned that the mayor was calling a meeting of city agencies to discuss the possibility of summer violence. Belford hurried to write another memo, this one a five-page document on the subject of "potential summer unrest" that reflected ideas developed by Belford and John C. Daniels, the CEO's deputy director, while they had attended a national conference on conflict.

The second memo, addressed to Mayor Lee, Rezendes, and Melvin Adams, suggested that "some steps can be taken at this time to ease the tensions and to alter the conditions in the more sensitive neighborhoods (such as the Hill and Legion Avenue areas) so as to minimize the conditions which may produce a riot." The suggestions, said the CEO staffers, were not "important long-range programs to bring about social change," but rather temporary steps that might be taken to meet "the immediate problems of this summer." They suggested, among the short-range steps, that the city install more street lights in the ghetto; clean the streets (and hire local residents to help clean them); hire, on a preferential basis, young people from the slums for summer employment; and improve relations between the police and the community by raising police salaries, allowing policemen to volunteer for patrol duty in the ghetto areas, urging them to participate in neighborhood civic affairs in their spare time (and, possibly, compensating them for this), and establishing programs whereby civilians could accompany policemen on foot and motor patrols.

The meeting of city agencies was held, and Mayor Lee discussed the Belford-Daniels memorandum. "He expressed anger and hostility over the fact that we had sent the memorandum," recalled Belford, although "he did not disagree with any of the proposals in the memorandum." Mayor Lee was critical of the CEO for waiting so long to initiate a discussion of summer conflict; "He stated that . . . we should have started discussing the problem five or six months ago," said Belford, adding that that was exactly what had happened.

The CEO director said Mayor Lee delivered himself of several other criticisms, most of them without solid foundation, and that he did it "in this public way, in front of the other city agencies, with anger and hostility, and, in our opinion, undermined to some extent our relationship with other department heads and assistants." Belford said he started getting the impression that Mayor Lee had wanted the CEO as window-dressing, not as an agency that really produced action and certainly not as one that produced controversy.

Belford's narrative of the HPA-CPI controversy later that year repeatedly made the point, although not in so many words, that CPI was worried about the HPA proposals and did not want to fund them. Hill Parents Association, he noted, felt that CPI was "paternalistic" and "that any funds which CPI was prepared to give for these programs were being given as a dole." HPA wanted Mayor Lee brought into the negotiations.

The Commission on Equal Opportunities sided, in the main, with HPA, and it used what good offices it had left to try to effect a meeting with the mayor. The HPA proposals sounded to the commission very much like early attempts at people's controlling their own destinies. Belford entered the HPA-CPI controversy on June 9, 1967, when Fred Harris called him and said he was having difficulty with CPI. Through the intervention of CEO, discussions were started, and on June 12, Harris reported success: "It looked as if their requests were going to be honored," said Belford's narrative. On the following day, negotiations broke down. By June 14, "Hostilities were high" in the Hill, "tensions were rising, and there were threats of violence."

Hill residents, who apparently had given up on CPI, were demanding a meeting with Mayor Lee, who was out of town. Finally, a meeting with the mayor was promised for the following morning. A little after midnight, about a dozen officials from the city and CPI started a five-hour meeting to formulate the recommendations they would make to the mayor later in the morning. Some of the topics of conversation, according to Belford, were these:

• Should the proposed programs be accepted as written by HPA, "without critical analysis?"

• One of the programs seemed to call for more staff members than was necessary. "Is this an attempt by HPA to create a patronage base for future organizing, and, if so, should we resist it?"

• "If these programs are accepted and funded as requested by HPA, will this set a precedent for other neighborhood groups to submit programs?"

• Item Number 5 for discussion was: "In view of the earlier threats of violence, should we agree to the HPA requests, thereby appearing to be intimidated?"

Belford noted that at about the time Item Number 5 was being discussed, fire trucks arrived a few doors up the street, at the Dixwell office of CPI. The city officials went outside to see what was happening. The window of the office had been broken and two firebombs had been thrown inside. Then the officials learned that another CPI office had been attacked earlier. "We went back inside . . . to continue our discussion," recalled Belford. "Question Number 5 above received more emphasis at this time."

The group finally decided to recommend to the mayor that the programs be accepted as drawn up by HPA; that HPA be allowed to run the programs as it saw fit, including the hiring of staff, and that when the mayor met with the neighborhood people later in the morning, he should start things off by stating his agreement with the proposals.

All of this came to pass, and representatives of HPA, CPI, and other city agencies adjourned to work out details. Belford noted that the final agreements "were identical" to those proposed a week before. The difference, of course, was that a week before the city would have nothing, or at best very little, to do with HPA. It took pressure, it took violence, and it took a crisis to get the city to move.

Richard Belford was asked, some time after the $32,120 deal (as it came to be called), why he thought New Haven had failed to become the model city it once was hailed as being. He replied:

"I think there are perhaps a number of reasons for it. I think one of them is that we make the mistake of operating from crisis to crisis with a view toward putting the lid on a crisis, or on an uncomfortable situation, when it arises, without making any real attempt to meet the underlying problems which have produced the crisis.

"And that, in turn, has made many people, especially poor people and black people, feel that there's not a real desire to meet the problem, because this kind of approach, I think, becomes pretty transparent after a while. It creates a situation where people who have legitimate grievances, legitimate points of view, and legitimate suggestions, find out that their grievances, their points of view and their suggestions are not going to be listened to or attended to when they present them in a nonviolent way.

"In essence, the message that comes through, the message that is really being transmitted to these people, is that the city administration will not really attend to the problems unless they're confronted with a crisis."

The upshot of the $32,120 deal, he said, "was that it was not until the city administration was literally confronted with a crisis and with threatened violence that they agreed to give the funds for these programs, notwithstanding the fact that they agreed in principle that it would be a good idea to give these funds for these programs. And it turned out that even our local newspaper, which is anything but liberal on these questions, complimented, eventually, the city administration and the grass-roots people for doing something for the first time in the history of our redevelopment and antipoverty program—namely, funding a program that was developed by grass-roots people themselves. This was in the summer of 1967, after we had had an antipoverty program for *five years!* And yet this was the first time that a citizen-inspired program was finally going to be financed. It was the first time that one was actually developed and planned by the residents of the neighborhood."

After the confrontation that resulted in the $32,120 deal, the city started paying more attention to the Hill. It seemed that if violence were to strike in the summer of 1967, the Hill would be the logical place for it. There were, however, a couple of things happening that might avert violence: The HPA people had gotten their money and were at work on their programs, the most highly visible of which was a park and playground on Congress Avenue. And the city seemed to be trying to avoid the sort of police-community frictions that had triggered riots in other places. A young, intelligent police captain named James Ahern was seen often in the Hill, wearing civilian clothes, talking with Fred Harris and others.

Peter Almond, one of those with whom Ahern talked a lot, recalled later that "After any small incident he would immediately appear. He would start talking; he would talk to anybody and everybody around. He would facilitate meetings between neighborhood people and police commissioners to get the process working so that there were always avenues for people to express their strong feelings about police brutality and all the other kinds of problems that had sparked riots in other cities."

Late in July the Hill Parents Association sponsored a meeting in the park it was building, and it invited neighborhood businessmen to listen to requests for help. Almond, who was there, remembered that "The purpose of the meeting was to bring together white businessmen from the Hill with neighborhood people, to talk about common interests and common problems, progress for the Hill and progress for business.

"That meeting was a bitter one and a fascinating one. It was held at dusk in this beautiful outdoor playground that the Hill Parents had constructed. They had some ten or twelve neighborhood people who gave arguments why white businessmen had to do more, and to get more involved in the life of the Hill, make more contributions to community projects, help out, donate sodas for children's outings, and so forth. There were implications, obviously, of a great deal more, but it was a public meeting and nobody had a gun against his temple."

Fred Harris, who also attended the meeting, said later that the sponsors had asked the white merchants for money, but not for money alone. "We were building a park," he said. "What the speakers were talking about was that those who could afford to give money, it would be gladly accepted. Those who could give other things, it would be gladly accepted—like food for the day camp, sodas, letting us use an apartment house's electricity for lights at night. Maybe a store would let us use their water for a fountain. This was the kind of thing we were talking about. And I think it wasn't asking too much. It was a very moderate position to take."

Some of the white businessmen didn't think it was moderate. They formed an organization called the Hill Businessmen's and Taxpayers' Association and later issued a statement accusing the city of "coddling" lawbreakers and following a "policy of favoritism" toward Negroes.

The park incident seemed to be forgotten, though, when the riot struck in August. What strides the city had made in avoiding police-community frictions were quickly wiped away. Mayor Lee, who had plenty of advisers telling him that Fred Harris was the logical man with whom to deal in the Hill, all but ignored that advice. The HPA issued a statement shortly after the riot that said:

> Why has an organization that has tried to maintain a public service for all, constantly come under fire from our City fathers? HPA has tried very hard in light of the recent disturbance to keep open lines of communication between the streets and the City, only to be confronted with, 'We don't need your help', and have guns stuck in our faces and told, 'This is the only help' . . . HPA has provided what it sees as a great service, but we need help. Who is to help us?

One organization that was not likely to help was Community Progress, Incorporated. Knowledgeable observers in and around CPI at the time reported that the agency, angered over having to deal with the HPA in the first place, became angrier over the situation involving the white businessmen and the park, and felt ultimately stung when the $32,120 failed to ward off a riot in the Hill. Yet the agency needed to use the HPA appropriation in its publicity as an example of CPI's renewed (or belated) interest in citizen participation.

Furthermore, CPI had been criticized from on high—from the Ford Foundation—for the way it had handled the HPA deal. CPI's annual report for 1967, which went to press shortly after the riot, gave an indication of the agency's dilemma. The preface was a well-nigh classic blend of confused antipoverty agency rationalization: There were "outside agitators" to blame (agitators made outsiders by their youth, in this case); the real residents were contented ("Our niggers are happy," they used to say in the South); the violence demanded a redoubling of efforts; but this in no way indicated that previous efforts should be condemned. *It seemed that young people had done the rioting:*

> Some of the "disadvantaged" are too young to know about the progress that's been made—or too burned up to care. They

live in the here and now . . . the evidence indicates that it was some of the angry young who fused the four nights of disorder that broke out in New Haven on August 19, 1967. To some it was a rebellion; with most others, the violence reflected more of a thirst for revelry than a social protest. The rebels made up only a tiny fraction of the Inner City population. Much of their following comprised teenage hooligans more bent on "fun" and vandalism than possessed of a cause.

Those who sated their thirst for revelry did not speak for the majority:

Few if any of the incidents of the four days bespoke any widespread discontent. There is no basis for reading into the four-day flareup (as a few have done) an Inner City-wide indictment of the physical and human-renewal efforts of fourteen years. . .

The real *militants in New Haven were CPI and City Hall:*

. . . the strife notwithstanding, New Haven is farther along the road to human and social progress than the vast majority of communities. Had there not been a CPI (and its partner agencies in New Haven's human-resource effort), the August violence could quite conceivably have flared into a Newark or Detroit. Without CPI, the ranks of the rebels would have been swelled by thousands who HAVE found genuine opportunity through community action.

CPI and a handful of allies cannot singlehandedly wage or win the war that needs to be won.

The loudest voices of protest are mostly directed at City Hall and CPI. But the fact is that City Hall and CPI are the chief militants in the Inner City crisis. . .

CPI will "accelerate and intensify" its efforts in the field of community participation:

Starting this fall, CPI hopes to earmark specific sums in the Community Services Division budget to enable existing and specially formed neighborhood groups to launch new services. In some instances they may even take over programs now operated by CPI or delegate agencies. . .

The new departure in CPI programming is based on the conviction that, in many instances, neighborhood residents are best able to determine their most pressing needs...

But CPI had learned some lessons from its first hesitant dabblings in community participation:

In this experiment in self-determination and self-help, no neighborhood group will receive substantial funds until it has demonstrated its capacity to run programs which meet the most urgent needs of residents of the areas they serve.[7]

After the summer, Hill Parents Association received no substantial funds from Community Progress, Incorporated.

In early October of 1967 Peter Almond was approached by the young, intelligent police officer who had been helping to keep things cool in the Hill. James Ahern, said Almond, telephoned and "said he wanted to pick me up and talk about some things. What he told me was that I was likely to be subpoenaed before a federal grand jury investigation against certain Hill leaders into conspiracy to commit extortion."

Almond said he testified before the grand jury for two and one-half hours, "being really ruthlessly examined by a prosecutor whom I will never really forgive. The whole grand jury system is such a perversion of justice. They called all the Hill leaders to testify, although it's interesting that they had me on the witness stand like three times as long as anybody else. Maybe they were thinking that a white kid who sounds fairly rational and who yet appears to be a radical type, to this average-age-about-seventy grand jury would be the turning point to convince them that there was really something wicked that had gone on in that meeting. They were really trying to make a conspiracy to commit extortion charge *stick*."

Almond was asked about the racial composition of the grand jury. "It was roughly 100 per cent white," he said with a grim

---

[7] Community Progress, Incorporated, "The Human Story: 1967," 1967.

smile. "Grand juries are really scary things. This was a frightening experience because, you know, you cannot have a counsel with you. It's behind closed doors. I had things done to me like this: The prosecutor smiling and asking if I realized what it means to commit perjury; asking if I realized that what I had just said could be used against me, and stuff like that.

"They were trying to pin me down to state that I had heard certain language used that amounted to threats."

Almond said he felt at that time, and was certain afterward, that a concerted effort was under way to suppress the HPA leadership. "I believe there was a rather conscious decision," he said, "to pursue any real—and to create or fabricate other—situations where they could use the law to limit and to discredit the activity of the Hill neighborhood leadership."

From the beginning the grand jury action had the smell of phoniness. Extortion, in most parts of the United States, is considered a local problem and it is dealt with by local or state laws. But in New Haven the probe was undertaken by a federal grand jury which supposedly was investigating possible infractions of Hobb's Act, which makes it a federal offense to destroy or threaten to destroy merchandise transported across state lines. In the end, the investigation was dropped.

"I had the feeling," said Almond, "that they went as far as they did with the investigation because the Hill white politician types were saying to the authorities, You'd better do something because these guys have been threatening us, and the riot had happened, and they had *had* it. The city officials had had it. They weren't going to coddle the neighborhood any more. The summer was over, so the threat of further trouble was diminished. And I think they went that far just to please the white business leaders."

Almond, however, was anything but pleased. He had gone to the Hill as a white liberal, trying to help in the war on poverty, and he had seen those who had power engaged in a fairly naked attempt to suppress those who believed in citizen participation.

"What so disturbed me," he said, "was that because those guys had the law in their hands—and in the context of this federal grand jury investigation, they actually had the *processes* of law, of 'justice,' in their hands—that they could use this for what was just a different interpretation of the facts from my own. In a lot of these situations, they pushed me into a much more favorable interpretation of what was going on in the Hill than I would have had on my own.

"Remember: When I was talking initially about going to the Hill in '66, I didn't go there with any ideology. I went there sort of to see what was happening. I was out of the real Bureau of the Budget, high-level, bright-young-man, Sviridoff-aide school. But what I saw is really one of the things that makes a young and committed and naïve man like me a radical. Sort of in spite of myself."

Not every white liberal in New Haven had a chance to be radicalized by witnessing a grand jury at work, but in the weeks and months that followed the abortive investigation, many others did have opportunities to sense that something strange was going on.

• Early in the morning of October 26, 1967 policemen entered Fred Harris' apartment and arrested him on charges of possession of heroin and possession of stolen goods. The officers said they found the heroin stuck under a trophy with chewing gum, *The Register* reported. The newspaper also quoted policemen as saying "fresh needle marks" had been found on Harris' arm—a piece of alleged information that few respectable newspapers would print, whether the police said it or not, because of its prejudicial impact on any future jury. (Harris later acknowledged that he had used narcotics in the past, and that there was a mark on his arm that was "an old track" made by a needle.) Also allegedly uncovered in the raid, which was conducted with a warrant, was a typewriter that had been reported stolen from a Yale student about a month before.

Partisans of Harris charged that the raid had been a frameup, and that Mrs. Harris had been forced to dress in front of male policemen. Francis V. McManus, the chief, denied this. Harris' friends also argued that he had received the typewriter at a surprise birthday party not long before, and that anybody could have "given" it to him—even someone bent on framing him.

In March 1968 a superior court jury found Harris guilty of the narcotics charge and innocent in the matter of the typewriter. Harris started the process of appealing the conviction.

• A few minutes after Harris had posted bond in the October narcotics arrest, he was arrested again and charged with breach of peace. A landlord alleged that Harris had spat upon him and berated him.

• In mid-November 1967 Harris and another HPA leader, Willie Counsel, were sentenced to 30 days on breach of peace charges that had grown out of the 1966 demonstration at the state welfare department offices in Hartford.

• On December 23, 1967 HPA leader Ronald Johnson and four others were arrested and charged with plotting to blow up the police station and two downtown banks and to murder several policemen. Bond was set at $100,000.[8]

In the trial, which took place in early 1968, a Negro undercover agent from the Federal Alcohol and Tobacco Tax Division testified that he had written a memorandum for a superior in which he had said that while Johnson was the apparent director of the plot, Fred Harris was "the real ringleader."

In March 1968 Johnson was found guilty and sentenced to eight to twelve years. He appealed the verdict. He also was found guilty, in another court, on a charge of possession of marijuana, which police allegedly uncovered in his home while searching for dynamite in the bomb case.

• In April 1968 charges of loitering, which had been brought against Harris after the 1967 riot, were dropped when he pleaded guilty to the charge of breach of peace and paid a $25 fine.

Mayor Lee and the official side of the city, with the exception of the police department, the courts, and the grand jurors, continued to ignore and/or minimize Fred Harris and the sort of

---

[8] In this case, *The New York Times* did no better than *The New Haven Register*. *The Times*'s headline on its story reporting the arrests said "New Haven Foils A Bombing Plot."

leadership he represented. "Fred Harris is not a leader in the real sense," Lee said some time after the riot. "They've tried to *make* him a leader. It's hard to single out what the Negro table of organization is. No one really knows, and no one who is white really knows it, no matter what anybody tells you."

A visitor commented that it was hard to tell what the white table of organization was, too, and Lee quickly replied: "No, you begin with City Hall. That's easy."

Lee and City Hall seemed to be using a rather simple formula to assure themselves of their own popularity and Harris' lack of it. Harris didn't get many votes when he ran for office, and Lee did. Harris had been accused of having needle scars all over his arm and Lee hadn't.

There was some indication, however, that the formula might be misleading. In early 1968 a study was published by Dr. Louis Goldstein, a professor in the University of Connecticut school of social work, that indicated that the majority of a sample group of Negro teenagers in New Haven thought Harris was the most important and powerful person in the black community. Asked which black leaders had the greatest following and support among Negroes, the teenagers picked Harris again. He was followed by Martin Luther King, H. Rap Brown, and Stokely Carmichael.

Furthermore, the teenagers, when asked which person, black or white, was doing the most for Negroes, chose Harris and Mayor Lee in almost equal percentages. And, when asked which level of government they thought could do the most to improve their living conditions, the young people listed the office of mayor above the offices of both the President and the governor.[9]

---

[9] Louis Goldstein, Ph.D., "Ideologies and Institutional Forces: A Study of the Attitudes and Aspirations of Negro Teen-Agers, New Haven, Connecticut, February, 1968." Dr. Goldstein's survey was initiated by the Episcopal Church Mission Association of Greater New Haven as an effort to gather "some organized information on Negro young people involved in the disturbances in New Haven of August, 1967." The study sample was quite small, and Dr. Goldstein cautioned against generalizing the findings "to the wider universe of all Negro teen-agers . . . At best, this is an exploratory study which will provide some reliable information on certain categories of Negro teen-agers in New Haven." He did conclude,

Fred Harris, discussing the busy fall, winter, and spring that followed the summer riot, said he had changed a little. He no longer believed that integration was possible, and he said that the time he *had* spent believing it had probably been wasted.

"I guess that the mistake I made," he said, "was to try to understand where they, the whites, are coming from—why they are the way they are—and that gets in the way of militancy. I guess most people would just say To hell with them, you know, and just go on and do their thing.

"I tried to understand them, which I guess is really fruitless. But I always hoped that there was a way that they could be changed, and I guess that deep down inside I know there isn't. But the other thing I try to think about is that there is going to be a revolution in this country. The black people will be the vanguard of that revolution, but if white America would give up their racism, we would stand a chance of people's unifying themselves on different class levels. I guess this is the same kind of thing the Panthers are talking about, but it makes sense."

Harris, who at that time was in the midst of appealing his heroin conviction, said he was doubtful that he would end up a free man. "I think the man recognizes one thing," he said, "and that is that as long as I'm out here, he knows I can't be bought. He knows that I'm going to work until I'm dead. And he knows that I'm sincere. And he knows that as long as I'm out here, there'll be some kind of something going on."

---

however, that "There is no evidence that the fundamental conditions of society are being altered to remove the mainsprings of Negro protest and rebellion. On the other hand, the study reveals that the attitudes and feelings of Negro youth are primed and ready to be touched off with the slightest provocation, accidental or deliberate."

VII

A Feeling of Repression

It's the feeling that something may—may happen to you.
—Mrs. William Ryan, a white resident of New Haven

THE RIOT, and the associated events of 1967, seemed to waken something in a small, and previously silent, group of white New Haveners. Like Peter Almond, they became radicalized.

The phenomenon was occurring, or soon would occur, in cities across the nation as persons who had been content to think of themselves as white liberals learned—usually through the blunders of the police, of municipal executives, and of others in positions of power—a lesson that black Southerners had had beaten into their skulls long before: that peaceful protest, peaceful petition, peaceful negotiation did no good.

Undoubtedly some of those who were radicalized in New Haven, as elsewhere, were motivated at least in part by a sadistic urge to see their city in trouble. Fourteen years of good publicity, more than a decade of reading about your model city in newspapers and magazines—and knowing that the description was far from accurate—has a tendency to create resentment in the best of people. Relocation was an "opportunity," it was said, but the members of this small group of citizens knew it wasn't. They knew about the highways and shops that had been built where people had once lived. They lived with the knowledge that the low-income housing that was being built was not for black or other ordinarily poor people, but for the elderly. Some of these whites saw some justification in the riot, and they received some satisfaction from it.

Mayor Lee, in explaining how he was able to win reelection in 1967 despite illness and a near-total lack of campaigning, demonstrated an understanding of this feeling: "The radicals," he said, "probably wanted to see me take a fall because I'd been riding too high for years. When they saw me flat on my face, they said 'That's good enough for him,' and then when I got up with a broken arm, they felt sorry for me and they went out and voted for me and said 'He's a better man now.'"

Others, however, seemed to be reacting not so much to the riot as to another quality that had manifested itself during the spring, summer and fall of 1967—a quality that they invariably referred to as *repression*. When asked about this repression, they recounted the legal difficulties that seemed to descend with such regularity on Fred Harris, Ronald Johnson, and other leaders of the Hill Parents Association. They reminded visitors that HPA had been the only black organization that had asked New Haven's "executive-centered coalition" for citizen participation; the only one that, when rebuffed, had counter-attacked; the only one that had resisted co-option.

Coincident with the feeling of repression, or perhaps part of it, was a feeling of general distrust on the part of these whites against practically everything the city did and said. Every statement from the Redevelopment Agency was scrutinized in the belief that the precise opposite might be true. A visitor to the city who said he planned to speak with Mayor Lee was warned: "Watch out. He'll charm you. He comes on like a good guy, and in ten minutes he'll have you in his pocket. It's happened before, many times." It was as if the dissenters felt that Lee had some sort of supernatural power.

The feeling of doubt and distrust extended to the mayor's health. Lee, of course, had a long history of debilitating illnesses, and he was known to be supersensitive about matters of health.

But the dissenters thought there was more to it than that. They thought Lee got sick *most* in times of crisis, and that he avoided the necessity of speaking out on controversial issues in this manner.

They distrusted the newspapers. In New Haven, this was not difficult. *The Register* and her morning sister, *The Journal-Courier,* were widely suspected of suppressing most of the news and distorting the rest. Despite the fact that the newspapers disliked and disputed most of what Lee did—and therefore might be expected to go overboard in terms of printing news that would be embarrassing to him—their coverage of the local scene was so skimpy as to be uniformly pathetic. There was no local printed competition that might make the newspapers work harder, and television and radio in New Haven, as in most of the rest of the nation, offered no challenge.

Worst of all, the intellectual and intellectually-influential people in New Haven, especially the members of the Yale community, appeared not to really *care* about the quality of the local press, since they got their news from *The New York Times,* which was delivered and sold in New Haven in large numbers. *The Times* had a correspondent stationed in New Haven, and he could be counted on to supply information of interest to the intellectual community such as important events at Yale, news of elections and truly important confrontations, crises and natural disasters, but he could not provide information on the day-to-day happenings of redevelopment, CPI, and politics.

There is no way to utilize hindsight to measure such things, but it is very likely that the sense of distrust and repression increased dramatically during 1967. Richard Belford, who came to feel a bit of repression himself, explained it in terms of citizen participation:

"I think there's a certain relationship that should have been developed between the Establishment and the people living in the slums, a relationship in which the people would have the opportunity of a meaningful involvement in the affairs of the city that affect them. There must be not just a *statement* of citizen participation, but a sincere desire to *establish* this kind of relationship. And only if it's done sincerely do I think it has any kind of meaning. Otherwise, the hypocrisy becomes transparent, and people distrust."

The former director of the CEO had some experiences of his own that led him to distrust what was going on in New Haven. In September 1967, shortly after the disturbances, Belford resigned from his position. The reason, he said, was the overwhelming accumulation of evidence that the city and Mayor Lee wanted the commission to function entirely on a non-controversial basis. There were comments from City Hall from time to time, he said, "which sort of indicated to us that since we're 'part of the family,' or 'part of the team,' that our first and only loyalty lay in maintaining the mayor's image in the community, and that everything had to be geared toward that kind of activity.

"We on the commission refused to consider this the sole part of our activities, and we felt that it was our duty, if we wanted to do any kind of meaningful job, to size up each situation on its merits and do the kind of thing that the ordinance creating our commission provided for in the whole arena of equal opportunities."[1] There were several incidents, he said, that built up to "what I felt was the necessity of resigning because of the inability to be allowed to do the job:"

• The report of the CEO on police-community relations in April 1966, following the Arena case, did not sit well with City Hall. Lee and the police department soon appointed a community relations officer for the department, but denied that they had done so because of the CEO's urging.

• In November 1966 the social action committee of a synagogue, to which Belford belonged, held a panel discussion on race relations. Belford was to be the moderator, and the panel was to include Fred Harris. (In the end, Harris did not actually participate.) The next day, said Belford, Mayor Lee, who did not know that Harris had not spoken, summoned the CEO director

---

[1] The ordinance was an exceptionally strong one. In addition to instructing the commission to do what it could to "achieve harmonious inter-group relations," to establish programs and to study problems, the law also gave the agency the power to subpoena witnesses.

to his office for a bawling out. Lee, said Belford, considered the invitation to Harris a "personal offense toward him. . . . He stated that Fred Harris had been on his back for a considerable period of time, and that he felt that Fred Harris should not be considered an important person because, in his quest for the state representative's spot on an independent ticket, he did not poll very many votes.

"As a result, he should not be considered as a spokesman for anybody, and therefore the synagogue and the rabbi had no right to invite him to be a member of the panel; that he considered this as a personal offense to him.

"He then went on to say that the city is spending about $40,000 a year on the Commission on Equal Opportunities, which was our approximate budget, and that it was my job as executive director to quote keep down unquote people like Fred Harris.

"So that," Belford said, putting down his neatly-typed narrative, "was another situation setting the tone for our relationship with the mayor and also indicating a very significant difference in philosophy and approach between the way the mayor sized up the function of the Commission on Equal Opportunities and the way I did. Unfortunately, it was an irreconcilable kind of difference."

Belford finished his recitation of the incidents which led to his resignation, replaced the narratives on his desk, and concluded: "I suspect that the role which was intended for us was to be window-dressing, a showcase to look as if we're providing equal opportunities, but really as a pacifying agency so we can absorb the shock of any kind of protest without embarrassing the city. After a while, we were looked upon as the enemy, an agency to be fought."

Needless to say, Belford thought all this was wrong, and he blamed Mayor Lee for it. "I think that in the political system under which we operate," he said, "there is, first of all, a duty on the part of elected officials to take positions and exercise leadership on controversial and important issues, regardless of what their position happens to be. Another important aspect is to let people know how they stand on those issues and help to set the tone of the community on the issues.

"I also happen to think—although better politicians than I would probably disagree—that it's good politics to let people know how you stand on the issues. And I think, in the main, if you're sincere about it, this will show through, and people will respect a politician who does express his opinions, even if they disagree with him.

"I think it's still incumbent upon a politician to take that risk, and if it turns out that I'm wrong, and a person loses politically by doing the kind of thing I'm suggesting, I think it's less important that he gain politically than it is to have a better society in which to live. I think that's one of the risks a person ought to be prepared to take if he's going to go into politics as a statesman, as distinguished from a politician."

There was no mention in the 1967 annual report of the City of New Haven of the work of Belford or of the Commission on Equal Opportunities.

There was an uncounted but significant number of citizens outside the official government who shared Richard Belford's feelings of distrust and repression. One group of them, named the American Independent Movement, was a predominantly white organization of radicals, headed by Robert Cook, a sociologist at Yale (and an unsuccessful candidate for Congressman Giaimo's seat in the 1966 election, the one in which Fred Harris ran for the legislature). The group published the AIM newsletter, a periodical usually devoted to such topics as the war in Vietnam, the emerging Third World, and domestic radicalism, every two or three weeks.

There was another group of New Haven whites, many of them, like AIM, members of the intellectual community but perhaps less radical, that entered the picture during the fall of 1967. The Coalition of Concerned Citizens was formed as a result of Fred Harris' arrest on the narcotics charge. Members of the CCC, said a publication, "are united in their concern about the unchecked continuation of injustice and inequality in this city and are committed to action in order to change these conditions." The publication continued:

> The Coalition is concerned about injustice, discrimination, and harassment; but these are only symptoms of the real disease that grips New Haven: the decline of democracy. Coalition members are alarmed about the inability of citizens—particularly Black and Puerto Rican citizens—to participate in community decision-making and to protect themselves against the irresponsible and repressive activity of police and other agencies. . . .

The publication asked, and then answered, the question, "Why does the Coalition support groups such as the HPA?"

> The Coalition believes that groups such as HPA provide significant leadership for important segments of the Black and Puerto Rican communities, and that they therefore deserve support to enable them to continue to function. These organizations provide programs for and by Blacks . . . that are free of the emasculating paternalism so common in white groups that are supposedly trying to "help the Blacks."
> Genuine grass-roots organizations must not be allowed to fail, whether or not they represent their entire community or only a portion of it.

The coalition sponsored a rally on November 5, 1967 at Lee High School to protest the city's treatment of Harris and to hear and endorse various resolutions. An estimated 800 persons attended. The major piece of business was the reading of the "Report of the Committee to Enumerate Harassment and Repression," which recounted some of the things that had happened to the black community during and since the riot, and which charged that "there exists in the City of New Haven a system of harassment and repression being exerted against the black community and its outspoken leadership." The community and its leaders were subjected, the committee said, to "questionable use of legal process; public unsubstantiated accusations by police against black leadership; personal degradation, indignity, and humiliation; intimidation; broken promises; alienation," and "forced isolation from the decision-making processes of government."

Two early organizers and spokesmen for the Coalition of Concerned Citizens were Dr. and Mrs. William Ryan, a white couple who had moved to New Haven not long before from Boston, where they had been active in civil rights work, and where Dr. Ryan, a psychologist, had written an article condemning Daniel P. Moynihan for a survey he had compiled while an Assistant Secretary of Labor—the document that came to be called "The Moynihan Report."[2]

Now, in New Haven, Dr. Ryan was a psychologist at the Yale Medical School and the Connecticut Mental Health Center; Mrs. Ryan was the acting steering committee chairman of the Coalition of Concerned Citizens.

Mrs. Ryan, in an interview, said that two factors had been most important in the creation of the coalition: the mayoral election of November 7, 1967, and the arrest of Fred Harris on October 26. The election was a factor, she said, because so many white liberal New Haveners had become accustomed to voting for Mayor Lee on the lesser-of-two-evils rationale, and the coalition wanted at least to ask the candidates for their positions on matters of interest to the group before Lee's inevitable reelection.

As for Harris' arrest, Mrs. Ryan recalled: "Word of this spread like wildfire around the black community, especially word of the manner of his arrest: the Gestapo-like qualities of the policemen coming in and so forth." She recounted the report that Mrs. Harris had been forced to dress while policemen were in the room. "The

---

[2] The report, which achieved some fame, was officially titled "The Negro Family: The Case for National Action," and it stated that "the fundamental problem" behind the gap between black and white Americans was "that of family structure. The evidence—not final, but powerfully persuasive —is that the Negro family in the urban ghettoes is crumbling." Dr. Ryan's response was privately circulated, then printed in *The Nation* (November 22, 1965). Lee Rainwater and William L. Yancey, in their book, *The Moynihan Report and the Politics of Controversy* (Cambridge and London: The M.I.T. Press, 1967), referred to the Ryan essay's "singular importance as the best-known critique of the report." Moynihan's work, said Dr. Ryan, "draws dangerously inexact conclusions from weak and insufficient data; encourages (no doubt unintentionally) a new form of subtle racism that might be termed 'Savage Discovery,' and seduces the reader into believing that it is not racism and discrimination but the weaknesses and defects of the Negro himself that account for the present status of inequality between Negro and white."

quality of this got all over town, quickly, and by nightfall what we had planned as a small, sort of figure-out-what-the-problem-is meeting had turned into a large group, a group of some 50 people.

"Their conviction that there was police harassment in this city, and that Lee was a bad guy, and that he wasn't doing anything about the harassment, but was in fact allowing the police to run rampant, is supported by the fact that 3,000 bucks was raised that night. And that's a serious conviction."

White people raised the money, she said: "White people, exhorted by Fred Harris and Ronnie Johnson, who were there, and that night Ronnie predicted very much the course of what his own history with the police was going to be. He said publicly that he was being followed, and that he thought the harassment of black people was going to increase, and that the white people had better look to themselves—that they themselves were in danger if they didn't move."

Those present at the meeting started wondering about how to deal with the problem, the Ryans said, and they decided that one way would be through large, public rallies. But when it came time to decide who would sit on the platform, and who would deliver the speeches, some New Haveners started backing out.

"This theme came up," said Mrs. Ryan: "It was before the election, and people were saying 'Can we really say these things about Lee? I know they're true, and I guess I'll speak, but, well, I guess I won't speak on the *platform*.' There was enormous anxiety on the part of many of the people. One of the principals who had been very verbal at the meeting was really anxious about speaking at the rally."

In Boston it had been different. "This town is so small," said Mrs. Ryan, "that most of the white liberals are *implicated*. For example, some of the people who were suggested to me as people to go to see to get active in the coalition were already implicated in the city administration. Yale is implicated."

Said Dr. Ryan:

"There's also the whole lesser-evil rationale that takes place in the white liberal community. So that the fact that the Republicans put up such atrocious candidates—and that can't be an accident—

leaves the white liberals saying 'My God, we can't vote for Whitney, that terrible man; we've *got* to vote for Lee.'

"And with many of them there was more than just this concern about 'Will we damage Lee?' The people at the meeting—the people who were reluctant about speaking at the rally—reported getting a great deal of direct pressure from whatever position they were in—their board, or their colleagues, or whatnot—including a great deal of pressure from downtown. At least two or three of the people who were in leadership positions in the pre-coalition group reported getting direct telephone calls from Mel Adams, the redevelopment guy, urging them to lay off and get out and not get involved."

Mrs. Ryan broke in: "This is another quality that I found so unusual here, and that is the bush-league quality of the intimidation. It's a coarse kind of business. If somebody wanted to survey our house—which they did on the day of the rally; there was a car outside with a guy in it with binoculars—he might have done it in a somewhat cooler way."

Said Dr. Ryan: "There is another theme. After the rally, which I chaired, some CPI officials were over at Yale on another matter, talking to the director of the Mental Health Center, and they asked why he let me chair the meeting. 'What *right* did he have to chair that meeting that was going to criticize us?' So there's this whole perverse, paradoxical philosophy about what rights are involved in these matters: What *right* do you have to criticize us, or to do this or that?"

"Again I must go back to the Boston situation," said Mrs. Ryan. "In Boston, there were lines of communication. Lines to the Harvard community. Tom Pettigrew [the Harvard social scientist], while he would never picket or do anything on that level—he always kept his participation very scholarly—it would never have occurred to him to be afraid to go and testify before the Boston School Committee. Never in this world. This *does* occur to people in New Haven. In fact, my husband, who is, you know, a pretty nice guy, and not at all a radical kook, is seen in *this* community much more in terms of his identification with the coalition in a kind of dangerous position."

"Yes," added Dr. Ryan. "Dangerous is the word that keeps coming up."

Another word that came up frequently in the Ryans' conversation was "fear." Dr. Ryan was asked for his opinion on why the fear existed. "My feeling," he said, "is that it's a combination of circumstances. It's a monopoly of monopolies, in a sense. The Lee administration has essentially a monopoly position. And Yale has a monopoly. And they are in many ways in cahoots with each other. And there's a monopoly in the media—one TV station, one newspaper. So that there are all the conditions for developing a really totalitarian atmosphere here.

"The fear that a lot of people have now, I don't think that they themselves would even define as fear. It's just a 'realistic assessment of the way things are.' It isn't fear that keeps them from crossing the street against the red light; they've just been conditioned into thinking that that's the way you do things.

"And that's the way you do things in New Haven. You don't cross the authorities. You don't criticize. You don't raise alternatives. You don't discuss matters. It just isn't done. And it's pervasive. You find it throughout many of the academic departments at Yale."

What, the psychologist was asked, was the ultimate punishment that people thought could be inflicted on them if they ignored that conditioning?

"They'll be excluded," he replied. "If you're involved, for instance, in the medical field in some way, you'll be excluded from the Yale medical community, which is the only respectable community in New Haven. There's no place else to be. If you don't have an appointment at Yale, you're of no significance in the medical field. If you're in the legal field, you'll be excluded from what lawyers get from one another. You'll be put out of the game, whatever the game might be, if you don't play the game. And if you're out of the game, certainly in any professional or academic field, you might as well start packing your bags, because there's nothing else to do here if you don't play that game."

Mrs. Ryan said she believed the penalty might transcend exclusion. "The possibility for some more punishment for the people who are involved," she said, "is not at all inconceivable to me. And I say this for the first time in my life. I don't know what form it would take. It's the feeling that something may—may *happen* to you.

"In Boston I used to be very directly threatened by phone calls from a particular person who would say 'I'm going to come to your house and rape you and kill you and kill your child,' you know, and I never experienced more than a fleeting anxiety. Here, I do. I think there's some evidence that this isn't a personality problem that I'm having—that it's a *quality*." Mrs. Ryan looked at her husband. "Do you feel that way?"

"No, not really," he replied. "But I think maybe I'm just able to deny those things."

"You're, I think, braver," she said.

The Ryans were asked if they didn't think Mayor Lee was sharp enough to understand, and to be horrified by, what was going on—by the repression they felt and experienced and documented. Dr. Ryan replied:

"I'm a poor judge of Lee and his character, but I've been impressed by the real Alice in Wonderland quality of a great deal that goes on in New Haven. Take the redevelopment issue as probably the best example: There, all the naïve rhetoric that has been built up, over the years, over redevelopment gets used around here, apparently, very seriously. I think Lee is perfectly capable of saying 'Look at this great program we've carried out in redeveloping the Oak Street area,' when he *knows,* in another part of himself, that all you have to do is take a cab drive from the railroad station to see what a disaster area it actually is. So that they're able—Lee and his crew, his sort of non-political crew, are able—with a very straight face, to keep describing these magic community events and these imaginary wonders, and they don't really seem to believe that anyone will notice.

"I think Lee's in the pragmatism bag: that he's gotten to the point where he's persuaded himself that if he's going to do all these good things he dreams about, he's got to be pragmatic. He's got to work with these forces and those forces and the other forces. One of the problems in New Haven is making believe. Everybody makes believe that certain things are so which aren't so. And when they make those assumptions they are led to certain other kinds of action. And the central core of the making believe is that New Haven was in a terrible state of decline and now it's been saved and it's flourishing and it's growing and it's going to be a great metropolis. 'You have to give Lee credit for that,' they say. And actually it's ridiculous. That's not happening."

The Oak Street project, he said, was an example of this kind of fantasy. "They say, 'Well, maybe it was too bad that all those people had to be relocated, but, gee, we got something great out of it.' So they have to make believe that what they got out of it was good, too. They have to make believe that the Chapel Mall will soon have a branch of Lord & Taylor in it, and this sort of thing. There's this whole quality of making believe on both sides; making believe that things aren't so bad, but also making believe that at least we're getting something out of it. And that at least we're growing; we're thriving; we're coming to life, and we are therefore more secure. And this is a lot of *nonsense*. It simply isn't happening.

"So I think this is one of the major dynamics going on inside New Haven. People can't believe either side is the truth because they've got a complicated myth about the revival of New Haven that they're clinging to."

It appeared, after the riot and especially after the city's rather crude attempts to silence Fred Harris and remove him from the scene, that fewer whites were clinging to the myth. Perhaps the myth was not rejected as quickly and as totally as Dr. and Mrs. Ryan, fresh from more sophisticated battles in Boston, would have liked. But there was a change.

Whites—liberal and radical whites, at least—started scrutinizing what the city did. Of course, there had been some degree of scrutiny before, as when the residents of a pleasant neighborhood would wake one morning to find that the Redevelopment Agency or the State Highway Department had aimed a road at them and had neglected to inform them. The new awareness, however, was directed at projects and proposals that affected the entire city, or that affected neighborhoods so poor, so black, or so black and poor that they had never summoned the energy to protest before.

With the increased scrutiny came a decline in what Mrs. Ryan referred to as "this kind of gradual accommodation that is in the end what dehumanizes people," and what her husband described as a city-wide disinclination to take the initiative. ("I was surprised," he said, "to find out that no one involved in what you might call liberal civil rights work had ever seen one of the urban renewal project grant applications. It never occurred to them to *ask* to see the public documents.")[3] With a fervor that had not been there before, whites and blacks in New Haven started asking questions about the destiny City Hall had been planning for them. They found, some of them, that the Redevelopment Agency had been proceeding in utmost quiet with programs involving the displacement of families and the expenditure of millions of dollars; when public hearings were held, they were held too late, the critics said, for anybody to do anything about them.

A great deal of dissent was focused on the city's remaining massive redevelopment projects, foremost of which were the Route 34 proposal, the State Street project, and the coliseum. The

---

[3] Even the mainstay of dissent, the mimeographing machine, was under-utilized in New Haven. Mrs. Ryan, commenting on what she called "the lack of information about the most ordinary kinds of things," recalled that when she had been in Boston, she had been confined to bed for a period of time, and her friends suggested that she write a book about the use of public relations techniques in the movement. "I thought: 'That's silly; everybody already knows about that,'" she said. "But when I came here to New Haven I discovered it was as if a blanket had been put over this town. I mean, the simple matter of double-spacing a news release; knowing the way things work; knowing deadlines and how a wire service can be used and what it's for. Nobody ever gave a release to a wire service here. It's a sort of invincible ignorance. That's the whole phenomenon of New Haven—of not knowing the information. It's like going to a store and what you want isn't there, and you accept what they have, and if you buy it and it's bad, what can you do about it?"

critics raised their voices as never before against these programs, on the grounds that they made life easier for the suburban commuters at the expense of New Haven's residents, and in some cases they were able to cause changes in the plans.

Route 34 was to be an extension of the Oak Street Connector out past a peripheral road named the Boulevard, where connections could be made to the Naugatuck Valley suburbs. Forty-five acres of populated land would be razed to make way for the highway, which would have a 480-foot-wide right-of-way. A group called the Anti-Route 34 Coalition was formed to fight the plans, and it charged that "The mayor intends to give . . . up [the land] to a concrete jungle to take suburbanites from the Valley to the Interstate highways."

The State Street project, a few blocks from the New Haven Green and the last remaining sore spot in the downtown shopping area, would result in a new city hall, police station, and main library; an art center; a six-lane roadway; and a six-block-long parking garage. The project, which had been in the planning stages for about a decade, would cost $48 million. Critics surfaced and fought it, and in the end the Board of Aldermen amended the Redevelopment Agency's plan considerably.

There was similar controversy over the proposed coliseum and convention center, although the critics were not so successful there.

They did have some luck in at least slowing down the city's plans to re-do the central portion of the Hill neighborhood. Apparently, the city thought it could get away with the Hill project without asking the residents what they wanted, and it started to go ahead with plans to build two new schools, a boys' club, some new housing, and a park. Louis Kahn, the famed architect, was hired to design the project. The plans met with objections in the Hill. Fred Harris told architect Kahn: "You first deal with the people who need housing, and *then* design your pretty neighborhood with parks that we can't live in and trees that we can't live under." Later on, the city indicated that it would not do anything about the Hill Central project until agreement had been reached with the citizens.

The rising dissent took other forms:

• The Coalition of Concerned Citizens, finding that the course in New Haven was toward "dangerous polarization between the black and white communities," asked the Commission on Equal Opportunities to hold public hearings on the city's educational problems, and the CEO responded by holding them. The commission concluded that there was discrimination in the schools, there was an appalling inability to read on the part of students, and there ought to be more community participation in the running of the schools (See Chapter V).

• The CCC accused the Redevelopment Agency, and particularly Melvin Adams, of coddling slumlords. The agency, said the coalition, was not living up to its press notices, including those which had stated that New Haven was vigorously prosecuting slumlords and sending the more recalcitrant ones to jail. Nor, said the coalition, was Adams living up to a verbal agreement, which the CCC had tape-recorded, to tell the coalition within a specified time "whether or not he would enforce the law by prosecuting slum landlords who fail to bring their property up to legal specifications" 60 days after being notified that their property was in violation.

It is difficult to judge the validity of the CCC's accusations, since it is difficult to measure or define "coddling." But it was apparent that the city had become less enthusiastic about prosecuting slumlords after its initial try at it. At any rate, the CCC mounted a picket line outside Adams' house and announced that "we are trying to bring the problem home to him."

Much of the dissent, and perhaps the most productive part of it, was aimed at supporting the emerging black leadership in New Haven—the leadership, exemplified by Fred Harris, that had not yet been co-opted and that was not co-optable.

The Coalition of Concerned Citizens raised money to back Harris and others in a lawsuit they filed against the city and the newspapers which alleged conspiracy, intimidation, harassment and violence. White sympathy played a part, too, in a storm that broke in the late fall of 1967 when Harris, along with several others of a liberal bent, was named by the Board of Education to an advisory committee which was looking into plans for a new community college in the New Haven area.

Harris, at that time, was finishing his 30-day jail term in Hartford and free on bond in the narcotics and stolen typewriter case. Arthur T. Barbieri, the chairman of the New Haven Democratic Town Committee and head of the party machinery, was incensed, as was Congressman Giaimo. Barbieri said the appointment of Harris and the others to the committee had been made by "a chummy clique within the local educational establishment notorious for its wild social experiments and contempt for majority public opinion."

Harris replied that neither of his critics had ever shown any real concern for the poor—even the Italian poor—[4] and he noted that Barbieri, who operated a travel agency and insurance and real estate enterprises in New Haven, had made money off the city and that Giaimo voted with the racist congressional bloc from the South.

In this controversy, as in others, considerable sympathy was generated among the white liberals and radicals for the HPA president, and they backed him.

When an organization called the Black Women of Greater New Haven was formed, in the spring of 1968, with the intention of starting an economic boycott of downtown merchants, the coalition supported it by urging its members to close out their charge accounts and turn in their credit cards. Said the coalition: "We hope that turning our charge cards in and withdrawing economically will . . . communicate that we believe there can be *no* 'business as usual' until the business community applies their power to the change-making process that will, for once, help, not hurt, black people."

For this sort of assistance and sympathy, the emerging black leaders of New Haven in late 1967 and 1968 were thankful. But they also had developed a sufficient amount of intelligence, experience, and what they called "togetherness" to know that white

---

[4] *The Register* was quick to catch this comment which, in heavily Italian New Haven, could easily make a lot of people angry. The headline helped make them angrier: "Harris Raps Italian Critics; Vows More Militant Stand."

people and organizations could not deliver the black community from its various dilemmas.

There was at that time, in New Haven and in the nation generally, a tendency on the part of the black leadership to be younger, to be more militant, and to reject, as a strategic if not a philosophical matter, white support. It became very important for whites to relinquish the positions of power they had assumed in the Movement. In some cases, the changeover was dramatic, as when the Student Nonviolent Coordinating Committee suddenly went from a black-and-white organization to all-black. The Congress of Racial Equality did much the same thing.

Some of the whites thus displaced, even those who had been in the Movement for years and who should have known and gladly welcomed what was coming, were confused and disheartened. Others left joyfully and went off to join the peace movement or to become engaged in programs designed to change the mood of the white community.

In New Haven, the transition appeared to be a smooth one, thanks largely to Fred Harris' tolerance for and understanding of white people. The Coalition of Concerned Citizens and similar organizations quickly understood that when they dealt with the black community in the Hill, their role was to support, not to lead.

Richard Thornell, the black Yale law student who was active in the movement in New Haven with his wife, Joan, and who at one time served as an informal liaison between the coalition and the HPA, commented that the coalition had "concerned itself with establishing an agenda of things that militant grass roots blacks and sympathetic whites could work on in dealing with the overall problems of repression.

"The very active people in the coalition," he continued, "have recognized that the basic design of the agenda has to be done by us, and they're sort of helpful supporters, and I think that so long as this is true, the coalition has some chance."

Although the Coalition of Concerned Citizens and other pre-dominantly white groups had little difficulty in understanding and appreciating the blacks' need for togetherness, the official city of New Haven showed no indications that it understood or appreciated either black togetherness or white dissent. To Mayor Lee and his lieutenants, to the Redevelopment Agency and CPI, the dissenters were, at best, misguided folk who didn't understand what was being done for them. At worst, there were some indications, voiced in private, that some of the people in power thought the dissenters were dupes of a foreign power, some alien philosophy. Such accusations might not be shocking in a backward Southern or Northern town which went for Goldwater in 1964, but in New Haven, with its progressive and enlightened reputation, they were.

On the record, the official reaction to the dissenters was somewhat paternalistic. Dennis Rezendes, the mayor's director of administration, commented: "You have a sort of psychology that has taken place that says whatever is proposed by the Establishment and the representatives of the Establishment—the first thing that you do is you take your militant position, you establish your 'previous position,' you make it known, and you make a lot of noise. That's done in a consistent kind of way. It's the same ones, constantly, all the time. The same names, the same people."

The dissent and the constant opposition to everything proposed by downtown, said Rezendes, were frustrating, "because principally we're action kind of people. We like to see things going, we like to see things moving. We all believe that everything should have been done yesterday. In that sense, it's frustrating. Sometimes it can be annoying, but on the other hand, we're talking about the democratic process. We believe that the public has to have the opportunity to respond, whether you agree with them or not. That's implicit in everything that you do."

For Mayor Lee, the dissent and the dissenters constituted more than frustration. There was also the question of motive. Lee was strongly concerned with people's motives. It was all right, in his estimation, to try to change a system from within, while playing by its rules; it was incorrect to try to bring the system down from outside. He said, once, when asked his opinion of the dissenters:

"I question the motives of a lot of people involved—the Coalition of Concerned Citizens, for one, who are angry whites who have subconscious feelings of guilt, or else they have political ambitions and attempt to coerce and threaten and divide in the very fashion that too many people of the militant left do. Actually, they're from the left, many of them."

On another occasion, the mayor was asked about the expressions of a specific white dissenter, John Wilhelm, who had written critically of Lee.[5] Lee replied:

"Ah, the radical left. The reformers don't have staying power. The two-party system is going to continue, and those who try to bring it down will be unsuccessful, because the country is built on it, and those who are trying to bring it down will be absorbed into it, and some will stand for election under it.

"Look. I grew up in the Thirties. I knew an awful lot of people who felt that the collapse or near collapse of our economic system meant that true democracy could not work. Some of these people were the true intellectuals of our time, and some were swept up into this whole movement, and in a sense, what happened then matches what's happening now. And when the dust settles, 30

---

[5] John Wilhelm, "The Tragedy of Richard Lee," *The New Journal,* October 15, 1967. Wilhelm was, at that time, a recent Yale graduate and a full-time volunteer for the Hill Parents Association. *The New Journal,* in Volume One, Number One of which his article appeared, was a publication of Yale and Yale-connected people. The theme of Wilhelm's essay was that Mayor Lee and his administration had employed "the liberal response" to everything, and that still conditions were bad. He wrote: "Lee's approach is the most comprehensive attempt in the United States to implement the basic liberal theory of change: that those in power will use their power to significantly improve the lot of the disadvantaged, once they are made aware that it is in their self-interest to do so. At bottom is the assumption that the entire community, rich or poor, black or white, shares a common interest. Fourteen years of redevelopment have yet to prove that this is true. . . . The implication, clearly, is that those who are poor now will remain that way unless the structure of the society is changed in some basic way. It is foolish to expect that programs run by those who have gained power in the present structure will do anything but perpetuate that structure. . . . The Lee administration has demonstrated that a determined liberal can do everything possible to rebuild urban America, so long as he does not challenge the right of those in power to make the crucial decisions on priorities. . . . The Mayor has used his political genius to wring everything possible out of those who hold power; but to step outside the existing structure simply does not occur to him."

years will have passed and we'll be a better nation and have better leaders for it."

One reason that Mayor Lee could afford to adopt such a philosophical attitude toward dissent in his city was that there was an alarming shortage of persons whom the Establishment might consider "respectable" dissenters. Of course, Fred Harris, Ronald Johnson, and Dr. and Mrs. Ryan were respectable people by any reasonable yardstick. But they were not accorded official respect any more than Martin Luther King was given the keys to the city of Birmingham. They were "trouble-makers"; they were possessed of "subconscious feelings of guilt";[6] most horribly, they had "political ambitions." And there was considerable reason to believe that the city's reaction to some of the dissenters by arresting and jailing them was not mere coincidence, but part of a planned effort at suppression and repression. Liberals and radicals all over the country, who had watched or participated in the civil rights movement from its beginning, had been warning since the middle of the decade that there would be an era of massive repression against dissenters, and that the reaction would manifest itself in the arrest of dissenters on narcotics charges and on conspiracy accusations. And this was happening in New Haven.

It is possible to theorize that it might not have happened, or that the city would have been considerably more careful about causing it, if the "respectable" white liberals had been more active. As it was, they were hardly active at all. Many of them were on the payroll of the city or of CPI, and thus were effectively silenced. Some of them were making nice speeches; Kingman Brewster, the president of Yale, was making perhaps the nicest ones. In September 1967, shortly after the riot, he welcomed the university's freshmen with these words:

> If human dignity is outraged by violence, by oppression, by squalor, by materialism, it is also outraged by those who seek escape from the world's anguish;

---

[6] Presumably Dr. Ryan, being a psychologist, had managed to bring some of *his* subconscious guilt feelings to the surface.

Escape behind the callousness of indifference;
Escape into a hedonistic self-indulgence;
Escape into panacea;
Escape into hate. . . .

But Yale had not yet figured out how to escape from the escapism it had enjoyed for so long, and which had been exemplified only recently by its refusal to provide temporary housing for the riot refugees. The university was aware of its need to become more relevant to the world around it, but it was not quite sure how to turn the trick. One surefire way to demonstrate relevance was to set up a center of urban studies. Other universities had been doing that for some time, and the foundations seemed eager to invest in anything with the word "urban" in its title.

Thus in the summer of 1967, Yale started setting up an urban studies center. Joel Fleishman, a young Southerner who had worked with former Governor Terry Sanford of North Carolina, was named to the newly-created job of associate provost for urban studies and programs.

The new program seemed to ignore the potentialities for university involvement in the community. A big portion of Fleishman's work, it was announced, would be devoted to coordinating and developing communications among Yale's departments that were performing research on urban matters. It had become apparent that many Yale faculty members were unaware of the work done by their colleagues.

Fleishman also would raise money for individual and group research. And he would "oversee and coordinate the university's growing extracurricular social action programs." The *Yale Alumni Magazine* said Fleishman "would very much like to see the tutorial and other social action work in which so many students now engage made more relevant to the classroom, and vice versa." And it quoted Fleishman as saying:

I don't know to what extent an institution like Yale can ever do strictly service operations because it has neither the mandate nor the automatic resources of a public university, but I don't see any conflict in shaping a program which will enrich our own teaching and research while also providing service to the community . . . We have to get as much as possible out of what resources we do have. Yale's research should benefit the urban population; urban programs should similarly tie back into education.[7]

Perhaps it would have been unreasonable to expect a university, and one with a history of aloofness and isolation, to engage itself in matters of the street in the summer and fall of 1967. But it might be expected that some of the more important and popular liberals at Yale would be involved. They were not. John Hersey, the famed writer, was the master of Yale's Pierson College at that time, and New Haven's riots happened a few blocks from his living quarters. Yet he chose to travel half-way across the nation, to Detroit, to write a book about the riot there.

William Sloane Coffin, the chaplain of Yale, and a man who had traveled as far as St. Augustine, Florida, to make his witness for human rights, was not involved in the New Haven situation. He spent much of his activist time fighting against the war in Vietnam.

Richard and Jon Thornell, who had a great deal of communication with the white liberal community, and in particular with the white liberal Yale community, said they felt the lack of involvement might have stemmed from Yale's being "sort of cocooned off" from the rest of the world. Said Mrs. Thornell:

"Some of us started out thinking that the white liberal community—as opposed, say, to the AIM community, which we would be inclined to put into the radical group—wasn't responding, and that maybe there's a job of education to be done with these people. People at Yale, you know, don't read the papers in town."

Her husband recalled a meeting that the black community and the Coalition of Concerned Citizens had held with the Rev. Mr. Coffin. Fred Harris had led the delegation. "We went to see him to apprise him of the oppression that militant black groups are facing in New Haven," said Thornell. "His reaction was one of, first, ignorance, and then secondly one of disinterest in becoming in-

---

[7] "At the University: An Important Step to Coordinate Urban Studies and Programs," *Yale Alumni Magazine*, October 1967.

volved in the local situation because of his involvement in the anti-draft movement. Mr. Harris pointed out to Mr. Coffin that it's all well and good to struggle for freedom in Vietnam, but idealism should begin at home; and that he had a responsibility as a so-called moral leader, as a religious leader, to confront immorality in this city.

"And he responded in a very peculiar kind of way. It's a way that, I would say, is peculiar to political moralists—that is, moralists who have their ear to the ground, moralists who want to be sure that while they appear to be radical, they're not really rocking the boats in which they reside.

"Coffin's taking on the city administration of New Haven would have involved him in rocking his own boat, because the university is very closely tied with the city administration; in fact, the mayor is a former employee of Yale. He's a fellow at one of the colleges at Yale, and he spends some time in the Yale University gym, and he eats lunch at Mory's, and he spends quite a bit of time in Woodbridge Hall, the president's office. So Mr. Coffin can be written off as being immediately indifferent to the problems here.

"Another thing," Thornell continued: "Another of the political moralist's problems is that when it comes to supporting a black cause, he wants to be sure that it's the perfect cause. That is to say that there's absolutely no risk involved in supporting the leadership of the cause. And he [the Rev. Mr. Coffin] said that before he could get himself involved he'd have to be sure that Mr. Harris was innocent and all this kind of thing.

"And Mr. Harris pointed out that it wasn't a personal cause that we were involved in here; it was a social cause. But, like all other political moralists, Mr. Coffin couldn't see the distinction, because he said *his* cause might be jeopardized by his involvement in support of Fred Harris. He also pointed out that he didn't like Fred's wearing dark glasses.

"I think it's interesting that Mr. Coffin should rush all over the South some years ago in the sit-in demonstrations, and yet he has not lifted a hand thus far in New Haven since systematic repression has begun. Even to speak out.

"We were particularly interested in having a dialogue with him because he had the national stage, and if he had tried to relate his struggle against the war in Vietnam to the struggle here at home, against the repression of black people, well, we think that he could have done a great service to the cause of social justice between the races. But he hasn't been able to see the forest for the trees here at home."

Thornell paused. "I'm afraid my remarks about Mr. Coffin could be interpreted as a personal assault against the man," he said. "They're not. I'm talking about a breed of white liberal."

If the white liberals in New Haven who had access to the national spotlight were unwilling, as the blacks said, to become involved locally, then an important source of pressure was missing. It was a source of pressure that, if it had been evident, might have guided Mayor Lee, the Redevelopment Agency, and Community Progress, Incorporated, in a direction more compatible with citizen participation.

The fact that this pressure was missing might explain—but not necessarily justify—the disinclination of the city to deal with, and to recognize the leadership of, groups such as the Hill Parents Association and the Coalition of Concerned Citizens. Things might have been different if Kingman Brewster had recognized early on the need for Yale to serve as a constructive critic of the city; if William Sloane Coffin had made the point, in front of the television cameras whose attention he commanded, that freedom was lacking at home; if John Hersey had been reported to be gathering material for a book about city-community relations in New Haven. Much of New Haven's success at gaining foundation and government money and favorable publicity was built on *previous* favorable publicity. If the flow of nice words about the city could have been threatened, perhaps the city would have paid more attention to the dissenters.

Mayor Lee maintained that he *did* pay attention to the dissenters. A mayor, he said in the spring of 1969, before he announced that he would not run again, "has to have an ear for the demands of the multitude. I don't mean let them blackmail him into doing things, but he has to listen to them." Reminded of Mitchell

Sviridoff's suggestion in 1959 that a mayor shouldn't ignore the militants, he replied: "I *didn't* ignore them. I meet with them, listen to their requests. They come down without an appointment, and I see them anyway. I see them on the spur of the moment. You have to listen to *everybody* when you're mayor. If you don't listen, you won't be mayor very long.

"You have to listen to the PTA, to the self-styled radicals of the white community—everybody. You just listen to them all and what you have to do is decide what's best for the city and then proceed accordingly. I suppose that all adds up to eight two-year terms."

There was, though, another group of dissidents in New Haven that were extremely, undeniably respectable, an organization representative of the black community and full of the potential of communication. Most mayors would have given their eye teeth for an opportunity to deal with such an organization, but there is no record that Richard Lee paid more than passing attention to this one.

It was called the Black Coalition. The coalition was formed shortly after the riot. As one observer put it, the middle-class black community was beginning to feel personally the issues of black power and awareness that were surfacing nationally, and that had been surfaced locally by militants such as Fred Harris. A small group of people formed an organization called the Black Community Council because they wanted, according to one of them, "after they realized there was no broad-based community group, to set up one." The council petered out. A month or so later, a group connected with the Dixwell Community House, the focus for civic groups in the Dixwell neighborhood, started holding small discussions about the future of the black man in New Haven. They called their informal group "Heritage Hall."

Fred Harris remembered Heritage Hall's purpose was "to start a room, a library, or something of this type, dealing with black heritage and black people and all the important contributions that they gave to the world and to America." Hugh B. Price, who became the Black Coalition's executive director, recalled in 1969 that Heritage Hall developed into the Black Coalition because a need was felt for "a broader-based united black front in this city." The Heritage Hall discussion groups, Price said, were basically "a series of Saturday morning sessions where any black folks in the community, who wanted to, came together and sort of knocked their heads against each other to find out what this thing of blackness was all about—what it meant to be from the varying social and economic backgrounds, and what were the kinds of issues they could deal with."

The group found a few common denominators, he said. "Initially they found, for instance, the CPI ought to be decentralized. This was a project that they could all agree on. And they were very upset about the bomb plot conspiracy which had been alleged and charged against five people.[8] There were numerous outbreaks in the school system, and the police were being placed in the schools, and that was another area which they could deal with as a unit.

"And they also began to explore the entire feasibility of being a united effort, and that, of course, took quite a bit of time to resolve." When it was resolved, around January 1968, the group started calling itself the Black Coalition. An executive committee was set up, and efforts were made to secure funds.

The formation of the Black Coalition made several things clear. For one, the black leadership was obviously aware of the need for an umbrella-type organization that could speak for black New Haveners and resist the division that had worked for so long in the Establishment's favor. For another, the coalition was strongly for community control and citizen participation. And, finally, it exemplified the black need and desire for togetherness. A brief history of the coalition stated:

> The summer revolution of 1967 in New Haven shook the well-established political and social foundations of this city. New Haven had acquired a national reputation for urban renewal

---

[8] Actually, six were accused in the "bomb plot" case. One of them was white.

and antipoverty programs through the iron, one-man rule of Mayor Lee, his resourceful deputies, and his sophisticated public relations office. Only a few militant voices dissented from the veil of security and progress which shrouded New Haven. Black People as well as whites appeared to believe that this could indeed become the first slumless city.

The revolution permanently reordered the basic black-white and black-Negro relationships. Blacks throughout the city began to echo the previously "radical" contentions of black "militants" that black people and the poor in general must control their own lives and the government programs that affect them. The era of the anti poverty or urban renewal program designed and implemented by white planners yielded to that of black self-determination.[9]

It was a surprise to some when the funds did come in. In March 1968 the United Church on the Green, one of New Haven's oldest and most respected institutions, gave the coalition $10,000 for "neighborhood self-development." The coalition promptly formed a disbursement committee, made up of representatives of black organizations, to decide how the funds ought to be allocated. "The composition of this committee was revolutionary," noted the coalition, "in that organizations which stood to receive grants participated in the decision as to how the . . . grant ought to be shared."

The coalition was in the midst of its search for funds when the Rev. Dr. Martin Luther King, Jr., was assassinated. "The shock of Dr. King's death," said the coalition, "prompted a number of white institutions to re-evaluate their commitments to resolving inner-city problems and to recognize the Black Coalition as a viable organization with the potential to spearhead the drive for black self-determination."

In May 1968 Hugh Price, who had been one of those New Haven blacks with talent working for the city (a 26-year-old Yale law graduate at the time, he had worked for the Redevelopment Agency and the New Haven Legal Assistance Association), joined

9 "The Black Coalition of New Haven—The First Year," The Heritage Hall Corporation, 1969.

the coalition as its executive director. The chairman of the board was Henry E. Parker, the owner and director of a nursery school who had come to New Haven in 1957 as a program director in one of the community schools. The coalition's umbrella covered such diverse black groups as the Urban League, the National Association for the Advancement of Colored People, the Hill Parents Association, the Opportunities Industrialization Center, Muhammad's Mosque Number 40, Kappa Alpha Psi, the Progressive Democrats, the Farnam Courts Tenants' Council, the Knights of Ebony, and the Elks.

The coalition set about drawing up what it called the Blueprint for Black Dignity and Equality. Price explained:

"What we've done here is try to isolate the major problem areas that the black community has to deal with, and we've gotten literature on the programs that black groups are attempting to undertake and the kinds of programs that we think ought to happen in the city. We want to secure independent funding for them so that the black community can set its priorities and run its own programs." At first, he said, the coalition was looking into programs involving education, community awareness and organizing, voter education and registration, community service projects such as teenagers' lounges and narcotics assistance, and economic development. In other words, the Black Coalition was proposing to do the things that Community Progress, Incorporated, had promised seven years before, and that a lot of people thought CPI had already accomplished.

The Black Coalition grew rapidly. Its growth was aided immeasurably by the 1967 riot and the sudden realization by many New Haveners that things weren't perfect; by the repressive events of the fall of 1967; by the white community's almost desperate need for a black counterpart with which to communicate; and by the genuine white fear that followed the death of Dr. King. If the Black Coalition had any problem with respectability, that problem was solved when various white institutions recognized and financially aided the coalition. Yet the people in City Hall acted as if the Black Coalition never existed.

"If we're talking about the traditional city power structure," said Price, "our dealings with them are minimal. They recognize us; I don't know what they recognize us *as*. They recognize us as a group that's in the city.

"I think that the private sector, such as the foundations and the university, do recognize us as the group to deal with. The city doesn't want to do it, obviously, because it's the traditional kind of diplomatic recognition kind of thing: You don't want to give a person power by recognizing his existence. They've tended to deal with us when they thought the result would be beneficial to their situation. Our dealings with City Hall have been very casual and very minimal."

He was asked if City Hall wasn't looking for *some* group or individual in the black community with whom it could deal. "No," he replied. "I think it's fair to say that City Hall doesn't really give a hoot about the black community right now. They don't consider the black community to have any political strength, or any highly organized strength that they have to respect, to kow-tow to."

The reason for this, he said, could probably be found in the political personality of Richard Lee:

"I think Lee is a man who did an extraordinary job up until about three or four years ago, and then his political style was such that he wasn't able to make the shift into the mid-Sixties. There are a number of serious mistakes that City Hall made: Certainly the urban renewal program, which destroyed so much housing, was a serious mistake. I don't know that people were capable of perceiving that it was a mistake back then, but it's clear that it had become one.

"But the major problem is that the style of governing obviously changed. We didn't go all the way to the form of participatory democracy, but certainly the notion of decentralizing and sharing responsibility began to occur in about '64 or '65—questions of greater neighborhood participation in urban renewal programs, CPI programs.

"The city resisted it in the same way cities everywhere resisted it, and that was Lee's downfall. Whether it finished him locally, I don't know. But certainly as a national leader it was his downfall. He could very easily, I think, have been a hero. I think he could have made the adjustment."

But, Price was asked, making an adjustment means relinquishing power, doesn't it?

"I think he could have remained in power, kept his prestige, if he had made that adjustment. But of course that's all tied up in a person's own style of governing. And he couldn't do it. I don't think Lee's any great friend of the black community."

VIII
The Private Sector Moves

It's almost too late and we'd better get busy.
God help us all, we'd better get busy.
—Richard Lee on March 20, 1968

BY THE SPRING of 1968 hardly anyone who had paid a modicum of attention was still arguing that the riot of the previous summer, alone, had been the manifestation of some great change in New Haven's life. There was an acknowledgment among thoughtful people—aided, no doubt, by the report of the National Advisory Commission on Civil Disorders—that urban violence was a symptom, and not a cause; that it was a symbol of conditions that had been present all along, and that one of the conditions had been the racism of white society. Such arguments had been made for a long time by students and practitioners of the movement, and they had been accepted even by thoughtful political people— mayors such as Arthur Naftalin of Minneapolis, Jerome Cavanagh of Detroit, Ivan Allen of Atlanta, and John Lindsay of New York.

Of course, there were large numbers of New Haveners, and of Americans in general, who did not care in the least whether the riots were causes *or* symptoms. They believed, as did Mayor Sam Yorty of Los Angeles, that trouble was caused largely by Communists who were directing their recruiting efforts at "people who are excitable and some who are ignorant," a term he once used to describe Negroes. By and large, though, this segment of Americans had no real political leader. They had been all but ignored by the politicians, by the social welfare and the educational establishments, and by the press, and they felt that the riots, and the authorities' responses to them (which they considered too polite), were yet another indication of society's leaders' kowtowing to a minority group that was shiftless and that wanted everything for nothing. These whites later would make themselves and their grievances known, some of them by voting for George Wallace for President, others only slightly less dramatically by voting for Richard Nixon. But in the spring of 1968 they were just beginning to find their voices, and it was impossible to measure the power they wielded in New Haven or anywhere else, outside of the most reactionary Southern states and a few Northern centers of bigotry. But it is possible that, in the spring of 1968, they made up an unorganized and as yet unawakened majority of New Haven whites.

There was another category of New Haven whites, who probably made up a significant minority, who were characterized at that time mainly by their apathy—citizens who might readily have accepted the idea that summertime violence was a manifestation of something larger and more brooding, but who previously had done little or nothing about it. And, these citizens might have thought, there was little reason to try to do something about it, because Dick Lee was there in City Hall. All the magazines and government officials said Dick Lee was the best there was; how could anyone help in a situation like that? These citizens were not confined to any racial or class category; they could be members of the business Establishment, or the clergy, or the Yale faculty, or one of the prominent law firms; they even could have been Negro leaders of the more traditional variety.

Now, while a certain other segment of white New Haven was talking about repression, and seeing every arrest in the Hill as evidence of the tightening of a noose around the neck of dissent, and while a certain segment of the black leadership was talking most intensely about "getting ourselves together," this apathetic portion of the city seemed to be moving, too, away from its apathy.

It was common after the riot and after the events of the fall of 1967 to hear people (including the mayor himself) say that the city had been "Letting Dick do it" all alone for too long; that it was now time for others to pitch in and help. The theme was evident on March 20, 1968, in the ballroom of the Park Plaza Hotel, as the Citizens Action Commission gathered at a luncheon. The scheduled speaker couldn't make it, and Mayor Lee spoke in his place.

James Gilbert, the CAC chairman, and the president of C. W. Blakeslee & Company, a large construction firm headquartered in New Haven, opened the meeting with praise for Lee. "Tremendous advances have been made in New Haven over the past fifteen years," he said, "and the reason is Richard Lee." But "as a result of the initiative of Dick Lee," the citizens themselves had lost their initiative. "Are we, the citizens, going to abrogate our responsibilities to the special interest groups in the city?" he asked. He did not explain what those special interest groups were.

Citizens, ordinary citizens, could get involved, Gilbert said, by doing volunteer work—helping the elderly, tutoring at the schools. Industries should hire the "hard-core unemployed." People could patronize Negro-owned businesses: "Go out of your way to do something as simple as going by a Negro filling station for a tankful of gas." Go to hearings and meetings.

"One man has shown us the way," Gilbert concluded. "One man has breathed life and hope into the City of New Haven." Now, he said, it remained for the citizens to take over the job.

Mayor Lee rose to speak, looking small at the head table in comparison with the others there, looking trim and Ivy League in his pinched collar and tasteful tie.

"We're not a Model City," he said, "and we never have been. We have a long, long way to go. Each day . . . I wonder when, if ever, all the goals will be met and equal opportunity will be something more than an empty phrase. When I started out, in '53, I thought that by 1970 we'd have a slumless city. . . . We'd have rebuilt our city. . . . Have new schools.

"It's March the 20th of 1968, and when you look around you and you look at your city, and see how much we've done, and how much more there is tragically to be done. . . .

"Before we can solve our problems, we need the kind of commitment from business, and labor, and government, and from the two-party system, that'll really make these programs work." Mayor Lee talked about some of the things that had been done, and some of the things that should be done, "now, yesterday, five years ago." It is possible, with hindsight, to read into the things he said some indication that he was thinking about retiring from his job. But it is not recorded that anyone present at the luncheon interpreted his remarks that way.

"It's almost too late," said the mayor, sounding a bit tired, "and we'd better get busy. God help us all, we'd better get busy."

Before long, it was *de rigueur* for knowledgeable people in New Haven to repeat the theme about having let Dick do it all. Joel Cogen, who worked for the Redevelopment Agency for nine years, part of that time as its executive director and general counsel, offered a typical interpretation:

"One of Lee's problems in New Haven always was everybody said 'Leave it to Dick Lee.' The mayor came in and took a really moribund community, created this very dynamic government enterprise, which went about solving all sorts of problems, both physical and human. It wasn't just a big clearance program as some people say it was. There was a hell of a lot more to it than that. And everybody was used to letting Dick do it.

"The business community really wasn't doing much, nor was the organized civil rights community. Everybody always left it to the mayor.

"All of a sudden, the problems weren't the kind of problems that the mayor could solve alone. That was almost true by definition: When a part of the problem is that the black community wants to assert itself and make its own kind of determination and is looking for forms of expression and of self-implementation, there were no examples in New Haven to follow because everybody in New Haven had been letting the mayor do it.

"The tools that the mayor had been using for a long time, very successfully, all of a sudden really were not relevant to the demands."

Mayor Lee put it differently on another occasion, a little more than a year after the riot, when he commented: "I recognized a long time ago the social evils of a city, and the tragedy is that, like a voice crying in the wilderness, or the man who cries out too often, 'Help, help,' when finally the day of atonement arrives, no one pays any attention. Or people have failed to heed the warning until it's too late."

A visitor to the mayor's office mentioned that that had been a theme of Lee's in the past year.

"Not in the past year," he said. "The past five or six years. When I reached my tenth anniversary in this office, I guess, I began to realize that people just weren't paying attention."

"They were letting you do it?" asked the visitor.

"They were and they are."

There *were* people in New Haven who had been paying attention, and who had been offering help, and who had had their services turned down. Fred Harris had offered to help, in a way. He had offered it, perhaps, in an *unusual* way, but any experienced student and practitioner of social change, such as Mayor Lee, should have been able to recognize that Fred Harris had no alternative but to demand, to exhort, to be militant. Richard Belford had offered his services, and by his account and according to his voluminous narratives, they were similarly rejected.

Some attention must be paid to the notion, then, that it was not entirely a matter of an apathetic public's "Letting Dick do it." There were examples of persons' offering their help, and of City Hall's rejecting them. City Hall was, as before, a tightly-organized "executive-centered coalition." If the help that was offered did not coincide precisely with the sort of help City Hall wanted, then it was not welcomed.

Some observers of the New Haven scene attributed this situation to the sort of politician Lee was—a man not ordinarily given to sharing power. One former colleague of the mayor's commented that "The trouble with this guy is he enjoys playing the game, but he always has to win a hundred-to-nothing."

Another ex-New Havener, Mitchell Sviridoff, Lee's first CPI

director, put it a little differently when he recalled what it was like, trying to help Lee:

"It's very difficult for a political leader, who has built his strength and reputation and success on being *the* dominant leader, to share his power, to submerge himself into a power-sharing strategy.

"You know, when we worked for Dick Lee, there were several of us who were rather strong personalities in our own right. And we knew that we had to submerge our personalities to his. We knew that our talents had to be given to him. That's maybe one of the reasons why good, talented people couldn't stay in New Haven forever. Talented people aren't going to submerge themselves forever to another personality. They want to kind of make it out on their own. They want to be recognized for what they are."

It turned out, however, that a lot of people in New Haven who had been apathetic *did* start to get busy around the spring of 1968. It cannot be said, for certain, what their motives were. Whatever the reason, it appeared that white communities in other cities of the nation were reacting in pretty much the same way at pretty much the same time. Some white New Haveners, un-doubtedly, had truly been lulled into feelings of mistaken security by the awesome visions of physical renewal that seemed to become more magnificent every time they drove in to work from the suburbs. For these, the fact that violence had struck the Model City was shocking, and they wanted to do something about it.

Some, certainly, were motivated as much as anything else by fear of the black man. New Haven whites, like Northern whites in general, suffered from a debilitating complaint that stemmed from residential and social segregation. They knew few Negroes; the ones they did know were tokens of one sort or another; and, since they were *Northern* whites, their feelings about race were not influenced by the massive sense of region-wide guilt that influences the waking moments of white Southerners. Northern whites, in the spring of 1968, thought they had little reason to feel guilty about race. If they came from an old family, their grandfather was a

Union general; if they came from a new family, their father had been discriminated against, too, but he had pulled himself up by his bootstraps.

Some New Haveners, who could not be considered partisans of the mayor, expressed displeasure at what they considered Lee's lack of leadership during the "disturbances." It was, they said, as if the police had assumed control of the situation—although there was no way for them or anyone else to verify this. Lee said later that such an allegation was untrue, unfair, and totally wrong. "I *was* out there, and I *did* see people, and I *did* see community groups, and I *did* have confrontations with them," he said. To those who were skeptical of Lee all along, this argument carried little weight. The mayor's attempts at communication and confrontation, to them, were again a little too late.

Some formerly apathetic observers must have been touched by the sudden realization that Richard Lee, after all, was fallible, and that he needed help. And some, even those who thought that they personally had no reason to fear repression during the fall of 1967, must have heard about the harassment of Fred Harris and others at HPA and wondered if this was to be the reaction of a liberal Democratic city administration to pleas, and then demands, for citizen participation.

Lee's state of the city address, which he delivered in February 1968, was in part a request for help, but it had not helped to settle any white liberals' fears about the official reaction to the year of dissent. The speech was not at all in the tradition of liberal Democratic rhetoric. It did not demonstrate an understanding and tolerance of what had happened in the previous year. Instead it was defensive; it revealed that the mayor was still hurt by some of the criticism he had received. It was a call for unity, but the only sort of "unity" that could be inferred from the speech was unity behind what had been the status quo. Worst of all, it revealed that Mayor Lee either had no clear ideas about how to carry the city forward, or, if he did, that he was not willing to unveil them.

The speech, Mayor Lee told the Board of Aldermen, was about the spirit and morale of the city:

Tonight my remarks are directed to those whose differing views could tear this city apart. It is beneficial to have discussion in the marketplace of public opinion, but it is harmful to have so much negative and carping criticism, and planned divisive actions. We must recognize the harm which results from hostile, negative arguments, and seek instead new ways to bring people together in fruitful discussion of programs dealing with the future of the city.

I am not talking just about the deliberate fomentors of violence or those who are proponents of vigilante action and who would take the law into their own hands. These people are violators of the law and will be dealt with accordingly.

But I am appealing to the others—the responsible citizens, whose support and steadying influence this city needs badly. We need more citizens—black and white—who can join in our common work, unburdened by racial or ethnic prejudice.

I ask all of those who care about their city to stop this rancorous and hostile criticism of other groups, this tearing apart of our city in personal feuds, and this sweeping, unrestrained hostility to government on all levels. . . .

Tonight I ask you: How can we as a city, a people, a nation make progress in an atmosphere of mistrust, rancor, and continual bombardment?

There was, by tradition, a section of the state of the city speech that addressed itself to the future. But even there, Lee said little that had not been talked about before, and his audience could only speculate on how its mayor planned to get on with the solutions. He suggested a city-wide task force to find jobs; better utilization of the high schools for community activities; making 1968 "the greatest housing year in the history of New Haven"; improving police-community relations by opening more neighborhood police centers, and further improving parks and health services. There were a few lines about citizen participation: "We can make wise use of federal funds for our Model Cities and urban renewal projects and involve more people in the planning of programs which affect their neighborhoods."

"These are but some of the things we are setting forth as goals in 1968," said Lee in his conclusion, "but, as I said when I began

my remarks tonight, even more important than these specific programs and more important than more money for these programs
is the *spirit* and *morale* of the city."

It may have helped things, in the spring of 1968, that Fred
Harris was out of the picture temporarily, and that in his absence,
the black community was engaged in the serious soul-searching that
was to result in the formation of the Black Coalition. Crises, at
least those created by black protest, were at a minimum.

Harris had appealed his verdict of guilty in the narcotics case,
and he had gone to Daytop, the narcotics treatment center on
Staten Island, New York.

A high city official, asked at about that time about his feelings
about Harris, replied: "I haven't had any personal tensions with
him. Fred Harris is at Daytop right now; he's drying out from
narcotics. He claimed he was framed by the police when they
caught him with heroin and now, at the very time the appeal is
pending, he's in a private san drying out."

Harris had a somewhat different explanation. "When I went to
Daytop," he said, some time later, "I didn't go because I was
strung up on drugs. I guess I had four or five years of straight
grinding, night and day, and I guess I never knew much about
vacations and stuff like that. I never had vacations. I guess I felt
that my understanding was just, that's the way black people live,
you know—grinding and grinding and grinding.

"And not understanding that at different points you need to go
away and rest a little bit, take a few days off, something like that,
which I never did. I guess things had just gotten to the point
where my head was all knotted up, and I needed a place to go
which wouldn't cost me any money, and I talked to guys from
Daytop and I liked the way they talked, and it was free. Plus I
could learn about drugs. So I guess that's why I went to Daytop."

Was his head knotted up because of drugs? "Nah."

Because of being a black man in America?

"I think so. You know, wanting to take the hard, direct, black
route, but being confused at a lot of different points because I

knew that a lot of the people who really address themselves to our problem are *white* people. And that was very confusing. And I didn't know how to handle that.

"I think I know a little better now how to handle it, but it's still confusing. I'm not really concerned about integration now. I'm not *for* integration, at least not right now. I probably could be interested, once white people address themselves to their racism and begin to understand what it is and why it's perpetuated, and the danger of it. Then you stand a chance of at least coming together to address ourselves to the problems. But until that happens, I think black people will have to take the hard-nosed position. You know: separatism, or at least mental separatism."

When the apathetic white community did start trying to become involved, it was led not by the city but by what has come to be called the "private sector." The term may conjure up visions of bankers, lawyers, and owners of factories, and in New Haven it did mean this, but in New Haven "private sector" also meant Yale. Yale was the first in the private sector to become involved, and it is likely that it was the university's involvement that led the bankers, lawyers, and owners of factories to do something.

Yale had something of a record of being quicker than the rest in recognizing a problem and in doing something about it. It may be recalled that back in 1955 Yale had been among the first of New Haven's private institutions to recognize the value of physical renewal, and it had bought the three high schools from the city; again, in 1956, it had helped bail Lee out by showing interest in the Oak Street apartment complex.

Now, in 1968, Yale was the first of the private institutions to recognize the need for letting someone beside Dick do the job of "human renewal." Perhaps only an educational institution of high reputation could have afforded to be the first. Yale was thorough, competent, intellectual, decent, and gentlemanly. Everything it did was well thought-out, and when it did it, what it had done was explained, for those who were interested, in exquisite language on finely-coated paper. Yale's recent presidents had always been several steps ahead of society in general, and at least half a step ahead of the students.

When Yale undertook a project, its *modus operandi* was almost directly opposite that of a government agency. Government had a tendency to start poverty programs with speeches and promises, estimate that x million dollars would be needed, appropriate one-half x, shortly grow disenchanted with the program generally, re-fund it the following fiscal year for one-quarter x, and then declare the program a failure but retain the bureaucracy that operated it. Yale, when confronted with a proposal or a problem, would haggle with its rich, WASP soul for years, finally decide it would do something, and then do it, and do it in a way that it, and presumably a large majority of the white liberal society, thought was right.

What bothered Yale's more moderate critics, even her friendly ones, was not so much that the decisions were wrong. Demonstrably wrong and stupid decisions had been made at Columbia University and the University of California at Berkeley, but that was not Yale's big problem (the refusal to house exiles from the Hill during the riot was an exceptional blunder, and quite out of character for Yale). What irritated the critics was that the decisions often took so long to be arrived at.

Thus, during the period when the first rumblings of anger were being heard, when the Hill Parents Association was asking for participation and the city was denying it, when CPI was losing its grip on "human renewal" and slowly but surely disintegrating into a mere service agency like the United Fund, Yale was silent. It may have been haggling with its soul, but on the surface it was quiet. If Yale was asked why it was so aloof, the usual answer was that faculty and students were hard at work, on their own time, contributing their energies to the city. The problem, however, was that the city was co-opting Yale just as it was co-opting likely black leaders, and Yale's singular role as a powerful and valuable critic was compromised.

For those more intimately involved in the politics of con-frontation and protest in New Haven, Yale was not only aloof and slow, but it also was doing the wrong things. Spokesmen from the Hill Parents Association assailed the university's plans for a $50-million expansion of its medical center, situated in the Hill, on the grounds that an uncounted number of Hill families would be up-rooted. They also claimed that blacks and Puerto Ricans who were on welfare were discriminated against in the Yale-New Haven Hospital. And they were angered at the obvious lack of black faces on the Yale faculty—and, in fact, in most positions of employment except the menial ones.

There was, at the same time at Yale, a growing undercurrent of resentment from another area—Yale's own black undergraduates, of whom there were about 100 in late 1967. The blacks at Yale had formed their own organization, the Black Student Alliance, as early as 1964, but in those days there was still a great deal of talk about integration, and the organization was far from militant. Blackness had not yet become synonymous with "beautiful." The Yale students got together, some of them said, because they wanted better social lives.

Once the black students' organization was functioning, the students soon found, as others were finding all over the nation at that time in what was to become an important movement, that there were problems other than social that confronted Negro students. They wanted courses in black history; they wanted more black faculty members (Yale had one black professor); they wanted more black students; and, above all, they wanted somehow to re-move the stigma of being "different" in a situation where everyone made a great fuss of denying that they were different. But by that they did not mean that they wanted to remove their blackness and become white.

The students, who had been nine or ten years old at the time of the Supreme Court desegregation decision, and who had grown up watching and sometimes feeling their nation resist and flaunt that decision, were under terrible strains, not the least of which was the pressure to accept white liberal students and faculty mem-bers as their "equals" in their struggle for identity.

There were other, more specific, stresses, too. At Yale, campus policemen were in the habit of stopping black students at the college gates and asking them for their identification. The logic was simple:

There had been thefts from students' rooms.
Slums surrounded Yale.
Black people lived in slums.
Black people, therefore, were the thieves.
All black people look alike.
Therefore, the black students were suspected of being thieves.

To solve this problem, which infuriated the Yale blacks, some students took to wearing Yale sweatshirts all the time. After the issue reached the stage of protest, it was reported that the police had been instructed to try to memorize the faces of the black students.

Yale's attitude, for a very long time, was that black students were no different from white students, and therefore any argument based on an assumption of difference was not valid. It was, on the other hand, good for the black students to be there because their presence made the white students more tolerant. President Brewster said in 1967 that he didn't think white students needed that educational experience as much as they used to. "Nevertheless," he said, "I think for the average student it's a much more normal American life to have a fair representation of colored students in the class. It's like foreign students or any group that had distinctive attributes and qualities and capacities and limitations. It's nice to have students exposed to them."

One of Yale's deans followed that idea out the window by refusing two Negroes' request to be allowed to room together. He gave as his reason, according to one of the students, the explanation that "You're here to be an educational experience as well as to get an education."

Yale also was reluctant to move particularly quickly in the matter of hiring more Negroes to provide company for their token black faculty member. President Brewster said, though, in late 1967, that he was sure more would be hired. "I think it's very much like the problems of admissions," he said. "You can't do it by changing your standards, and I don't think you do it by having a double standard. But it's like looking for a house in a crowded town; you have to use the grapevine to try to find out about the best people but also let the best people available know that you're interested in them. The trouble, of course, is that there are such a darn few whom you would appoint without resorting to a double standard. You don't do the guy a favor, and you certainly don't do his race a favor, if you appoint him *just* because he's black and he turns out not to be as good as the others."

Prior to the spring of 1968, Yale had been more or less content to answer its critics with the rather standard reminders that it was doing its bit, intellectually and financially, and by reminding itself from time to time that it was an educational institution and not an experiment in community action. The school had had ample time to prepare this argument, for one of the few issues that the Republicans could come up with in their foredoomed mayoral campaigns was Yale: Mayor Lee was too chummy with Yale; the school paid little in the way of taxes, etc.

The university's financial contribution to the community *was* great. By 1969 there was an estimate that Yale was putting at least $78 million into the town a year.[1] And Yale drew industries to New Haven; it had a fine teaching hospital; the resources of its architects, libraries, museums, and theaters were part of the community's resources, too.

But suddenly this was not enough. Yale's critics recognized it, and Yale did, too. Intellectual ferment began at Yale, and this time it was aimed not at totaling up all the nice things the school had done for New Haven in the past, but at trying to figure out new nice things for the present and future. As one observer, an

---

[1] The university's payroll was $55 million a year; it spent about $11 million on supplies and equipment; students spent $7 million; visitors, alumni and parents spent $5 million, according to a market report by the Southern New England Telephone Company. ("Report Says Yale Pumps $78 Million To Community," *The New Haven Register,* July 26, 1969.)

employee of the city, put it: "Yale, I think, is trying to find ways that it can support and become part of the community and still maintain its primary function as being an institution of education."

Yale started, as usual, with pretty words printed on fine coated paper, but this time they were strong words. President Brewster, in a special message released in April 1968, let it be known that the university was through haggling with its soul. From now on, he said, Yale would help those who wanted to change things outside the campus. The message said, in part:

> There is an urgent and welcome call for the university to commit itself to do more about discrimination, poverty, poor education, poor housing, all of which deprive many of New Haven's citizens of the opportunities which America is supposed to stand for. Agencies of the city government and other public and private organizations have long had these concerns as their primary mission. This is the university's business also, not only as an institutional citizen of New Haven but as an institution devoted to the advancement of understanding and the education of young men and women who hope to make a contribution to the lives of others. The message of the Kerner Report applies to Yale just as it does to any other American citizen or institution. . . .

Yale already was engaged as an institution in various efforts at alleviating the city's problems, he said, but "We can do better and we can do more." In the field of employment, "our personnel office is designing programs which seek to recruit and train and upgrade people who heretofore were neglected as possible Yale employees."

There was a similar "opportunity and an obligation to do much more" in the field of secondary education. Joel Fleishman's work in setting up urban affairs programs was progressing, but it had become "clear that many initiatives may be frustrated by the lack of a central group with the resources to support planning and the power to seek more adequate funds from individuals and foundations in the name of the university." To this end, Brewster established the Yale Council on Community Affairs, to deal with "Yale's programs relating to human and neighborhood development in New Haven," and he set aside $40,000 to get the council started. (And, in June, Yale hired Peter Almond away from CPI to become the executive director of the council.)

Most important was Brewster's recognition that whatever Yale did, it had to be done in collaboration with the citizens. And he demonstrated that he had been sufficiently impressed with the Black Coalition to ask for its help:

> I am eager to have some non-Yale members on this Yale Council so that its thinking will have the advantage of community consultation throughout its deliberations. To begin this I am asking the Black Coalition if it will provide consultants to the Council. Other groups, including student groups, will be asked to consult and advise in whatever way seems most effective, depending upon the particular area or problem under consideration.

The Black Coalition, he said, seemed to be the likely avenue of citizen participation:

> Yale cannot solve the problems of New Haven, nor can it be its banker or redeveloper. It would be immoral to raise such false expectations. Also, we are aware that there is a widespread insistence by disadvantaged neighborhoods and the black community in general that they should direct their own destiny to a much larger extent than publicly financed welfare and community action programs have been able to permit.
>
> Until recently there has not been any group which could command the allegiance and respect of the great variety and broad spectrum of black groups, organizations, and neighborhoods. Recently a group—the Black Coalition—has come forward which gives promise of such comprehensive representation, and which at the same time is committed to local, neighborhood self-development. . . .
>
> Yale is prepared to put its faith in the Black Coalition.

The Yale Corporation, said Brewster, had "authorized me to respond favorably to any request for planning funds with no strings attached if the coalition should request them to supplement funds applied for and received from others."

The Rev. Dr. Martin Luther King, Jr., had been assassinated six days before.

New Haven had seemed close to serious violence; what saved it, many thought, was a memorial service on the Green, sponsored, conducted, and policed by the Black Coalition. Fred Harris spoke and said "The beast is ready to destroy us." Ronald Johnson said "Now is the time for revenge." Other speakers urged nonviolence. No top city officials spoke at or could be seen attending the service.

Nationally, there was racial violence in 125 cities, and at least 46 persons were killed. A few days after the memorial service, there was what *The Register* called a "night of restlessness in the city's predominantly Negro neighborhoods"; some fires were set, but there was little looting. Most of those arrested were charged with breach of peace, disorderly conduct, loitering, resisting arrest, and abusing a police officer.

Brewster's message was distributed to Yale's 15,000 students, faculty, staff, and other employees. With it was a blank for the recipients to fill out, asking for their pledges to help destroy white racism by volunteering their time or their money, by writing to their congressmen, and by working within their churches and organizations to make them more relevant to what was happening.

But there was some instant, material assistance, too. Soon after Brewster delivered the message, Yale gave the Black Coalition $100,000. A few weeks before, the United Church on the Green had given $10,000. Later in April, the New Haven Foundation provided $15,000 and a year later it gave another $15,000. In the summer of 1969 Yale promised another $50,000 and the New Haven Jewish Community Council promised $5,000.

By the summer of 1968 Yale was at work planning two new programs, one in Afro-American studies, and one in urban studies. There were 200 summer jobs at Yale for New Haven youths; fifteen Yale students, a dozen of them members of the Black Student Alliance, were assigned to recruiting and counseling in the city; Yale opened its athletic fields to city youth; there were a number of specialized summer programs; and the student radio station stayed on the air all summer, 24 hours a day, providing on-the-job training for two Negroes who wanted to learn the radio business. The station also played soul music for thirteen hours a week.

Yale accepted black students as never before, and Negroes were named to the faculty and staff in unprecedented numbers. In the fall of 1969 the Afro-American studies program was inaugurated, with the help of a grant of $184,000 from the Ford Foundation. The program was an interdisciplinary major, and it was possible to choose from more than 60 courses. Yale opened a new black cultural center. Black students helped plan all these programs and projects.

Also in the fall of 1969 the urban studies center initiated a new undergraduate major, "The Study of the City," leading to a bachelor of arts degree and allowing students to spend a year away from the campus, working in a city. The urban studies major, too, was interdisciplinary.[2]

Yale's new involvement was not accepted with universal praise. Ronald Johnson, of the Hill Parents Association, taking part in a news conference in the summer of 1968 at which militants called for a new black awakening in New Haven, said:

> As in every struggle, the enemy takes on many forms. There are the obvious enemies who hold public office. Perhaps the most difficult enemy to identify and deal with, however, is that enemy who comes disguised as a benefactor. Yale University, which until recently has ignored the *black* community, has now assumed the role of benefactor. But is Yale a true benefactor,

---

[2] Yale, in announcing the new program, commented that "The city is more and more the crucible of our times. . . Indeed its study is mandatory if we are to comprehend and then control the social forces whose currents often threaten to turn awry and challenge the possibility of civilization itself—a civilization whose purpose and destiny are now being judged in the city. As a great center for the discovery and dissemination of knowledge, and for the education of men and women for leadership in society, Yale has a special obligation to encourage, as well as to enable, the members of her faculty and student body to explore the shape and dynamics of our crucible."

or is Yale an enemy in disguise? We have looked this gift horse in the mouth and found that its breath "stinks."

Is Yale a true benefactor or does it have another purpose giving $100,000 to the *black* community? We think it is to buy off the *black* community and to buy security and protection for the thousands of white students and teachers, who invade this community every year, who though foreign to New Haven, receive preferential treatment here, and who require peace and calm in the surrounding *black* community in order to function. . . .

Using money, Yale is trying to play a ruthless game of pacification and political manipulation of the *black* community. The *black* community must be realistic in its dealings with Yale.

We also indict Yale because no amount of money they give to the *black* community can possibly be enough. We do not look upon Yale merely as a bank, but more importantly, as a powerful force in every aspect of New Haven life, especially in the political and economic areas. Yale has failed miserably to use this power to reform the racist power structure, of which it is a charter member, or to put its own house in order. Yale has acted *only* in its own self-interest. It has done us no favors and we owe them none. We will always look a gift horse in the mouth.[3]

Hugh Price, the executive director of the Black Coalition, said, however, that he had not been able to determine that Yale was an enemy in disguise. "There are no strings attached that I've been able to discern," he said in early 1969. "I think the cooperation between the two groups has been quite close. I think they're genuinely committed to this. Of course, if I'm wrong I'll find out, but I don't get that impression so far."

At that point the coalition and its parent group, Heritage Hall, were publishing a newspaper, *The Crow,* a twice-monthly tabloid.[4]

---

[3] Statement by Ronald Johnson, "Five Black Men Call for a New Agenda," *AIM Newsletter,* undated (but late summer or early fall, 1968).
[4] An editorial in the issue of June 7, 1969, explained that while the word "crow" had been offensive and derogatory to blacks, in actuality the bird was "large, majestic . . . smart, clever, prudent and can accurately judge the range of a gun and hence rarely gets shot . . . They rise early, provide for their families very well, and defend their young against enemies valiantly."

The coalition also was busy drawing up a set of proposals for community programs, planning to establish a black foundation, and in general behaving like a sophisticated, articulate organization.

One year after President Brewster's rather dramatic announcement, Yale again was asked for money. This time it was Mayor Lee who made the request. While the mayor was in the annual throes of formulating his new city budget—one that almost certainly would call for a tax rise, despite the fact that it was an election year and Lee was expected to run—he wrote a letter to Brewster asking that Yale pay the city $3 million a year over the following three years. This, said Lee, would be a gift from Yale to the city, in lieu of taxes, and it would be less than half of what Yale would be paying if its property were not tax exempt. The money, said Lee, would go into the city's education budget.

President Brewster was not enthusiastic about the idea. "Even if we wanted to," he replied to Lee, "there is a serious question whether we could legally reduce Yale's budget by millions of dollars in order to make a grant to the city. Our funds are held in trust for Yale's educational purposes."

Furthermore, he said, it would be a dangerous precedent. "I see nothing but trouble if Yale were to enter a relationship with the city government of New Haven which involved an annual payment which had no objective economic basis and no foundation in law," he told Lee. "It would be an invitation to constant haggling and bad faith, since both the city and Yale will always have more financial needs than they have income."

There was much speculation as to what, if anything, was between the lines of the mayor's request and the president's denial. Some observers suspected that Lee and Brewster had set the thing up in advance, and that the exchange of letters was a trial balloon. Others speculated that Lee was getting ready to run for reelection, and he wanted to beat the Republicans to the draw on the issue of Yale—that he knew Yale wouldn't supply the money, but that he asked for it anyway in order to show the voters that he wasn't Brewster's boy.

Still, Yale did not reverse itself in the months following the exchange of correspondence. One thing that was clear was that Yale had changed, in a relatively short period of time, from a very aloof, WASPish institution into one which could shower $100,000 on New Haven's black leadership, but which would not shower $9 million on its white leadership.

One day in the summer of 1969, Peter Almond was reminiscing on the Yale gift to the coalition, and on its refusal of Lee's request, and on his experiences as the head of the Yale Council on Community Affairs (a position he was then thinking of leaving). Work at the council, he said, was "fascinating, because the kinds of problems that come up range from things like trying to find $200 to help the Ebony Fashion Show get a good start to the question of whether Yale ought to give the city $3 million a year in lieu of taxes."

Almond had seen both sides of the picture, first as an employee of Community Progress, Incorporated, then as an employee of Yale. He said he had discovered a "very important distinction between the university administration at its top level—President Brewster, and one or two others—and the city people on the question of how you free up $200. The university people understand the subtleties and nuances and the importance of doing little things, and the importance of being flexible and doing it quickly, and doing it without a lot of messing around. And I didn't find this to be the case with the city, especially in the antipoverty program, where they would make the same fuss over a $200 item that they would make over a $200,000 one."

Almond was pleased that President Brewster had placed his faith, and his university's money, in the Black Coalition. The coalition, he said, was the logical black organization in New Haven with which the white community could hope to deal. "It does make the most sense right now," he added, "because I think it has taken the responsibility to provide general organization and some degree of coherence in planning and fund allocation for the black community. Now, that's taking a chance and a risk that an outsider would have to be a fool to take.

"If I were the mayor and a group offered itself to take on this kind of responsibility, I would do everything possible to link myself to them, to take advantage of their willingness to take strong positions in their own community—that is, to tell their own community 'The money isn't available,' or 'Here's what we have to do to gear up our programs in order to qualify for funds.' In other words, they're willing to take those kinds of tough responsibilities to do a long-range planning, to stick their necks out on the short-range gut problems, and they're able to keep most of the black leadership together on this."

But, he said, Lee had failed to link himself with that opportunity. "In fact, there's open misunderstanding and bitterness between Lee and Henry Parker, the Black Coalition leader; but it also symbolizes the failure of the city agencies, the city leadership, to relate to Black Coalition leadership. And I'm not saying the coalition is tried and true. I don't think their way is the only way to do it. But it's *there,* and it's doing some extraordinary things."

President Brewster took a definite risk, said Almond, in casting his lot with the relatively new coalition before he knew what it could deliver. "What he discerned, though, was that there was pressure on him, as a leader of a major American university, to do something about the city that was right under his nose. So he took a kind of a risk in acting definitively with this particular group. He committed Yale and himself to the Black Coalition, and he did it with that same style that he has of sensing a problem that he's falling a little behind with, and then going out and acting in such a way that puts him two steps ahead."

The mayor's failure to understand was not limited to the Black Coalition and the spring of 1968, said Almond. "I think even before that summer of 1967, when he was under the new pressure from communities to get some part of the action in the city, to get some control of programs, he failed to understand what it was about. And then the riot kind of sealed it up. It took his politician's suspicion of the new forces that threatened his power and turned it into blind spots about the black community. And all this was disruptive to Lee.

"His entire commitment and his notion of community change and urban renewal had begun and had been represented by a major kind of activity that focussed on strong central leadership, manipulation of power, dealing with the federal and state authorities and Yale—but all in a kind of massive urban real estate venture, as opposed to sensing the mood and spirit of a community that needed some kind of uplifting."

After Yale announced its commitment, and then backed it up with money, the other portion of New Haven's "private sector" started to move, too. In New Haven, as in America generally, business, industry, and organized labor had been reluctant to do any more than they were required by law to do to improve the lot of the slumdweller and the black. Business even had failed to recognize the potential in Mayor Lee's early efforts at physical renewal, much less human renewal.

Although Lee and his official programs had encountered little resistance from businessmen in the later years of his administration, it had been tough at first. He recalled an incident with a businessman that occurred back in 1954, about a month after he had assumed office:

"I took a distinguished citizen to lunch. He was a leader, a business leader. And I asked him to help me. I outlined what I wanted to do and what I thought should be done, and he listened impassively, and finally when I was through he said, 'Well, not only will I *not* help you, but I voted against you, I contributed to your opponent, and I think I was right. I thought then that I was right, and I think today that I am right, and what you're outlining to me is just the dreams of a young, inexperienced politician.'

"And I said, 'Well, if that's your decision, that's your decision, but that's not going to slow me up because I think I'm right, just as you think you are, so let the record show what you think and what I think.'

"So two years passed, and about a month and a half before the election I got a letter from this business leader, and he said 'Dear Dick: How you ever did it, I'll never know, but you were right and I was wrong. Enclosed is a contribution for your campaign. You'll be pleased to know that I'm voting for you also.'

"I tell you I was shocked when I got that check," said Lee. "Only a hundred dollars, but it was worth $5,000 to me as a reflection of his confidence."

That kind of business involvement came shortly after Lee proved, with highways and buildings and a parking garage designed by Paul Rudolph, that the dreams of a young, inexperienced politician were good for business. And it came when the business leaders allowed themselves to be named to membership on the Citizens Action Commission—an act which Lee later agreed was one of the wisest political moves of his career.

But the other kind of involvement—a recognition and public acknowledgment by the business leaders that they had a role to play in the solution of social problems, followed by action—was not forthcoming for a good long time.

As was the case with Yale's initial efforts at involvement, business, industry and labor engaged in long years of pretty talk before any action occurred. New Haven was not unique in this respect. In the early sixties, many businessmen subscribed to an equal employment program initiated by President Kennedy, called Plans for Progress, that was a fraud on the black people of America. Organized labor did no better. The AFL-CIO passed a resolution at its 1967 convention—one of a long series of such statements of principle—that said "Our goal is true and absolute equality of opportunity throughout America. We shall not rest until we achieve it." But on the local level practically nothing was done. A year later, George Meany sent a letter to the NAACP at *its* convention that could only be described as absurd. He declared that discrimination in local unions "has not been entirely eliminated yet. But with the aid of the federal [civil rights] law we fought so hard to enact, the few remaining abuses will soon be eliminated."

C. J. Haggerty, the president of the Building and Construction Trades Department of the AFL-CIO, a strong proponent of "voluntary action" in desegregating the rigidly segregated building trades unions, said in 1968 that if "qualified" Negroes had been discriminated against, "it hasn't come to my attention."

When the words started turning into actions, both nationally and, then, somewhat later, in New Haven, it was violence, as usual, that did the trick. At the end of the first nine terrible months of 1967, whole sections of Detroit and Newark had been burned to the ground and disorders had been reported in 162 other cities, including New Haven. A group of "leaders of American life," as they later were to refer to themselves (they were 1,200 persons representing business, the professions, organized labor, religion, civil rights groups, and government), met in an "emergency convocation" in Washington and got the Urban Coalition, which had been established a few weeks before, off the ground. Although they were leaders of American life, their organization came to be associated also with the notion of the involvement of white businessmen in the ghetto.

The convocation produced a "Statement of Principles, Goals, and Commitments," which called for a reordering of national priorities and added: "We believe the private sector of America must directly and vigorously involve itself in the crisis of the cities by a commitment to investment, job-training and hiring. . . ."

All over the nation, businessmen appeared to be getting busy. Once they convinced themselves that helping the ghetto was good for business, there was no stopping them or their publicity departments. It is still possible to make the sweeping, general statement that the typical American businessman likes to think of himself as hard-boiled and tough, not subject to the weaknesses that come with making moral decisions. In some cases the very top executives of the very top corporations became personally involved, a necessary step if all the verbiage was to make a difference.[5]

---

[5] One of them was Thomas Watson, Jr., the chairman of the board of International Business Machines, who served as a board member of Bedford-Stuyvesant Development and Services Corporation, a group of white businessmen gathered by the late Senator Robert F. Kennedy in 1967 to offer technical and financial advice to a parallel black organization, Bedford-Stuyvesant Restoration Corporation, in Brooklyn, New York. Watson put an IBM plant in the ghetto that was to employ 300 residents and that was expected to become profitable to IBM within a relatively short period of time. Said Watson, when asked about his experiences: "You've got to cure the ghetto, in my opinion, from a practical, hard-nosed point of view, rather than the point of view of too much do-goodism. . . . There are very few businesses in the United States which can afford to be do-goody. Therefore, for cures to come from business, it

These were the people, as one black economic developer put it, "who can move institutions." With the top executives involved, it was no longer practical for a middle-level executive to say that he would like very much to hire Negroes, but that there weren't any qualified ones around. A memo from the president or the chairman of the board could start a job training and talent search program that could *make* qualified ones.

Often a white business executive could become involved by simply being exposed to the ghetto for the first time in his life. Peter Libassi, who was the vice president of the Urban Coalition shortly after its founding, noted that "Bus tours are important" to acquaint the businessmen with the problems they had promised to try to solve. Libassi said he had seen executives after such tours who were "converted men; they've had religious experiences."

Religious experiences were in short supply among New Haven businessmen, however. Just as it took the assassination of Dr. King to really move Yale to start acting, it took violence to move the businessmen to start talking.

A few days after the March 1968 release of the *Report* of the National Advisory Commission on Civil Disorders, one New Haven businessman told his colleagues that the problems of the cities constituted "perhaps the most serious domestic matter this nation has faced since the Civil War." The speaker was Gordon Grand, the president and chief executive officer of the Olin Mathieson Chemical Corporation, which employed 4,700 people at its New Haven works. He spoke at the annual dinner meeting of the Greater New Haven Chamber of Commerce.

Only a few months before, Grand said, business had been pessimistic about the chances of its involvement in urban problems. But

---

can't be on a do-goody basis. . . . If you're talking about a total cure to hundreds, if not thousands, of ghettoes all around the world, or the United States, then it seems to me that you can only urge sufficient numbers of business people to go into those areas with their businesses if you can take them in on a practical, hard-nosed basis. If you just appeal to their charity, there are not going to be enough businesses doing it to make any real impact on the ghetto. . . . It doesn't take very much to engender pride in those people, it seems to me. Once they get a little bit of dignity and economic independence, the pride comes along pretty fast. Of course, that's what builds industry."

more recently, he said, there had been a "total commitment by business to work with the government to do what we can. . . . business is entering the arena as a full-scale partner in attacking the problems of the city. As a result, entirely new relationships will evolve between the business community and all other elements of society." Business had "no choice" but to involve itself, he said, because Negro leaders thought of business as their last hope for help.[6]

Grand pointed out that the fastest way to break through the "poverty cycle" was through employment, and that "obviously this is the area where industry can make its most immediate contribution." In addition, he said, industry could lend some of its executives and experts to organizations involved in fighting urban problems (a technique which seemed to be working in Senator Kennedy's Bedford-Stuyvesant programs).[7]

Immediately after Dr. King's death, the number of white businessmen who were viewing things with alarm underwent a pronounced increase. It was not surprising that many of those who spoke out used, as their basis for concern, the argument that a nation full of urban problems was bad for business—the money argument, believed by many to be most effective with businessmen.[8]

In mid-April 1968 Alfred W. Van Sinderen, the president of the Southern New England Telephone Company, which was Connecti-

---

[6] This point echoed one made in the Kerner Commission *Report,* which quoted, in an appendix concerning private enterprise, Dr. Kenneth B. Clark as saying: "Business and industry are our last hope. They are the most realistic elements of our society. Other areas in our society—government, education, churches, labor—have defaulted in dealing with Negro problems." (The National Advisory Commission on Civil Disorders, *op. cit.,* p. 313.)

[7] "Olin Head Tells C Of C: Urban Peace Up To Businessmen," *The New Haven Register,* March 14, 1968.

[8] Hardly a speech was made, or a report issued, on the subject of business involvement that did not have as its central focus the profit motive. The Kerner Commission's Advisory Panel on Private Enterprise, made up mostly of businessmen, reported not only that "maximum utilization of the tremendous capability of the American free enterprise system is a crucial element in any program" for setting the country straight, but also that "we believe that a truly massive number of companies could be induced to participate only if appropriate monetary incentives are provided by the federal government to defray the unusual costs of participation." (The National Advisory Commission on Civil Disorders, *op. cit.,* pp. 313–14.)

cut's third largest employer, said if something wasn't done about ghettoes there would be a "tremendous" increase in taxes to pay for more police, jails, prisons, and welfare.

"It has been true through history," he said, that "each generation draws an assignment. We have our assignment. It may not be the assignment we would have chosen, were we given a choice, but it is ours—and our children will judge us by our response to it." If nothing was done, he added,

> . . . we can retreat to the suburbs and prepare for the biggest shootout this nation has seen since 1861 . . . we will lose the peace, the comfort, the security, the prosperity that we have achieved—or that was achieved for us. If we do not help, we will carry an ever-increasing segment of the population that is an unproductive liability on our economy. And if we do not help, we will be encouraging a degree of wastefulness that should be abhorrent to any prudent man.

Van Sinderen, in acknowledging that the business community had not done nearly enough in the past, also admitted that his own business was behind. Only 5.5 percent of the telephone company's 12,329 employees were nonwhite, he said, but he added that he was going to do something about that.[9]

In the action department, the businessmen were a little behind their words. This was the case with the rest of the country, too; another sweeping, general statement that can be made about businessmen is that they often mistake their calls for action for the action they called for. But some progress was made.

A few weeks after the head of the telephone company had delivered his warning, the company announced that it was lending three of its experts to the Board of Education. The purpose, said Van Sinderen, was to help the school system utilize "sound man-

---

[9] "SNET President Warns Colleagues: Aid Ghetto Or Pay Staggering Cost," *The New Haven Register,* April 17, 1968. Van Sinderen did do something about his own company's hiring policies. By January 1970 he had raised the proportion of nonwhite employees to 9.5 percent. In 1969, he said, nonwhites made up 25 percent of all new employees hired by the company in Connecticut, and for New Haven-based employees the rate was higher than that.

agement planning techniques" and to establish better communication between the system and the public. The experts, who were lent to the school system on a part-time basis, included the company's business systems staff manager, a business office supervisor, and the urban affairs manager. (Urban affairs is a recently-coined industry phrase that apparently means public relations with Negroes.)

In January 1968 New Haven's commercial banks announced the creation of a $1-million loan pool that would help small businessmen, particularly in the ghettoes, establish themselves. The loans would go to businesses that ordinarily would not qualify for them; the repayment time would be lengthened, and the businessmen would be entitled to free advice from established experts. On the day after Dr. King was shot to death, the program made its first loan. A few days after that, a New Haven bank issued its first mortgage in a new program designed to make it easier for low-income families to buy their own homes.[10]

And, the Olin Mathieson Charitable Trust donated $265,000 to Georgia Institute of Technology and four black colleges to encourage more Negroes to become engineers, and the New Haven Foundation set up a $25,000 revolving fund to help low-income families make their downpayments on houses. New Haven businessmen became involved, eventually, in a number of nation-wide programs designed to make jobs available to the "hard-core" unemployed, notably the JOBS program.[11] But the most interesting

---

[10] The initial result of these lending programs, however, was probably more to make the bankers feel good than to help the folks in the ghetto. There was much chest-beating in the Bedford-Stuyvesant program about a $100-million mortgage-lending pool that Senator Kennedy's agents had talked 80 New York lending agencies into establishing; a Bedford-Stuyvesant Restoration official called it "the most significant commitment in the country." A lower-level and more cynical program official, however, called the plan a con game "because all those mortgages are insured by the FHA anyway. Those guys are only doing what they should have been doing all along." Of course, it can be argued that if any significant number of Americans had been doing what they should have been doing all along, race relations and cities would not be the problem they are today.

[11] JOBS (for Job Opportunities in the Business Sector) was established in 1968 after President Johnson asked the business community to do something about the "hard-core unemployed." The National Alliance of Businessmen came into being, with Henry Ford II as its chairman; created

and the most potentially hopeful example of the involvement of the white businessman in New Haven was represented by a small group of business leaders who got together on Thursday nights starting in the spring of 1968, who later started calling themselves the Urban Development Organization, and who finally incorporated under the name of the Urban Alliance of Greater New Haven.

One of the original participants in the Thursday Night Group, as it was informally called, was James H. Gilbert, the construction firm president and Citizens Action Commission chairman. Gilbert recalled, in an interview in late 1968, while the group was still in the formative stages, and while it was going under the name of the Urban Development Organization, that the Thursday night meetings got started in April of 1968. "I believe the idea started with the New Haven Community Council and the United Fund," he said, "with professionals who believed that there wasn't enough communication and coordination between agencies. It was agreed that it might be worthwhile for some of the presidents and executive directors of some of the private agencies in town, that were

---

JOBS; and said its goal was to find employment in private industry for 100,000 persons by June 30, 1969, and for half a million by the middle of 1971. By late 1968 the organization said it had found jobs for 84,000 persons, 61,273 of whom were still at work as of September 30. While JOB's own descriptions of what it was doing were full of praise for itself, others found it less dynamic. The National Committee on Employment of Youth charged that the program missed its summer of 1968 goal by 40 percent, and the New York City commissioner of manpower and career development, speaking also of the summer program, said "the private sector just didn't deliver." One possible reason for the summer failure was that the businessman-participants didn't have the proper "incentives"; there were no federal reimbursements for summer job placements. Businessmen got up to $3,500 per person to offset their training costs in the year-round program. The alliance, in its literature, used the term "hard-core" as a noun, and provided its participants with a good deal of advice, such as: "Many Negroes from poor neighborhoods believe a 'hat' is a sign of manhood and should be worn at all times. We know that manhood recognition is usually best achieved through a real job assignment. Through patience and persuasion, we must convince the Negro of this. The same holds true for the transistor radio. To the disadvantaged, music has often been a substitute for conversation. . . . The hard-core respond well to simple rules which are backed up with authority and immediate action if the rule is broken."

relating in one way or another to inner-city problems, to get together to exchange information."

The assassination of Dr. King had nothing to do with the formation of the group, he said. Nor was the group trying to force the city government to do what it had not been doing. "In no way did this supplant, subvert, or replace city government whatsoever. You don't have the top leaders of the city deciding they will sit down and take over city government," said Gilbert.

Rather, the group was founded on the notion of defense. It seemed to be a reaction to the dilemma that black leaders in the Hill had been creating for white businessmen when they asked, year after year, for funds to operate summer programs. The most recent example of that dilemma, which occurred in the spring of 1968, came locally to be called the "$107,000 Holdup." The Holdup consisted of a request from the neighborhood for the money, followed by a great deal of misunderstanding from the businessmen who were being asked for the money, followed by ultimata, followed by the money, followed by hard feelings on the part of the merchants.[12] Gilbert said the Holdup was not responsible for the formation of the Thursday Night Group, but that it did point up to the white business community the need for better coordination and communication in the area of meeting demands and ultimata from the black militants. "Never again will this happen," he said, referring to the Holdup. "The next black group that goes in looking for a particular contribution is going to have a lot more difficult time."

The problem that all this helped define for the white leaders,

---

[12] One interpretation of the Holdup was offered by Milton Brown, the director of Community Progress, Incorporated: "The business community was told in short by the summer planning group in the Hill to come up with $107,000 or else. Some people felt they should have stood up to the 'or else,' but if you want to say capitulation, $107,000 was produced. Subsequently, when they came back and asked for $135,000 for [another project], I recommended to them [the businessmen] to tell them to go screw themselves. If they want to riot, be my guest. Nothing happened. They were turned down and nothing happened. At some point you have to face up to reality. You can't continually come before a group of quote militants unquote and produce the dough they claim they need with no accountability whatsoever."

said Gilbert, was the problem of "identifying spokesmen for, in this case, the black community."

The Thursday Night Group met for several months. After the initial sessions, it was broadened to include representatives of the city administration. Then, during the summer of 1968, a rough sketch of the group's future was put down on paper:

> Recent events connected with development of summer programs in the inner city have pointed up certain basic factors which now need to be taken into account in efforts to solve problems of poverty and race. These factors include:
>
> 1. The growing desire and capacity of inner-city residents to define their own problems, determine how best to meet them, and share in the management of programs brought to bear on them.
>
> 2. The uncertainty and lack of coordination among community agencies and community leadership generally in dealing with inner-city problems.
>
> 3. The disparity between the magnitude of needs and the paucity or diffusion of resources available to meet them.
>
> 4. The crucial importance of developing an effective working partnership between neighborhood leaders and those in positions of leadership and influence in the community at large.
>
> Both the threat of aggravation of inner-city problems and the hope of alleviating them impel us to find newer and better ways to mobilize the necessary moral, professional, and financial resources.

The memorandum proposed that an organization be established of "top citizen leaders" and the top executive officers of local private and governmental organizations, and that among its purposes would be determining the differences between needs and resources; mobilizing the resources; sharpening existing programs and backing new ones that might be needed; and, forging "a new community consensus in support of all appropriate measures designed to solve what is, by common consent, the most urgent problem of our community." Added the group:

> It is not intended that what is proposed here be a super-agency. Rather, it should be a confederation of interests, each of which would retain its autonomy, but all of which would have the

opportunity to maximize their efforts by making common cause with those having similar objectives.

The group considered starting an Urban Coalition in New Haven, said Gilbert, but decided instead to try to construct a federation of groups that were already "trying to relate to the problems of the city."

Frank Logue, who had been listening as Gilbert talked, was asked how, then, the new organizations differed from two other New Haven groups—CPI and the CAC—that had been started with somewhat the same objectives. Logue, at that time, was the general counsel of CPI and the director of its Community Action Institute. Now, in October of 1968, he was on part-time loan from CPI to the Urban Development Organization as a consultant, and he was about to start a tour of similar organizations in other cities. The result of his tour would be a report, outlining to the UDO leaders what form the New Haven effort should take.

The federation would be unlike the Citizens Action Commission, said Logue, because it would not involve itself in the city's administrative functions, as the CAC had done. It would not be a substitute for, or competitor of, CPI, because CPI was dependent largely upon public funds.

"I would say," said Logue, "that the Urban Development Organization is looking, certainly at the beginning, anyway, at private sources. I think that the private sector has increasingly come to realize that it has reasons of its own for getting involved in the city. It's a conviction born of simple motives that they've got to get involved because they're affected by what happens in the city."

Once the decision was made to turn the Thursday evening sessions into something more formal and permanent, the group was faced with the problem of determining how it should deal with the black community and the black leadership. It also faced the problem of making certain that outsiders understood that the white businessmen were not establishing some sort of a new cornucopia to supply funds for community projects.

Obviously, thought Gilbert, the answer was to invite the black leadership to join the UDO. To his surprise, "the blacks indicated that they wanted no part of this; that they looked at it, Number One, as a subversion of the Black Coalition. Secondly, they didn't want to be a minority group in a white Establishment organization, to be again in a position where they were being dictated to and directed. Rather, what they wanted was to have this group formed —they were all in favor of *that*—which would then respond to the programs which were developed by the black and the underprivileged side of the community.

"At first, this was a bit of a shock to us, because up to that time we had naïvely believed that integration was the thing. But for the moment it isn't, and I think this is good, too.

"At any rate," Gilbert continued, "we told the representatives of the black community 'Great.' If they're going to develop their programs, this is fine, but first they must recognize that there's not enough money *anywhere,* public or private, within New Haven or within the state or within the country, that could fund all the programs they might develop.

"So one thing that they had to do was not just talk about the short term, not just the summer needs; but what they had to do— and they agreed to do it—was to sit down and develop long-term programs, programs for the next year and two years, in an orderly fashion. And we said that we would be willing, if our organization was in existence, to provide professional help to them, at their call. Our group would provide a human bank of resources as well as monetary resources, which would then be on call by them."

One of the reasons that money from private sources had been so limited, Gilbert felt, was the "absolute total chaos and lack of coordination" that had been the rule in New Haven. "We hope that if we can put together some general package, we will be able to get more money from the city, and also be able to go outside the city—to foundations, et cetera—and find it, and help the black and other disadvantaged communities."

A visitor remarked that Gilbert was saying "black" instead of "Negro." At that time, it was not yet universally fashionable for whites, particularly white businessmen, to say "black."

"I've quit saying 'boy' also," he replied. "I got called on that three or four times."

He was asked how he felt, as an integrationist who was accommodating himself to the notion that integration might not be the goal at that particular moment.

"I think we have to have integration," Gilbert said, "and I think we're going to get it. Basically—I don't know a damn thing about it; I'm a contractor—but as far as I'm concerned, these people need to establish an identity, and they're not going to establish an identity through integration.

"They want—and I think this is great—they want to establish the fact that they're *equals,* and they want to establish the fact that they're *black* equals. And once this is recognized—and we're seeing it happen already—once we say 'All right, you're separate and you're equal, and you can perform the job maybe as well as we can,' then the dialogue starts again.

"This just points out the need for this organization: a dialogue between groups. And another thing is happening in the other direction: We're all being educated. Those who know the least get the most education. I've got a lot. One thing that interested me in one of the meetings with the blacks was that they looked at us and said, 'Well, you people just don't understand the blacks. How can you talk to us when you don't understand us and our problems?'

"And we finally agreed that that was the case. But we said it was also just as true that they didn't understand the whites. This was new to them, but they don't. They absolutely don't. The more working together, the more integration there will be, in the good sense of the word. The more we'll understand each other."

Gilbert was reminded of what he had said when he introduced Mayor Lee at the March 1968 Citizens Action Commission meeting, the one at which he had urged an end to "Letting Dick do it."

"He's no longer able to do it," said Gilbert now. "Absolute power is followed by an absolute vacuum. We don't have either, now. When Dick Lee's health gave out on him, we were rudderless. I think it's no longer fair to ask one man to shoulder the whole burden."

IX

The Public Sector

. . . we've never put on the packaging that we have in these last two projects.
—Melvin Adams, New Haven's development administrator

BY LATE 1968 some of the observers, activists, and movers and shakers in New Haven felt that the "private sector" was really making progress; that no longer was New Haven generally content to "Let Dick do it" (or, as Mayor Lee preferred to put it, "Let Dick do it *alone*"). Except for Yale's gifts to the Black Coalition, there was little physical evidence of this commitment, but there was enough earnest-sounding talk to convince some spectators that things had changed, or were changing, or would change soon.

Joel Cogen, the former Redevelopment Agency executive, was one of those who felt that things were happening. By now, Cogen had gone into business for himself, as the head of a program-development agency that specialized in advising public and quasi-public organizations on how best to set up programs of social change, and then on how to get the money to run them. Cogen said he was certain that in New Haven there had been "a lot of significant change. The white Establishment has really made concessions," he said, "and is prepared to make more concessions, in terms of what the black man really wants, which, as much as anything else, is involvement in making his own decisions."

Others expressed their pleasure, especially with the Urban Development Organization, the white business group. Milton Brown, the head of CPI, called the white businessmen's group a "movement," and added that "I'm real stimulated by it. It's hoped now that the black community will sit down with this powerful group of top leadership in the white community—and in the black community, too, because *I* belong to the UDO—and we will put our collective heads together and see if we can't come up with something.

"The Black Coalition will present the problems of the poor; the white group will listen and then see what can be done in a constructive way to provide jobs, housing opportunities, to provide some answers to these problems that will be presented to them, rather than have more of the $107,000 Holdup type of thing."

Why, Brown was asked, had CPI not participated in such an exchange with the black, poor, and business communities all along?

"I'm not sure CPI could have done it that way in the beginning," he replied. "It's only been in the last short time that the business community has even spoken to us on equitable terms. Two years ago, the business community would have no truck with CPI. We were a socialistic, almost anarchistic, kind of operation, as far as they were concerned. But certainly in the past year or so there's been an almost abrupt about-face in the attitude of business. It's exciting; it really is, because here, for the first time, we have this group of high-powered people talking and concerned and really committed to building something, but not quite sure of what they want to do."

Some of the others in the black community were considerably less excited. Willie Counsel, of the Hill Parents Association, when asked about the white businessmen's organization some months after it was founded, said he really didn't know much about it, nor had he made much of an effort to find out about it; he doubted that "anything will come out of it."

"I just don't feel, you know, that white America really cares about social problems," he said. "You've got gouging slums, white slum-landlords, you've got gouging, bloodsucking white merchants in the community who are taking money out of the black community, taking it into the white suburban areas. So I don't see business as playing a greater role in bringing some changes. I think, you know, it'll be the everyday thing: Tokenism. It's the same thing the mayor has done. He has done this great job in the city, and all over the United States, in brainwashing people, making them think in terms of the great job the city has done."

The Black Coalition, the black community's obvious counterpart to the white business group, was less cynical, but still not quite as excited as the head of CPI. Hugh Price, asked about the white organization, responded, "I think it's potentially useful. We're watching it very closely. I'm naturally skeptical about an assortment of folks like that. I wonder what their motives are. I'm wary of them; it's obviously a group what's very much tied to the Establishment. I don't know the extent to which they're going to try to undermine the thrust of the Black Coalition or of the black community generally."

As both the black and white communities started to figure out what the white businessmen's group was up to, other elements of the "private sector" started moving, too. The National Association for the Advancement of Colored People, which locally had had the same problems of relevance that its national parent had been having, started trying to get itself together. The local chapter in 1969 started making plans to revive interest in itself and to determine ways it might become pertinent to the new mood of the movement.

Even organized religion, which nationally was excruciatingly slow in becoming involved as an institution in the most pressing moral question of our times (its involvement was, and still is, for the most part, limited to individual clergymen's risking their lives and their jobs), did a few things: An organization of clergymen announced in the spring of 1968, for example, that it was setting up a revolving fund to help New Haven Negroes expand business ventures.

Clergymen and suburban white liberals of the League of Women Voters variety were instrumental in April of 1968 in starting

Project Concern, a program designed to "integrate" suburban school systems by bussing in small numbers of Negro children from within the city limits of New Haven. Although public hearings in the thirteen suburban towns were heated, nine of them agreed to take part in the program.

The debate over Project Concern made it possible to assess yet another element of New Haven's "private sector," one that had long been derelict in its duty: the press.

The press, in New Haven, at least until *The Crow* started publishing, meant *The New Haven Register* and the *Journal-Courier,* the afternoon and morning papers owned by the family of John Day Jackson, an iron-collar Republican who had bought *The Register* in 1907 and edited it personally—very personally—until shortly before his death in 1961. Both newspapers were "sharply etched with the convictions of the owner," said Robert Dahl, in an understatement that might be humorous to any regular reader of the New Haven press. *The Register* and the *Journal-Courier* had, and still have, a tendency to confuse editorials with news stories and, furthermore, to simply not print a great deal of news. "A more adventurous publisher," wrote Dahl, "might have sought ways and means of mobilizing public opinion; Jackson was more interested in immobilizing it. To achieve his purposes he did not have to initiate new policies; he had only to veto policies initiated by 'spendthrift politicians' and 'pressure groups.' "[1]

The history of American journalism is replete with scars left by publishers who used their newspapers, from cover to cover, as instruments of their own personal opinions, but in recent years most of these old men have died, and their newspapers have at least started to make the change—to recognize, with the help of competition from television, that you can't fool all the people all the time. In New Haven, this change had not taken place by the end of the sixties. Under the direction of Jackson's sons, the newspapers continued along in pretty much their old way—not *sensationally* bad, in the manner of Hearst or the New York *Daily News,* but just bad in a mediocre way.

---

[1] Dahl, *op. cit.,* pp. 256–58.

The Register did escape from its mediocrity for a brief period, however, when it was covering the Project Concern story. Public hearings were covered thoroughly; background was presented; reporters were sent to Hartford, which already had a functioning Project Concern, to find out about that city's experiences.

The reason for all this became apparent when the newspaper finally ran an editorial on the subject and revealed that it favored Project Concern, apparently because it was a nice, safe, token that wouldn't inconvenience any white people. The editorial said, in part, that ". . . it might be that transporting those 200 or 300 children, and scattering them two or three youngsters per suburban classroom, could demonstrate to the black community the genuine concern of the white people of greater New Haven for accomplishing the kind of changes that are essential if jobs, and housing, and vocational training, and good education in well-run schools down the street are to become available to the Negro or the Puerto Rican."

The Register's attitudes on such matters as education, taxation, bureaucratic idiocy, and political expediency might be shared by many a liberal or even a radical. But the newspaper consistently presented those views in such a way as to alienate anyone whose opinions were to the left of Barry Goldwater's. Time after time, the New Haven press proved itself capable of pointing out deficiencies, but totally incapable of understanding why those deficiencies existed.

Thus a news story on a state-wide tax battle (one of many that complemented *The Register*'s editorial stand on the matter) could declare, in its first paragraph, that "The Connecticut public next Tuesday will start picking up the bill for the General Assembly's 1969 tax-raising spree that finally came to an end at 1:30 A.M. today." But nowhere in the paper, in its news columns or on its editorial page, could *The Register* summon the energy to explain in anything approaching neutral terms *why* there was a crisis in Connecticut (as in the rest of the country) over governmental revenues.

This fatal flaw, and variations on it, were evident in almost every issue of *The Register* during the crucial years when New Haven was trying to learn to cope with such important problems as dissent, citizen participation, and a definition of the term, "model city." It could be speculated that, if the press in New Haven had done its job properly, the city might still be referred to as a "model city."

But as far as *The Register* was concerned, CPI was a "funding fountain." (That was in a news story, not an editorial.) Behavioral science research into the problems of poverty was "a mountain of mumbo-jumbo," according to the editorial writers. And Negroes who were charged with crimes were identified by race in news stories even when their race was not a factor. This was a practice that even a lot of Deep South newspapers had had the decency to discard, but *The Register* was still practicing it in 1969.

There was movement, too, in the public sector—very gradual movement, very cautious even in comparison with that of Yale; perhaps *normally* gradual and cautious when compared with the movement, or lack thereof, in other cities. But New Haven was supposed to be better than other cities.

Some of the movement came from Mayor Lee. Although he was reluctant to acknowledge that he had changed in any basic way, the mayor did demonstrate an apparent shift in attitude from his February 1968 state of the city speech, the one in which he called for an end to acrimony.

In March of that same year, Lee wrote an introduction to the city's "Community Renewal Program," a fifteen-year forecast of municipal needs and plans, and he included in his introduction indications that citizen participation was heavy on his mind:

"This report . . . has a message: that in New Haven's past, change has not always meant progress. In years to come *change can benefit our people*—but only if we harness it, only if we plan for it, and make it conform to the needs and wishes of all our people."[2]

---

[2] New Haven Redevelopment Agency, City Plan Commission, and Citizens Action Commission, *op. cit.* Unfortunately, the remainder of the report did

In their public utterances, Lee and his admirers and fellow city executives were wont to talk more and more about citizen participation and to reply, if asked whether there had been too much concentration in New Haven on physical renewal at the expense of such participation, that it had been necessary to use the bulldozer to expose the human problems.

In an interview in the fall of 1968, Lee elaborated on this:

"In 1968 and thereafter," he said, "the important thing *now* is neighborhood and community participation. People become involved in planning their own destiny and working out their own problems, neighborhood by neighborhood, and this can be the most exciting and perhaps the most rewarding of all.

"We did do this in the beginning, back in 1957 and '58. We were trying to instill into this somnolent public of ours the idea that they should get in and take an oar and help paddle the canoe.

"But the motion was not real; the motion was all mine, running all over the city. We would get these crowds of people out and I would exhort them, and they would applaud and smile and we would have coffee and cake and I'd pass out certificates, but there was not as much involvement as I thought, not as much as I wanted, not as much as is necessary."

Did Lee mean participation by business and industry?

"No. By the people who live in the community, themselves. I mean people who may live in the Hill, or Wooster Square, or in Dixwell, or in Dwight, or in Newhallville. We've been trying to do this for years, but the kind of participation we got, to some extent, was artificial participation.

---

not demonstrate that its authors considered citizen participation to be of more than passing importance. Four paragraphs of the 91-page document were devoted to the subject, and even they were disappointing: Under "Citizenship Participation," the report said: "Formation of the Citizens Action Commission in 1954 was one of the first actions taken in establishing New Haven's development program. . . . In addition to the CAC, neighborhood groups operate in every neighborhood throughout the city; they participate actively and effectively in the renewal planning and have often taken the lead in encouraging new plans and programs. There has also been outstanding citizen participation in the sponsorship of non-profit, moderate-income housing. . . . Voluntary rehabilitation by private property owners . . . provides other concrete evidence of the participation in renewal by thousands of New Haven citizens."

"We were *selecting* people who were members of the Establishment, I suppose, in one sense, to provide the leadership on the grounds that we had no other leadership to turn to. And the people in the individual neighborhoods, to a certain extent, were accepting this passively. There was some involvement, to the degree that people improved their homes, and there were many participants in the neighborhood improvement programs, but there wasn't any *real sense* of involvement.

"Everything, in a sense, came from City Hall. The thrust today, which is just getting under way, is from the neighborhood to City Hall."

Lee was asked if, when the sort of involvement he was talking about came to pass, he might find himself threatened politically.

"I think a person like me can adapt," he replied. "I'm more thoughtful than people appreciate, and I recognize the need for adaptation to different approaches. I've been preaching it, and I believe in it."

What, Lee was asked, did he know in 1968 that he had not known sixteen years before?

"Well, I know an awful lot. When I first began, I thought of changing the city in terms of brick and mortar and steel and concrete. I learned that a city is far more basic. It's people first. I found, as I really dug into it, for instance, that this nonsense of high-rise public housing for low-income families, without social services, is hogwash. We need scattered-site, low-income public housing. We need rent certificate public housing, where people can literally fade into the woodwork and not have anybody recognize that they are low-income families.

"We need all kinds of special programs aimed at the low-income family, or the marginal-income family, or the family with social problems. The problem of physically restoring a city is almost secondary."

Gradually, in 1968, the official tone began to change. People in and around City Hall started explaining that the physical renewal had been necessary in order to expose the great need for human renewal, that there had been a period when citizen participation, even if it had been seriously considered, would have been an impediment to physical renewal. Physical renewal had been necessary in order to convince the businessmen—the bankers, the planners, the officials from Washington—that New Haven indeed meant business. And the people who were squawking about physical renewal now were the same ones who had been silent, or who had welcomed it, when the renewal projects were being planned.

Said Joel Cogen: "Part of the problem—and this is a real problem in a democratic society—is that people don't respond when they should. You have a public hearing and people don't understand the issues. They only understand that the road is going to wipe them out when they see it coming right at their noses."

In the meantime, there was some evidence of action. The Board of Aldermen, long considered a lethargic body that existed largely in order to rubber-stamp Lee's ideas, showed signs of independence. The Citizens Action Commission, the organization which in the early years had been New Haven's idea of citizen participation, and which Dahl had astutely identified as a device for avoiding, rather than settling, disputes, went out of business in 1969. Its passing was rather pathetic: the CAC's leaders said the reason for its dissolution was that it had fulfilled its purpose.

At about this time, as both the public and private sectors were talking more, and in some cases even doing more, in terms of citizen participation, and as more citizens were beginning to demand the right to participate, the major source of financial assistance in community action programs for New Haven and all other American cities started drying up. President Johnson had become disenchanted with the war on poverty he had started, and President-to-be-Nixon was revealing, in his campaign speeches and in his choices for Vice President and attorney general, that he did not have the sort of sympathy for or understanding of the black and the poor that his two predecessors had had. Congress had come to identify community action with riots and radicalism; the popularity of George Wallace and the emergence of his constituency of "forgotten Americans" was not lost on the Senators and Representatives (nor was it to be lost on Nixon and Agnew when they took office). The war in Vietnam was sapping more of the country's energies than most people realized; when budgets had to be cut, it was the budgets of the domestic social action programs—already under-funded and already the subject of increasing criticism—that went.

By the fall of 1968 the nation's mayors were getting the word: The dream, the experiment, was dying, at least as far as Washington was concerned. Some urban leaders and experts felt that the cutbacks were coming just at the point when some of the programs were showing signs of success. Mayor Lee, in October of 1968, expressed dismay at the actions of Washington and at the hints of even more severe cutbacks in the future that were coming from the Nixon Administration, and he said:

"You *can* rebuild a city. You *can* provide the social opportunities in a city, despite what Nixon says in his campaign—that he's going to stop this dribbling of many millions of dollars down the drain in this poverty program, which is a monumental waste of effort. It is *not* a monumental waste of effort. People are feeling their way in these programs.

"Let's face it: In experimental programs, you're bound to make mistakes, and in programs dealing with people, you're bound to create frictions, and in programs dealing with people, you're bound to find the hard-core unemployed, the hard-core unwed mother, the hard-core illiterate, the hard-core people with criminal records. And in trying to rehabilitate them and develop in them a sense of public responsibility and a desire to improve their lot, it's going to take a lot of time and it's going to take a very real effort by people who are mayors and by community leaders to get them into the mainstream of society."

As New Haven began to receive less and less assistance from the federal government, the city's officials found it more and more possible to speak critically of the bureaucrats in Washington, the people who once had welcomed them with open checkbooks. Thus, in the fall of 1968, Milton Brown, the director of Community

Progress, Incorporated, could comment that "the promise to eliminate poverty was a very improper promise, given the resources that have been committed to the program to date."

Fortunately, for CPI and for the rest of the city, there was a source of funds that took up some of the slack occasioned by the massive federal retreat from the war on poverty. The Connecticut legislature had passed the Community Development Act and created, as of July 1967, a State Department of Community Affairs. This department took over much of the major funding of anti-poverty and human renewal programs.

The act established programs of community development, almost all of which were to provide financial assistance to communities in the form of state grants. The act also required that municipalities wishing to receive the state aid must complete a Community Development Action Plan—a survey of community needs and resources and a schedule, running over at least five years, of anticipated improvements. There was also a vague requirement for citizen participation. The legislation establishing the Department of Community Affairs also created a state Advisory Council on Community Affairs. There were no provisions for insuring representation by the poor on the council.

The Connecticut agency, then, must be considered as something less than revolutionary—as another agency, created, as dozens of others had been before, in order to disburse funds, guided by confused and token ideas about citizen participation. And where the state failed to insist on the proper degree of citizen participation, it was certain that the municipalities would not volunteer it. The executive director of a housing agency criticized the City of New Haven in 1969 for preparing its Community Development Action Plan without involving the citizens—it was a case of "professionals planning in conjunction with other professionals," he said. And *The Register* noted that despite all the nice guidelines on citizen participation that the state had sent out, New Haven, when it was establishing its Action Plan advisory committee, had tried to get the Citizens Action Commission certified as the proper agency to do the job. The failure of this attempt, said the newspaper, was instrumental in the eventual disbanding of the CAC.

The state agency did, however, serve as a source of funds at a time when federal funding was disappearing. Community Progress, Incorporated, reported in early 1969 that the funds it was then receiving from the state exceeded those it was getting from the Office of Economic Opportunity, the federal agency that had been patterned after CPI in the first place.

One by one the public agencies started coming around, years late, to the idea of at least talking about citizen participation. When the State Welfare Department decided to build a branch office in the Hill neighborhood, it printed broadsides in English and Spanish asking Hill residents to come to meetings and help in the planning.

When the director of New Haven's Head Start program, who had held the post since the pilot program was begun in 1963, announced her retirement, it was also announced that parents of Head Start children were helping to designate her successor.

Mayor Lee appointed two public housing tenants as commissioners on the Housing Authority, and when the city drafted a $5 million proposal to the Department of Housing and Urban Development for the modernization of low-income public housing units, many of the specific proposals had been suggested by tenants themselves.

The educational Establishment reacted to the new demands for citizen involvement in a predictable manner: It studied the problem. A committee of the Board of Education met from the summer of 1968 until the summer of 1969 to try to formulate ways of giving citizens—in this case, parents and students—a say in the operation of the schools. The committee came up with the suggestion that councils be established in each school, composed of parents, teachers, non-instructional school personnel, students, and representatives elected at large from the community served by the school. The councils would help establish codes of discipline, help write and revise the curriculum, and assist in the selection of school personnel. Said the committee when its report was finished:

"The ultimate goal of citizen involvement in the schools is the utilization of all resources within the community in order that education equip our New Haven children to develop their individual potentials and enter society as mature, self-sufficient human beings."

The Register was not impressed. "It is believed," the newspaper said in what had the outward appearance of a news story, "the method proposed . . . could lead to certain organizations taking over in each community."

Soon after the committee handed in its recommendations, the City Plan Department decided to study the problem again. It gave $40,000 to an organization of educators and consultants to study the needs of education, including the question of citizen involvement.

The police department was long overdue for serious changes. The excesses of individual policemen at such events as the rock music concert frightened some city officials and others who had long ignored the way the police functioned in less visible sections of the city. What frightened them more, according to one of them, was the indication, after the 1967 riot, that Francis V. McManus, who had been the chief for thirteen years, wanted all sorts of new police hardware to deal with future disturbances. In March 1968 McManus left the force and a bright, young policeman, James Ahern—the man whose omnipresence Peter Almond had noticed in the Hill—was named chief.

The circumstances of McManus' retirement were somewhat unusual. The city gave him a pension of $14,000, which *The Register* quickly figured out to be 77.8 percent of his normal salary. In addition, the departing chief got $6,230.76 for 90 days' accumulated sick leave and $1,384.60 for four weeks of vacation. McManus said he would spend the first few weeks of his retirement catching up on his sleep and fishing.

Ahern, the 36-year-old new chief, lost no time in reorganizing the department. It was a tricky job, without doubt, because the new chief had to try to please two critical audiences. A growing portion of the public was losing faith in the police as a symbol of much of anything except repression, and they were demanding that the department be run intelligently, with respect not only for law and order, but for justice, too. And the department rank and file were doubtless feeling the waves of emotion and self-pity that were running through police departments all over the nation—the feeling that they were misunderstood and falsely maligned, that people wanted to handcuff them. Ahern somehow had to keep both sides happy, and he did about as good a job of it as anyone could have done.

One of his first acts after becoming chief was to relax the departmental rule that forbade a policeman's smoking at all during his eight-hour tour of duty. He reorganized the schedules so that more men would be on patrol at night. He sent a budget request to the Board of Finance that asked for almost $1 million over the previous year. And, during the first days of his administration, the police commissioners announced that 98 men had passed the examination for sergeant.

The examination was nothing new, but the results, and the way they were used, were. Two Negroes placed among the top eleven candidates. The results of the examination were announced the day after Martin Luther King was assassinated. *The Register's* Frank Whalen, writing in his "Around the City" column the following Sunday, noted that "The action became immediately suspect, because it was the fastest reporting back of any promotional examination here in memory (about 90 days from when the test was taken in January). Some results have been held up two and three years before being announced." The test scores, Whalen pointed out, were not totally objective, but rather represented the combination of a written civil service examination and superior officers' views of the candidates. Inasmuch as no Negroes had made it past the rank of patrolman during Chief McManus' tenure, it might be assumed that the examination results meant a little more than they appeared to mean.

Two weeks later sixteen of the candidates were promoted to sergeant, and two of them were Negroes. One of the new black sergeants, Burton V. Gifford, continued what can only be called a meteoric rise through the ranks; he soon became a supervisor in the patrol division, and in May 1969 Chief Ahern appointed him a deputy chief inspector. At the same meeting of the police commissioners at which Gifford was appointed, the regulations were changed to allow policemen to wear mustaches if they had the chief's permission. Soon afterward a motorcycle patrolman turned up with one of the handsomest cop mustaches east of San Francisco.

Ahern reshuffled 50 patrolmen, detectives, and supervisors, cut back on the issuance of pistol permits, and issued a new policy to his policemen that forbade them to use guns as weapons of fear. Firearms shall be used, he said, only "after all other means of apprehension fail." He also told his officers that the department must work to "diminish . . . hostility about law and order." In a restatement of the department's policy on police conduct, Ahern said:

The policeman "must be civil and orderly. In the performance of duty he must maintain decorum, attention, command of temper, patience, and be discreet. . . . Discussions and conversations in the precinct by members of the force or others in relation to nationality, religion, or party politics will not be permitted." Complaints from the public "will be investigated no matter how minor in nature. While I have the obligation of protecting from unwarranted accusations and charges both the men and the department itself, I also have the responsibility of insuring that individuals are not subject to the misuse of police power, personal abuse, or arrogance by police."

When the Black Women of Greater New Haven mounted a picket line in support of their boycott of downtown stores, Ahern responded with police protection for the demonstrators. In the first days of the boycott, a motorcycle gang descended on the pickets and beat them with baseball bats. After the incident, the police started providing more protection, and *The Register* thought this was worth a headline: "Police Protect Picketers." Joan Thornell said she felt "understanding" by the police had "grown immeasurably in the past day or so."

In the meantime, Ahern was proving that he was not *too* soft, either. When a black student at Yale referred to the chief in a public meeting as a "white racist," Ahern filed a $100,000 libel suit. In it, Ahern said that such an appellation would mean that a person had "mental and emotional disabilities," and that those disabilities, "if true, and such accusation, if true, would require the separation of the plaintiff [the chief] from any properly conducted police department."

The chief, according to one of his civilian employees, managed to bring a considerable degree of success to his job because "He's aware of problems that are not specifically police problems." The civilian, one of many hired under the new administration, was Jay Talbot, a young man who had the title of "program analyst" for the department, and who not long before had been hired from CPI, where he had been an assistant to the executive director. Talbot's new position at the police department replaced the old office of "administrative assistant to the chief;" changing that title to "program analyst" seemed symbolic of the reforms Chief Ahern was attempting to bring about.

"I think his view is a lot broader than most policemen," continued Talbot in an interview at the police headquarters. "And yet he's a tough cop; he's a 'good cop' in police department terminology. And yet he's a good cop in terms of people who are outside the department, too. I guess he is, in a way, kind of what you would want all cops to be."

Under Ahern, New Haven was not nearly so excited about stockpiling police hardware to deal with potential rioters as it was interested in the causes of riots. When the Safe Streets and Crime Control Act was passed, and municipalities began lining up for money, New Haven asked for around $170,000. Less than $20,000 of the request was for hardware, said Talbot, "and the rest was for prevention, detection—not control—of riots or civil disorders. We put in for money for an auxiliary police force, and for additional support for neighborhood police centers, and for some computers, and for some radios, and for some administrative and civilian employees. . . .

"I think the department's position is that it's very difficult for the police department alone to prevent riots. That's the job of other agencies. And yet we may be able to do certain things that would help create an atmosphere that would prevent riots and make the community a better place. And one of these things is to have a police department that's sensitive to the needs of the community." The department was at work, he said, on a sensitivity-training program, and was consulting with Mrs. Fred Harris in its design.

While Talbot had been talking, Chief Ahern had walked in. He was young, bright-eyed and intelligent-looking, and he appeared very mature, probably because his hair was stark white.

Police departments, he said, "should be kind of prevention-oriented. They should provide a service to the community. They should have the support of the community. In some ways, police departments have grown more efficient. They've done a number of things in terms of technological improvements, but they've lost the support of a good percentage of the community in the process. I don't think all the answers lie in getting patrolmen back on the beat.

"In some ways, it's the police departments' fault. Let's be very honest. They haven't been particularly honest. They haven't done the job that they probably could have done, over the years."

Ahern said his biggest task was to build the community's trust in the police department. "There's real suspicion," he said, "and there's real mistrust, and there's a real question whether police departments in urban centers really serve the black community. They see the police as an occupation army; they don't see them as their police department."

What did the new chief think of Fred Harris? Most of the rest of the city officials, from Mayor Lee on down, had demonstrated, either by their words or by their actions, that they had failed to appreciate Harris for what he was—an ethnic politician; perhaps a politician of the future, but nevertheless an ethnic politician, not really too different from the Irish and Italian politicians of the recent past and the present.

"From my personal point of view," said Ahern (he did not stop and think out his reply the way most of the other members of the Establishment did when asked about Harris), "as a citizen of New Haven and as a policeman, I've seen him make some very irresponsible statements, and I've seen him make some very responsible statements. Militancy doesn't bother me. Maybe extremism does, or maybe revolutionaries do. But I have no problem at all with him.

"He's looking to create social change, and you can't do that very easily without being militant. I don't have that many problems with militant people. I have a problem with them in the sense of *demonstrations,* in the sense of *threats.* You can talk about militancy and sometimes it borders on intimidation and extortion and such, particularly when you're talking about raising funds.

"I may have a problem with that, but I just don't have a problem with what his goal is, and that's to create some change in the structure of the city government. I may have a problem, at times, in how he tries to do it."

In the city's other departments and agencies, the reaction to the demand for change (or perhaps it was the reaction to Dr. King's death) was far less dramatic. There were more words than actions. But, theoretically at least, the Redevelopment Agency and CPI didn't have as far to go as the police department.

The Redevelopment Agency, long considered by some of its critics as little more than an evil conspiracy against the powerless people of New Haven, became more defensive and started including, in almost every press release, broadside, and newsletter, some evidence that it thought the bulldozer approach was a thing of the past. (Of course, at the same time it pushed ahead on projects such as Route 34 and State Street.)

Neighborhood corporations were established in the renewal neighborhoods (and citizens were involved in their establishment), and the members of those corporations were asked, for the first time, what they wanted in the way of redevelopment. Still, the agency's overall philosophy seemed to remain one of *giving* people something rather than helping them *get* what they wanted. As one official put it in a seminar in 1968:

Our goal is to upgrade conditions in housing and human relations. We want to bring a house up to the level where it will be
a beautiful site in the community. To do this we must put
pressure on the landlord. Then we must put pressure on the
tenants to maintain the work the landlord has done. We must
make the tenant see that *he is being given dignity* as well as
better living conditions. [Emphasis added.]

It was interesting that the neighborhood chosen by the Redevelopment Agency to serve as its flagship in matters of citizen
participation was not the Hill. Residents of the Hill were already
getting dignity on their own, and the sort of dignity they were
getting seemed to make the downtown officials a bit uncomfortable.
Newhallville, a far less blighted neighborhood, with upwardly-
mobile black residents who already had most of the qualifications
for middle-classness except the money, was chosen.

Visitors who several years ago might have been shown Oak
Street on their tours of the city were shown Newhallville now. The
agency's literature was filled with news of citizen participation in
the neighborhood. Said Melvin Adams: "I like always to refer
people to another neighborhood than the Hill; one which, I think,
from my limited point of view, is a more productive neighborhood,
and that is Newhallville. It's more of a middle-class neighborhood."

When renewal came to Newhallville, the residents were asked to
help plan the $7.9-million undertaking through a neighborhood
corporation, the United Newhallville Organizations. One of the
results was far less destruction of existing housing; in fact, there
would be a net gain of 68 units. The Redevelopment Agency
called this sort of cooperation "a milestone in citizen participation."

Melvin Adams, the quiet, scholarly-looking development administrator, commented in an interview in late 1968 about the
work of the Redevelopment Agency, citizen participation, and dissent. He was asked why, with all the money New Haven had
received to rebuild itself, there were still problems.

"Money is part of the answer," he said, "but money isn't all
of the answer. An analogy might be someone coming from a family
with a lot of wealth, but the kid goes bad. Well, it's certainly not

the money that caused him to go bad. The kid who comes from a poor family thinks that a lot of his problems would be solved if he or his family had money. That doesn't always do it.

"It's easy to say that we've had a lot of money, but it's nowhere near enough. But I think that's true. But the whole focus of the conversation on money overlooks a lot of other things that have an effect on people's lives. One is how people are treated, not only by government, but in their day-to-day relationships. There *is* unequal treatment, and all the money in the world won't in and of itself change that fact. I think some of our problems in New Haven have been the unequal treatment that black people have.

"In terms of what's worked, I think rehabilitation has worked. Neighborhood rehabilitation. It's a never-ending process. On housing, I think we've only scratched the surface. I think the community school program, the idea of having community schools in each neighborhood, is a very good program."

It was very important, said Adams, to come up with programs that were successful. "You have to produce success, and you have to demonstrate that it succeeds. And everything doesn't always succeed. The trouble in public life is that you've got to talk about success or somebody will accuse you of being a complete failure."

One of the city's areas of least success, of course, was in the field of low-income housing. "Hand in hand with the cry that we need more low-income housing, which I agree with," said Adams, "is the cry that people ought to have more involvement in determining their future. A neighborhood ought to determine its future more. I agree with that. In case after case, these two things come into conflict, because as we go into the neighborhoods and propose low-income projects, they're rejected, whether it's a white neighborhood, whether it's a middle-class black neighborhood, whether it's a low-income neighborhood.

"It's almost a class problem, as far as public housing's concerned. Now, we go into the same neighborhoods with what I call economically integrated projects—low and moderate income, mixed—and there isn't the same opposition."

Adams was asked about the accusation, leveled frequently by

people in the low-income neighborhoods and their sympathizers in such organizations as the Coalition of Concerned Citizens, that the agency did a lot of its planning in secret, and that the citizens were hardly ever consulted.

"We had a public hearing a couple months ago on a plan for Newhallville," he replied. *"The New Haven Register,* which hardly ever has a good thing to say about redevelopment, thought it was an excellent hearing. The plan was developed by the neighborhoods and the Redevelopment Agency. The neighborhood committee held five meetings with the neighborhood to explain the plan, and then had a big public hearing on its own, where they said 'This is the plan we want.' The Redevelopment Agency's public hearing was held in the neighborhood. It was approved by the aldermen with no opposition, and everyone said this is the way it should be done.

"We're doing the same thing in Fair Haven. We've had two neighborhood meetings and about three to four hundred people attended each hearing. At the end of the hearings, they'll tell us exactly what they want in the plan, and that's what we'll do.

"I personally feel that that's what we've done in the *other* areas, too, but we've never put on the packaging that we have in these last two projects."

Community Progress, Incorporated, started doing some packaging of its own. Despite the fact that CPI was *the* human renewal agency in New Haven; despite the fact that it had had longer to learn about citizen participation than other, more recently-founded antipoverty agencies; and despite the fact that CPI had witnessed and participated in many confrontations with citizens demanding participation, the agency had a long way to go—considering its tendency, in its 1967 annual report, to blame the city's troubles on hooligans and fun-seekers and to identify itself and Mayor Lee as the "chief militants in the Inner City crisis."

CPI's first post-riot actions in the direction of citizen participation had been to help organize its *own* "militant" groups. On the Hill, CPI support went to the Hill Action Group, "apparently," as *The Register* observed, "as a counterfoil to the controversial Hill

Parents Association." But that clearly didn't work; before long, the Hill Action Group was acting just as militantly as the other, home-grown organizations.

As the summer of 1968 approached, CPI convened a committee of 30 persons from slum neighborhoods and asked them to return to their communities and find out what the citizens wanted in the way of summer programs. Milton Brown, who at that time was the director of CPI's community services division, told the representatives that he didn't know how much money would be available, but that the seven neighborhoods should think in terms of developing programs for which either $50,000, $100,000, or $150,000 could be split seven ways.

One reaction to CPI's new and somewhat conciliatory attitude toward the neighborhoods was a demand for more power. Six black organizations, including the Hill Action Group, said they wanted control over all of CPI's manpower programs. CPI, they said, should become an agency for disbursing funds, rather than for drawing up plans and running programs.

In addition to its troubles with the neighborhoods, the agency was simultaneously battling for its own life on another front. In the previous year Congress had passed economic opportunity legislation which required, among other things, that New Haven designate as its official community action agency either the existing outfit, CPI, or a new agency, or the city itself. Congressman Giaimo urged that the city take over the function, citing CPI's record of inefficiency and wasteful spending. CPI eventually won the designation.

All this, coupled with other evidence that the black groups in New Haven were not going to be satisfied with continued co-option of their leaders and tokenism in the name of citizen participation, led the CPI executive director, Lawrence N. Spitz, to declare that it was time for CPI to decentralize itself. Programs of human renewal, he said, could be run by local corporations in the seven renewal neighborhoods.

In May of 1968 Spitz resigned from his post and returned to work with the United Steelworkers of America, where he had been employed before his arrival at CPI in November 1966. In the announcement of his resignation, Spitz repeated the call for decentralization. The agency's programs should gradually be phased out, he said, although a "large number" of services could be spun off immediately. CPI, he suggested, would remain as a "planning and funding" agency, with operations of much smaller scope.

In response to a question from a CPI board member about the dangers inherent in neighborhood control, Spitz said: "Sure there will be failures . . . but a failure is not necessarily a failure. I subscribe to that. Sometimes a failure is an important part of the training process."

The CPI board, at the same meeting at which it received Spitz's resignation, adopted a set of guidelines—minimal qualifications for neighborhood agencies that wanted to become neighborhood corporations: They must be broadly representative of the neighborhood; they must be operated under "democratic processes"; they must have fiscal responsibility; they must guarantee that they will continue to provide services to residents; they must promise to retain current CPI staff members for six to nine months; and they must adhere to the larger planning body's formula for distributing funds throughout the neighborhoods.

A few days after this meeting, CPI found $150,000 for summer programs for the neighborhoods.

As the search for Spitz's successor was started, a new controversy developed. The Black Coalition offered its services to help screen candidates for the job, and said it would hold meetings in the poor neighborhoods, at which the candidates could speak. "The screening committee would determine the consensus of opinion and then inform your board of which candidate or candidates received the most support," said the coalition to CPI. Community Progress, Incorporated, said it would adopt the coalition's offer "in principle"; this the coalition interpreted to mean CPI had no intention of involving the community, or the good offices of the Black Coalition, in the selection of a director.

Eventually Milton Brown was selected. Brown, a light-skinned Negro (but one who said "I've been a Negro all my life") with a background in social work,[3] appeared to have the backing of a broad spectrum of neighborhood organizations.

By the fall of 1968 Brown had gotten out his first annual report for CPI, and it was chock full of talk about citizen participation, although a good deal of what it talked about was only a reflection of mandates from the Office of Economic Opportunity. The sixteen-member board of directors had been enlarged to 21, and, in line with OEO rules, there were seven representatives from the neighborhoods, seven "from private groups which reflect more black and Puerto Rican involvement," and seven appointees of the mayor. Said Brown in his message from the executive director's office:

> By far the most exciting development at CPI during 1968 has been the evolution of the concept of the neighborhood corporation and the practical steps undertaken to achieve this goal. The involvement of hundreds of neighborhood leaders in the summer program and their success at "doing their own thing" has confirmed a conviction I have always held—that given the resources and the authority, neighborhood groups can operate their own programs with great success . . . with more success than a series of programs and services imposed from "on top" by a centralized administration.

And the major section of the annual report was devoted to bringing the word of "a new era in community action"—CPI's neighborhood corporations:

> From its start, CPI has been concerned with "full and meaningful participation" by residents of its neighborhoods in planning and running services and programs. In the year ahead— if plans now being carefully laid work out as expected—CPI's byword will be decreasingly mere participation. Instead the

---

[3] He started out in pre-medical training at Temple, then switched to teacher training. Because "in those days a Negro had a hell of a time getting into the educational system," Brown went into social work. In 1945 he started work in settlement houses, was the first Negro to work on the staff of the National Federation of Settlements, and was also the first to head the Health and Welfare Council in Washington. He went to work for CPI in 1962.

emphasis will be on neighborhood direction and control of the community-action program.

This would be accomplished, said CPI, through the establishment in the next one or two years of neighborhood corporations which not only would dispense services, but which also would be " 'umbrella' agencies in their agencies for other groups. They will approve or reject programs proposed by these groups, subject to the rules and conditions laid down by funding agencies." Once this is accomplished, CPI would become "a broker rather than a deliverer of services."

Although what CPI was proposing was said, on the one hand, to signal a "new era," the agency didn't want anyone to get the idea that it was *too* new. The annual report contained a history of CPI's efforts since its founding to insure citizen participation—a history somewhat at variance with the recollections of people like Peter Almond and Fred Harris.

> CPI declared as long ago as 1963 that "full and meaningful participation (of the people served) is central to the neighborhood approach" to community action. The CPI creed of today —that actual operation of most programs is best left to the people who understand neighborhood needs best, those who live in the neighborhoods—is a natural outgrowth of that affirmation.

From the beginning, CPI's offices and service centers were oriented to the neighborhood, rather than downtown, said the report. The Neighborhood Services division was at work back in 1963, trying to get the neighborhoods moving.

> Not all the objectives . . . were realized as quickly as the planners hoped. It was hard to convince some residents that "the system" could be so completely overhauled that the fate of neighborhood services and programs could really be determined by neighborhood residents and not by "downtown." No city had ever attained this degree of autonomy and self-determination in its neighborhoods. But New Haven had chalked up many other "firsts" in physical and human-resources develop-

ment. Why could neighborhood self-determination not be another?

In 1965 (in keeping with the federal law), spokesmen for the poor were added to the CPI board and the Residents Advisory Committee was established.

> From then on—to the extent that neighborhood representatives were active and vocal—CPI programs and policies more and more reflected the felt needs of the neighborhoods. No longer was the determination of services and programs the exclusive domain of an "establishment" board and of the staff. . . .
>
> Still, it is a long jump from neighborhood representation at the policy-making level to actual operation of programs by corporations. This was the jump the Board decided to make in the spring of 1968. . . .[4]

At about the time CPI was beginning to sound the trumpet of citizen participation at louder and louder volume, Milton Brown, the new director, was asked about the agency's problems and successes. It was his opinion, he said, that it had been unfortunate that New Haven had gotten the nickname, "Model City." "I don't see that New Haven is any different from any other urban area," he said. "The problems plague us all over the country, and they're the same problems."

Was militancy one of the problems? he was asked.

"I guess that militancy, if you want to use that phrase, is a euphemism for what's happening over most of the world today. It's dissatisfaction with the governing order. I don't think it's any different from what's been expressed by many, many people in different eras in history. It's dissatisfaction with the status quo. But even more than that, I think, it's a feeling that people want to be involved in what decisions affect them."

Had there been such involvement in New Haven all along?

"I'd be remiss if I said yes. Of course not. This started as an

---

[4] Community Progress, Incorporated, "Human Story: 1968," 1968.

executive-centered coalition. It was planning at the upper level *for* people, basically. And it stayed that way until about '65, following the mandate from OEO for maximum feasible participation. But the executive-centered coalition purported to do *for* people, rather than *with* people. I think there's no gainsaying that."

New Haven, he said, had not yet been able to achieve the maximum in citizen involvement. "You don't have any such thing as instant citizen participation. It takes a hell of a long time to build this kind of understanding and strength on the part of people. I can't tell you how close we are to it. We're as close to it as our resources will allow us, in a very limited way, to get to it. If they give us the wherewithal to help implement it, over the next five years, come see me in 1972 and I'll tell you. I don't know now."

In the meantime, Brown said, CPI was doing what it could. "We're developing neighborhood councils. We're developing neighborhood corporations. We're developing block groups. We're developing neighborhood groups. But they've got to coalesce. You've got to develop the group first. You don't just go out and wave a wand and say 'People, organize,' and all of a sudden you have a whole bunch of neighborhood and citizen participation.

"You can't go out and hold elections and expect people to relate to something that they have no participation in or know nothing about. It just doesn't happen that way. It takes long, tedious and tough community organization programs at the neighborhood level, tied to something pretty specific, to get people to participate.

"You can't go out and say you're going to hold a meeting at *x* school just to have people come out and listen to a whole lot of hot air when there's a good TV program or a good movie on, or 19 million other things to attract people.

"But if you have an issue, a specific issue—around the school problem, for example, or around the lack of adequate recreational facilities—you organize around these particular issues, and you get people to participate in their area of interest, and then you develop specifically something for them to do, to become a part of it.

"And if a problem gets solved, you have to be smart and astute enough and clever enough to come up with something else that's going to keep people's interest up. This is not easy. It's very difficult.

"I think the thing that *doesn't* work is a paternalistic attitude on the part of anybody. People don't want to be told what to do or handed things on a silver platter. Things that do work are where you involve people in planning for their own self-determination. These things work: when they have a stake; when they participate; when they make decisions—and I'm not just talking about loose decisions, but decisions in terms of how money is expended, what leadership is involved, hiring their own staff, doing their own thing. These are, for me at least, things that do work."

Had New Haven been too paternalistic in the past?

"I think that New Haven is no different, no better, no worse, than any other territory or city or state or subdivision you identify in these United States," said Brown. "I think there has been too much of a paternalistic attitude. In the very beginning, the planning was done by the executive-centered coalition in terms of what that group felt was good for people.

"This may be great, and if it hadn't been for this in the beginning, we probably wouldn't be where we are today, if that means anything. But somebody has to take the bull by the horns and get the thing moving, and that's what the executive-centered coalition did here. It got millions of dollars when other cities were sitting on their royal derrieres, doing nothing.

"But there comes a time when this kind of attitude has got to stop and when the people have got to be wrapped in more closely, more tightly, with planning their own thing for themselves. If there's one criticism I have, it's that this wasn't done early enough in New Haven. This is the one criticism I would put forth. It could have happened—it should have begun to happen—in 1962. Unfortunately, it didn't until 1965. We lost three years, it seems to me, that we could have used in making inroads into involving citizens in making decisions for themselves, rather than sitting here in our benign benevolence, planning *for* them."

X

Momentum

If I don't run again it'll be because . . . I will have created in this city a momentum that can't be halted. —Mayor Lee, spring of 1969

Democratic politics are dead. I say that it has not worked for over 400 years, and I don't see no great dreams that are going to make me believe that it is going to work in the next 400 years.—Willie Counsel, chairman of the board, Hill Neighborhood Corporation

NINETEEN-SIXTY-NINE CAME, and with it arrived a new administration in Washington, and it was possible to detect in the nation and in New Haven a tendency among involved people to speak and think less of race relations *per se;* to speak and think more of politics. Nobody knew what the new Republican Administration was going to do. For some, the truly big question was whether the new Republican Administration understood even that it needed to do something at all. Clearly its most urgent priority was the war in Vietnam, and this both dismayed and encouraged the onlookers who saw things in the context of urban America. Nixon had better stop worrying about Vietnam and worry about the unfinished battles here at home, they said. They also felt that when the war *was* ended, it would free billions of dollars for use in rebuilding the cities.

Nixon took a long time letting the nation know what his domestic priorities were. For those who thought he had none, it was a bit of a shock when Nixon appointed Daniel P. Moynihan, a liberal Democrat who had worked for John Kennedy, to be the head of his Urban Affairs Council, with cabinet rank. As Nixon introduced the new members of his official family one night on television, Moynihan loomed in and out of the camera's range, much taller and more Irish-looking than any of the others, looking a little lost in the crowd of Republicans. The liberal onlookers started placing bets that night on how long Moynihan would be able to stand Nixon, or vice-versa.

While the spectators continued waiting for action from the new national administration, there was politics at home. Nineteen-sixty-nine was an election year in New Haven. Richard Lee was expected to run again, and to win.

An announcement of his intention to run again normally would come late in the spring or early in the summer, and Lee told friends and colleagues that he would have a statement when he finished work on the city budget. If he announced anything before that, he said, every addition to and subtraction from the budget would immediately be interpreted as a political move.

The hints that Lee gave were interpreted by many observers as subtle indications that, despite a certain amount of weariness and frustration, he would certainly run again. Asked once whether he thought cities could be governed democratically, Lee replied:

"I think so. It all depends on the quality of the candidates who stand for office under the two-party system. You can't have 1928 candidates running in the Sixties. You can't have 1928 philosophies burdening candidates now. There are too many people today who still feel that a city should be run in ways which, happily, have long since disappeared—the idea of a city as a source of jobs for friends and patronage for the faithful, and a mayor who has no understanding or concept of the social ills of the city.

"The mayor is perhaps the most important single social force for good or evil in America today. You can't just have ordinary citizens standing for office, which, tragically, more often than not, is still what's happening.

"I don't know what's going to happen to the two-party system in the next five years on the local level—or the next *decade* on the local level—especially with elections in New Haven every two years," said Lee. "I think it will be in a state of confusion, frankly. I can't run forever. But I have no qualms about running again and being re-elected. The question is really whether this increasing burden on my shoulders will deplete my physical reserves. And the question is, after sixteen years, do I really want to do that again?"

On another occasion, as the time for Lee's announcement drew nearer, the mayor was asked again about reelection. It had been rumored that the Lee forces were conducting polls, especially of Negro voters, and it was understood that the results had been favorable to Lee—that 87 percent of the black voters questioned had said they would vote for Lee if he ran again. This was an increase of three points over those who had voted for him in 1967.

Lee did not answer the question directly. His announcement, he said, would still have to wait until after he finished work on the budget. On Church Street, outside his office, a police car with its siren on screamed down the street, and Lee instinctively got up from his desk, walked past the telephone with twenty-odd buttons on it, past the unabridged dictionary and the small bust of John F. Kennedy, and looked out the window. "Sometimes," he said with a chuckle, "I think they turn those things on when they're going past here just to get me excited."

Back at his desk, he continued the conversation, but in somewhat of a rambling manner. Black separatism, he said, was "just so much hogwash. People today in America are beginning to understand that the answer to all our problems is to understand what each of us wants, and to learn to live together better than they're doing now." A militant black organization, he had just learned, had an assassination list, and he was number one on it in New Haven. He was obviously in a mood of mellowness, of retrospection, and it seemed that his mood had been brought on by talk of his future.

What, he was asked, would he best like to be remembered for? "Involvement," said Lee, without hesitation.

What kind of involvement?

"The best kind: Involvement by people in planning their own plight, their own destinies, their own futures."

If he decided not to run again, what would that signify?

"If I don't run again, it'll be because after sixteen years, I will have created in this city a momentum that can't be halted, won't be halted; one that has created permanent involvement in the life of New Haven."

He toyed with the pens on his desk. "Do I need the status of the job? Is it for ego? Or is it for the money? Or a springboard for something else in '70?" He answered all those questions in the negative. "It's a matter of not wanting to leave the job," he said, "until I'm sure that the momentum I started will be carried on."

If the momentum were there, and if money was one of the yardsticks by which momentum might be measured, then New Haven had a great deal of momentum. By the end of the Lee era, no one could be quite sure how much money had been invested in the city's rebirth, but everyone was sure it was a tremendous amount.

It was, perhaps, typical of Washington's approach to urban problems that no one there had the slightest idea of how much federal money New Haven—or any other city, for that matter—had received. Individual federal agencies did not know. One of them, the Department of Housing and Urban Development, apparently was embarrassed enough by its ignorance to hire a consultant to try to find out how much money had been spent in one city, Fresno, California. One source within HUD said the consultant reported back that he could not find out.

The Bureau of the Budget was supposed to be the federal government's watchdog over all spending, but it didn't know, either. Partly because Congressmen and Senators had been hounding the Bureau for statistics (so they could brag to their constituents about how much federal money they had brought home), the Bureau started late in the sixties to find out. Two years later, according to a spokesman, "We've barely gotten to the state level. It's a monumental task."

Some rough and incomplete estimates can be found for New Haven, however. *The New Haven Register* reported early in 1970, in one of its rare articles friendly to Lee, that his administration had "put about $180 million in public funds to work" in the city, and the newspaper cited an unattributed estimate that "as much as $250 million in private funds have followed this into a revitalized New Haven."

From public officials in New Haven, a partial breakdown of funds received and spent could be obtained, but even that was incomplete. For the sixteen years of the Lee administration, it went something like this:

• For *urban renewal:* Federally initiated renewal grants, including the portion anted up from local sources, for such purposes as land acquisition, demolition, site improvement, streets, sewers, relocation, construction of parks, interest and staff, totaled $175.8 million.

Approximately 26.5 percent of this sum went to the Church Street project; 25 percent to State Street; 21 percent to Wooster Square; 13 percent to Dixwell; 9 percent to Dwight; 3.5 percent to Oak Street; 1.5 percent to Temple-George; and 0.5 percent to the Hill.

• For *housing:* The total amount of federal money spent on building new housing (completed or under way as Lee left office) was $22.7 million.

Of the total, 44.5 percent went to build 720 units of low- and moderate-income private family housing; 23 percent went to build 380 units of public housing for low-income families; 22 percent went to build 333 units of public housing for the low-income elderly; and 10.5 percent went to build 142 units of public housing for moderate-income families.

• For *rehabilitation* of residential and commercial structures: Public monies contributed $6.3 million.

• For *human renewal:* One top CPI official estimated that $18 million had gone to CPI from all sources since the agency's beginning. Another top CPI official estimated $28 million.

The $28-million estimate is probably more nearly correct. Of the total, approximately 45 percent went for CPI's manpower programs; 30 percent for community services; 15 percent for delegated programs, and 10 percent for administration. Those percentages reflect the breakdown of CPI expenditures during its entire existence from 1962 until 1970; toward the end of that period, a substantially greater percentage of the total was spent on delegated programs.

When CPI began, the agency considered that the 90,000 people who lived in the seven "inner-city" neighborhoods were its "targets." By 1970 one official estimated that 18,000 persons had been involved, in one way or another, in the agency's manpower programs, and that 10,000 to 15,000 had been involved in community service programs. (Some of the 18,000 found their way into the manpower programs through the community service programs, so there is an unknown amount of overlapping there.)

The statistics and estimates cited above, in addition to being rough ones, also fail to take into account a number of other ways in which New Haven received money, or benefited economically or in other ways, during the Lee administration. It would be difficult, for example, to put a price tag on private, voluntary rehabilitation, just as it would be impossible to calculate the benefits incurred by the city when a housing contractor, impressed by the city's architectural experimentation, decided to hire an architect of his own rather than build a standard, dull apartment building. It would be hard to determine the number of jobs that were *not* eliminated when businessmen and industrialists, encouraged by the physical activity going on in New Haven, decided *not* to move somewhere else. Another impossible statistic would be the number of people who were moved by all the talk of citizen participation and physical rebirth to protest the lack of action behind the talk, and who thus became radicalized and organized—and therefore forced the city to make a little more progress.

At any rate, it would not be unrealistic to suppose that New Haven, a city of less than 150,000, had spent in sixteen years a minimum of $200 million in public funds for physical renewal and at least $30 million for human renewal, with literally uncounted other millions coming in simply because the physical and human renewal programs were there.

The great bulk of that money flowed through two agencies which were under Lee's strict control—CPI and the Redevelopment Agency. If New Haven and the Lee era had produced momentum, it should be found in those agencies. But by the end of the era, the mayor's critics were saying that all the momentum had been designed to serve either the business interests, the motorist, or the status quo, or all three.

The Community Action Institute, the agency of CPI which had served for four years as the training center for New England poverty professionals, announced in May 1969 that it was changing its approach from one of services to one of organization—to teaching the poor how to organize to get their own services. One month later, however, the Office of Economic Opportunity notified the institute that it was out of business. A group in New York got the OEO contract for the New England region.

Further evidence of the decline of CPI and its influence as a social innovator came during the summer of 1969 in what by then had become part of an annual nationwide controversy over anti-poverty funds. New Haven was preparing to mount a summer program that utilized approximately $1.25 million in funds, which CPI would distribute. CPI, by now, was an old hand at getting involved in bitter battles over summer money. To this history was added, in 1969, a slightly new dimension—battles over funds of any sort, regardless of the season. When the federal government announced that New Haven was one of twenty cities eligible for funds to repair riot damage, the Hill section received $280,000.[1] CPI officials and others had expressed their fear, at the time of the

---

[1] The city had to go through considerable soul-searching before it decided to admit that it had *riot* damage, but finally decided to seek the money. *The Register* had trouble with the concept, too; in a news story about the city's decision to apply for the money, New Haven was termed a "disturbance-scarred" city, and the neighborhoods which had been disturbed were called "disturbance-troubled areas."

$32,120 Deal, that if the Hill's militancy led to concessions, other neighborhoods might get the idea that they could be militant, too, and that there would be no end to the demands from the citizens. Sure enough, when the $280,000 in repair money was announced for the Hill, a committee of Fair Haveners got together and demanded $200,000. "The Hill got $280,000 in federal funds for riot-damaged areas and we got none," said the committee's chairman. "We would like to know why."

A battle over state funds started after the State Department of Community Affairs announced that all recipients of its assistance would have to tighten their belts, because the state was tightening its. Governor John N. Dempsey, who at that point was facing a taxpayer revolt in Hartford, was asking for only $13 million for the entire state for "human resource development." This rankled community organizations in New Haven, who said the city alone needed almost twice that much.

The community agencies turned their rage on City Hall, which told them it didn't have any money, either; that funds would have to come from the state or federal governments. CPI, at this time, was placed in the somewhat sensitive position of being a part of the bureaucracy that was handling the money even while it was trying to convince the local organizations that it was one of them. During one tense meeting, CPI Director Milton Brown was moved to make the absurd statement that he was not there to represent the city.

"CPI is not a city agency," Brown was quoted as saying. "CPI is a private, nonprofit organization which works closely with the city as with many other agencies. . . I want to make it very clear that I don't represent the city."

Because of the lack of funds, and because of the need for dramatizing that lack, eighteen summer programs shut down for two weeks, including a day camp in the Hill that had served about 500 children. Six busloads of the children held a camp-in on the New Haven Green, across the street from Mayor Lee's office.

At the summer's end, the neighborhoods got some of the money they asked for, and New Haven had avoided another riot, which undoubtedly provided extreme comfort for the officials in City Hall and at CPI, inasmuch as that is what summer programs have been all about since the Harlem riot of 1964.

New battles were started on the citizen participation front with the emergence of the state as a major source of money. It turned out, in the summer of 1969, that the steering committee that supervised the allocation of about $10 million a year in state funds to New Haven programs was about as representative of all the citizens as the Citizens Action Commission had been years before. Representatives from neighborhood organizations in the seven poor communities, who called themselves "Seven Together," disrupted one meeting of the steering committee. At the next meeting, the committee voted to enlarge its membership to include neighborhood representation.

Then Seven Together tackled the problem of citizen participation on CPI. The group announced at the end of the summer of 1969 that its constituent organizations, each of which had representatives on the CPI board, were seeking to recall those representatives. Such action would hasten the decentralization of CPI, it was reasoned, by forcing the funding sources to send money directly to neighborhood organizations rather than through CPI. One of the directors recalled was Harry D. Jeffreys, who represented the Hill Neighborhood Corporation. This was sticky, inasmuch as Jeffreys had been elected the president of the CPI board.

Milton Brown said the recall move had "no validity at all." Jeffreys said he would stay on as president of the board and that he would not be "bulldozed" by a handful of people. Shortly afterward he was reelected to his post by the other CPI directors.

It was obvious by the end of the summer that once again New Haven had done very little until it was faced with a crisis. The city could expect similar situations, perhaps worse ones, in subsequent summers, unless it worked out a better way of coping with the demands of the neighborhoods. And a way could not be worked out until the city recognized the legitimacy of the citizens' demands.

For another thing, the argument that militancy paid off more than moderation was again proven. And the city still had not devised ways to cope with that militancy—either to accommodate itself to the demands, or to learn how to talk the militants into accommodating themselves to the city's situation, which was one characterized largely by lack of money.

Donald Dallas, in a news analysis article in *The Register* during the height of the 1969 summer controversy, noted that the $107,-000 Holdup of the previous summer had "set a precedent which is continuing to have effects."

> The money was contributed, some critics say, primarily due to fears of—and threats of—violence on the Hill. It was not given entirely out of altruism or compassionate concern, but it was in many ways a "pay-off."
> It had two effects:
> One, it automatically boosted Hill annual summer financial requirements. It got the Hill used to increased spending plans that were self-administered.
> Two, it "legitimized" the "militants."
> By succumbing to its fears, the community coalition that provided the funds gave the most angry and vocal Hill spokesmen an increased status, power, and "legitimacy" in their own and in Hill residents' eyes.
> The move also made the "militants" heroes in the view of a sizeable corps of the "liberal" community here. A notable number continues to follow them, in somewhat romantic fashion. . . . Forgotten during the romance, unfortunately, were priorities.
> The need, while great, is a community need—or rather a New Haven area need—not just the Hill's.[2]

Some help for New Haven, in its battles over decentralization, citizen participation, summer funding, and relationships with new sources of funds, might logically have come from an element of society that was moving, in 1969, for the first time—the business community.

The Urban Alliance of Greater New Haven, it may be recalled,

---

[2] "The Hill Program Fund Controversy: A Problem Involving Nearly Everyone," *The New Haven Register*, July 10, 1969.

was initiated back in the spring of 1968 by James H. Gilbert, the former head of the Citizens Action Commission, and others, and was formed in apparent reaction to the $107,000 Holdup. The alliance had gone through some name changes—the Thursday Night Group, then the Urban Development Organization—and it had hired Frank Logue as a consultant and sent him out to do a study of what was needed.

Before he left, Logue had said it was his feeling that the Urban Alliance had been started by men who were interested in co-ordination, but that it seemed to be heading more in the direction of businessmen's wanting to "concert their resources."

"If they take the view that they *don't* want to concert their resources," he had said, "then I think just the information-exchange function is not a sufficient one for an organization."

Logue spent five days touring the country, checking into urban alliance– and Urban Coalition–type organizations in Washington, Detroit, Los Angeles, San Francisco, and Oakland, and when he returned to New Haven he interviewed 30 or 40 leaders of business and minority group organizations. Then he wrote a thirteen-page report, with appendices, entitled "New Haven—Where We Are," and submitted it to the men who were organizing the Urban Alliance.

The report demonstrated its author's sensitivity to the problems that had been forming in New Haven for so many years:

> New Haven has perhaps done as much as any city in the nation to improve educational, employment, housing, and other opportunities for disadvantaged people. Nonetheless, spokesmen for the intended beneficiaries frequently maintained that nothing has been done. . . . We are also at a point, in New Haven and in the nation, where many complain that too much is being done for the poor. . . . The interests of such groups must be clearly represented and expressly recognized in mobilizing community-wide support for dealing with critical urban problems.

In addition to the fact that the "disadvantaged" were increasing in number, in percentage, and in volume of protest, there was a further and dangerous problem:

At the time when neighborhood residents are approaching a position in which they could begin to exercise some control over the services furnished to them, there is the serious possibility that funds for such services will be reduced or eliminated.

Logue proposed the creation of an organization along the lines of the Urban Coalition model—that is, one in which "neighborhood and minority group leaders join government and private sector leaders in a single organization, often functioning through task forces in such areas as employment, housing, education, economic development and the like." The organization, he said, should subscribe to "sustained, patient commitment," and it should try to find ways "to move the community as a whole in directions that necessarily represent choices between conflicting claims for attention."

To do this, the "very top echelons of leadership" in the public and private sectors would be tapped for membership, along with the "broadly representative minority and neighborhood leadership." The staff should have a minimum of salaried persons and a maximum of experts loaned from member organizations.

The chief functions of the organization would be to serve as an agency for receiving and disbursing funds; secondarily it would serve as a clearing house for coordinating action and facilitating communications. The agency must immediately select the areas it wishes to emphasize, said Logue; otherwise it will only react "as one or another of the community's urgent needs claims its attention."

Nowhere in the Greater New Haven Region is there a structure which is a natural forum for broad communication in times of crisis. Neighborhood, minority, government and private sector leaders need a community resource to which they relate in a continuing way. When the need is urgent, that resource, whatever its day-to-day concerns, can be the vehicle for prompt communication—and possibly for a unified community response. It is likely to be effective in a crisis to the extent to which its constituent members have communicated effectively on a year-round basis.

The businessmen's reaction to the Logue report was not immediately clear. As the Urban Alliance became incorporated in

March 1969 it declared that it would not act as an "action agency" or a "super-agency," but "rather as a supportive agency with the basic purposes . . . of helping the community provide a forum, a clearing-house and a resource bank to identify, agree upon, and respond to priority needs."

According to most observers, Logue had been the logical man to become the executive director of the new alliance. But this possibility faded as the incorporators continued to give evidence that they were not terribly excited about his suggestions. So Logue became the director of the Urban Fellows Program, which was sponsored by the National League of Cities, the U.S. Conference of Mayors, and Yale, and which was designed to place potential urban leaders in on-the-job training with present urban leaders. Not long after taking the new position, Logue was asked to comment on his experiences with the Urban Alliance.

The response to his report, he said, "was that we'd better go a little bit slower than I had suggested. And, having received that response, which a group of people made, I decided that this wasn't something that I wanted to do. I had some views, which I had expressed. It wasn't so much that these views were disagreed with, but that they just thought that it would be better to have something a little bit later and a little bit less."

Since the businessmen received his report, said Logue, they had been looking for a staff director, "and I hope they'll do good things, and I wish them well. I think there is some commitment in the private sector in New Haven. I don't know how much there is, and whether the Urban Alliance achieves anything or not depends on the extent of that commitment. That's something that I don't feel in any position to assess. As I say, I wish it well; I hope there is commitment. There are certainly some people, and there is some money available, and I think that they can put together an effort from the private sector which can make a good contribution."

But, he added, "They have used the phrase, 'clearing house,' and that doesn't seem to be enough of a role for an organization. Usually it means finding out what people are doing and communicating and exchanging information. That's the minimal function, and that's not enough.

"The evidence I have," he concluded, "would indicate that they're about like the people in the rest of the country. There are some who want to do good, and there are some who are beginning to understand that it's rather complex, and there are some, I guess, who are not very much involved."

In the spring of 1969 the Urban Alliance sent letters to legislators asking them to provide more money for the state's attack on poverty. That was about all the news the alliance made, at least in its initial months as a functioning organization. All this led one observer, Peter Almond, to conclude that the Alliance could not be considered an important actor in the city's efforts to rebuild itself socially.

"It would be one thing," said Almond, "if they just simply did nothing—if they met no longer, if they showed absolutely no interest. It's somehow more discouraging when they continue to meet, when the meetings prolong the agony of leadership's coming together, in effect, to say 'This is a problem but we really are not all that interested, and one way we'll handle it is to meet irregularly, once every four to six weeks, and set up a lot of committees and some kind of mechanism which sounds impressive and tries to reach all groups in the city.'

"What has also struck me is that they have failed to respond to any real or immediate demands on them, or pressures on them, to do something the right way. When the Black Coalition stated fairly clearly that it had a fund shortage, the leadership of the Urban Alliance failed to respond. They just talked about the importance of a long-range program and project development and longer-range organization."

Some evidence of fresh momentum might be expected in New Haven's Model Cities program, since it was new and not burdened, as CPI was, by a rocky history. Theoretically, Model Cities should have started off as the beneficiary of a lot of painful experience, particularly experience in the realm of citizen participation. Model Cities, according to the Department of Housing and Urban Development, was designed to show "how all urban resources can be combined into a massive onslaught on city problems."

In its first phase, the massive onslaught consisted of federal grants to cities of 80 percent of the cost of planning and developing "comprehensive city demonstration programs." About 150 cities started such planning under the Johnson Administration, but the original plan was that truly comprehensive attacks on the problems would be mounted initially in only five or six of the cities.

In addition to taking advantage of a more coordinated system of existing federal grants and programs, the Model Cities areas would be entitled to federal block grants, which could be used as local agencies saw fit. President Johnson had asked Congress for $750 million for these grants.

Under the Nixon Administration, the program was changed considerably. Nixon reduced the block-grant request to $675 million, and it was further reduced by Congress. As fiscal year 1970 approached, HUD was talking in terms of $515 million, and in the fall of 1969 it looked as if $300 million might be spent on block grants. Congress also enlarged the plan to cover not five or six cities, but all 150. The new administration made benefits under the program available to all poverty neighborhoods within a city, not just one "demonstration" neighborhood, and, most importantly for proponents of citizen participation, Nixon made it plain that under *his* Administration City Hall would be in charge. The Model Cities program, said a HUD aide, would "not be controlled by citizen groups."

Back in 1967, though, when planning for the Model Cities program was just beginning, the word was that citizen participation was to be a vital part of the concept. New Haven, which in November of that year was to be selected as one of 63 "first-round" participants, started planning well in advance. The city selected the Hill as its Model Cities neighborhood and city agencies started drawing up initial proposals.

To meet HUD's requirement of appropriate citizen participation, the planners suggested the election of neighborhood representatives to the City Demonstration Agency,[3] public meetings in the Model

---

[3] The City Demonstration Agency, according to HUD's original Model Cities guidelines, would be the local agency through which funds flowed from Washington to the neighborhood. The CDA, said HUD, could be

Cities neighborhood instead of "downtown," and "a good public information program." On that last point, the Model Cities planners noted that the Redevelopment Agency and CPI had had "good success" with their publications programs.

When it came time to put its money where its mouth was in the matter of citizen participation, however, New Haven exhibited the same reluctance it had shown before in CPI and the Redevelopment Agency. Some observers, though, were inclined to believe that a new wrinkle had been added this time: They charged that when some degree of citizen participation finally was incorporated into the program, the city then methodically and deliberately tried to sabotage the entire effort.

At stake, to begin with, was New Haven's designation as a Model Cities participant and a $105,000 planning grant from HUD, to be followed, the city hoped, by a $1.8-million grant to start the execution of the plans. The Board of Aldermen, in March 1968, set about deciding on the composition of the Model Cities agency. A majority report of the aldermanic Committee on Urban Development came up with a proposal rather distantly removed from citizen participation: The agency should have fifteen members, with five of them from the Hill. Interestingly enough, what seemed to intrigue some observers about the majority report was that it bypassed City Hall to a considerable extent. These observers saw in the report fresh evidence of the growing feud between Mayor Lee and Arthur Barbieri, the Democratic Town Committee chairman, who was in much closer touch with the aldermen.

A minority report from the committee recommended a 21-

a city, county, or local public agency established expressly for the purpose, or it could be an existing agency, "broadly representative of physical and social concerns." A CDA, among other things, should have sufficient power and authority to run a coordinated program, free of fragmentation and duplication; should be "closely related to the governmental decision-making process in a way that permits the exercise of leadership by responsible elected officials in the establishment of policy and in effecting coordination," and it "should provide a meaningful role in policy-making to area residents and to the major departments and agencies . . . which must participate in order to carry out a successful program." (U. S. Department of Housing and Urban Development, "Improving the Quality of Urban Life: A Program Guide to Model Neighborhoods in Demonstration Cities," December 1967.)

member agency, with the majority of them elected from and by residents of the Hill. A quickly-organized group of about fifteen Hill residents who were active in agencies there, who covered the entire range from moderator to militancy, and who called themselves the Hill Ad Hoc Model Cities Steering Committee, issued a statement saying that neither the majority nor the minority reports were acceptable, inasmuch as neither gave assurances of neighborhood participation.

As the aldermen stewed and argued about the makeup of the agency, Washington announced that time was running out for the city that once had been at the head of every line for federal funds. H. Ralph Taylor, an assistant secretary of Housing and Urban Development (and former executive director of the New Haven Redevelopment Agency), said the city had a deadline of April 20, 1968. Other cities were interested in getting the money if New Haven couldn't make up its mind, said Taylor: "There are serious questions here in Washington as to how long we can hold the money aside for New Haven."

A few hours before the deadline, the aldermen acted. After a three-hour, closed-door meeting, they voted to set up an agency in which the Hill residents would have control. Rather suddenly there was created an organization called the Hill Neighborhood Corporation, which more or less duplicated the Hill Ad Hoc Model Cities Steering Committee, and whose membership would be open to all Hill residents aged sixteen or over. The City Demonstration Agency would consist of 21 members, eleven of them named by the Hill Neighborhood Corporation; four named by the mayor (and three of those from city agencies); one from the Greater New Haven Chamber of Commerce; one from the Central Labor Council; one a state official, appointed by the president of the Board of Aldermen, and three aldermen (two of them from the Hill).

The agency, it was quickly noted by those who study such matters, completely bypassed the Redevelopment Agency, whose chief, Melvin Adams, was quick in reacting. He said he doubted that the agency would get Washington's approval, since it didn't follow HUD's guidelines. For reasons that were not entirely clear, Adams shortly changed his tune. In a letter to Joseph B. Goldman, the assistant regional administrator of HUD for Region One, the New England region, Adams said: "Mayor Richard C. Lee has asked me to urge prompt approval of our Model Cities program. We wholeheartedly and enthusiastically support it and will use every resource at our command to assure its success." Further surprises were forthcoming when Congressman Giaimo endorsed the agency and when Mayor Lee broke a long silence to promise he would make technical help and facilities available for use in the planning period.

In May 1968, HUD approved the New Haven agency. Willie Counsel, the vice president of the Hill Parents Association, was elected chairman of the board of the Hill Neighborhood Corporation, and the planning started.

In March 1969 troubles developed. Housing and Urban Development, it turned out, was holding up $15,000 monthly planning allotments to the corporation on the grounds that HNC was not providing sufficient information on how it was using the money. HNC, meantime, charged that both federal and city officials were holding up the funds for silly reasons. "Emergency meetings" were held all over town; HNC, faced with the distinct possibility that it would not be able to meet its payroll, asked for cash advances from the city. The city refused.

At almost literally the last minute, the money started flowing again from Washington, and HNC began turning out drafts of its proposals. The proposals concerned Hill residents' desires in such areas as education, renewal, health, employment, economic development, welfare, recreation, cultural activities, law enforcement, and day care. One of the draft proposals, for example, in education, suggested that the schools be made "responsive and responsible to their clients. . . through progressive localization of control," better efforts at early childhood education, more experimentation, imaginative curricula, a reduced pupil-teacher ratio, and the employment of residents in the schools. In law enforcement, the Hill planners wanted a civilian advisory board to relay the citizens' feelings and desires to the police department and to help the department recruit, screen, and train policemen.

Not long after the proposals started coming out, Joseph Goldman, the regional HUD executive, was asked about New Haven's program. The structure there, he said, "has been very unique in the Model Cities program, certainly in this region, and probably throughout the country." The rules, he said, called for "widespread citizen participation;" in New Haven, it may have been *too* widespread. "We are very interested in looking at New Haven as a demonstration," he added.

"In most cities," he continued, "we had to go out and make sure there was citizen participation; here we had to be assured that the *city* was involved. If it was just turning the money over to the Hill Neighborhood Corporation, we couldn't accept that as part of Model City planning. So for months we've struggled to tie the city in closer with the Hill Neighborhood Corporation."

As the HNC's proposals emerged, some of those who had been studying them were struck by the conventionality of the citizen-written suggestions. One of those observers, who was sympathetic to the cause of citizen participation, had commented: "I'm struck by the fact that, if anything, they're more limited, or more conventional, than what everybody else comes up with. This is a problem you hear from professionals who work carefully and professionally with neighborhood organizations—that the organizations that are dominated by non-sophisticated or non-trained people come up with ideas like, say, in education, where they want more teachers. They're not talking about challenging the conventional assumptions of what a school is, and that kind of thing. Another thing is that it's just kind of sloppy. It's not well done, it's not imaginative, it's not rigorous in any way, and it represents the sloppiness of the process that put it together. You can argue, of course, that it's valuable psychologically because it's *theirs*."

And another sympathizer remarked that he had made the same disappointing discovery. He added: "During those years when CPI and other groups were getting such great experience in proposal-writing and money-getting, apparently, the people from the neighborhoods were not getting any of this education at all. It was the professionals and semi-professionals who were getting the education."

As the Hill Neighborhood Corporation continued writing its proposals (which seemed to become less sloppy and more sophisticated as the agency gained experience), there were further difficulties, financial and otherwise. There was a great deal of staff turnover, and attendance at meetings of the CDA was so poor that the 21-member group had to change its rules to make seven members a quorum.

The executive director of the HNC was ousted in a battle, apparently with proponents of the Hill Parents Association philosophy. He charged that they were bent on destroying the program if they could not gain control over it.

Melvin Adams said the administrative structure of the Model Cities agency had broken down. He added:

> The neighborhood corporation has complete responsibility for planning, and also for involving the people in the neighborhood. and meeting all the federal policy and procedural requirements. At the same time, there are pressures on the corporation to hire neighborhood people for paid positions.
> The result—and this isn't any criticism of the people involved —is that the HNC staff does not contain the technical competence either to prepare the technical reports that are part of the plan, or to meet the very complicated procedures of the program.

To this, the Hill Neighborhood Corporation replied that "Mr. Adams is only recollecting his long-held view that community people should have a minimal role in planning programs."

More than one observer commented that the city's enthusiasm in turning over control of the Model Cities program to the neighborhood, coupled with its resistance over making technical and financial assistance available, was evidence of deliberate sabotage.

If the city had to allow citizen participation, the reasoning went, the city would destroy the program in the process.

It was a diabolical plot on the part of the city, said the critics, to assist in the establishment of a program that the city knew would not be successful (and that therefore would demonstrate the futility of citizen participation) and that would not receive the continued blessings of the officials in Washington.

Such accusations might sound like typical radical paranoia. Strangely enough, however, they were partially confirmed by persons of the highest authority whose views reflected precisely those of City Hall. This, they said, is what happened:

• It became obvious to Mayor Lee that a group of people, those whom City Hall called "critics," wanted control over the Model Cities program. "They would take it away from the 'power structure,' " one official said, sneeringly. The "critics" got enough support from dissident aldermen to pass legislation setting up a program that kept most of the control out of the hands of City Hall.

• Lee pledged his cooperation, but he didn't really mean it. When the neighborhood ran into its first siege of troubles in getting the program rolling, it asked Lee for help. Lee replied, according to the city official: "What do you want from us? You've got what you call the ideal citizen participation program; run it."

• The neighborhood said that it needed help because it was in trouble. "And Lee said, 'As they say in the old country, t.s.' Lee was not about to pull them out of the hole they were in. This is the nut element," said the official.

• It was all an exercise in demonstrating to the neighborhood people the impropriety and foolishness of attempting to run their own program without accepting the direct involvement and control of City Hall. "These people thought they'd pulled a coup on City Hall," said the official. "Well, to a certain degree they did. But the coup they pulled was self-defeating, because they won a battle, but they lost a war. And all they proved, to everybody who could see or was interested, was that they can't run a goddamned thing."

Willie Counsel, 28 years old at the time he became the chairman of the board of the Hill Neighborhood Corporation, had never heard of Richard Lee until 1960, when he left Tuskegee, Alabama, and came to New Haven. By then, many of Lee's physical renewal projects were already finished.

One of Counsel's first impressions of the city, he said some years later, was that the black community was not very much together. "I found New Haven a very unique city," he said. "The place really didn't have any type of black awareness or leadership. I found out that you had the NAACP and CORE, but they weren't really getting to the grass roots of the *problem* and making the public aware of the problem and making *people* aware of the problem and giving them hope that something could be done."

Counsel got involved in the Hill Parents Association, and he soon met Fred Harris. He, and the HPA, were incensed at the situation at a local school where, Counsel said, the books dated back to 1938 "and the teachers were ruler-beating black kids and calling them black niggers and ignorant stupid animals and they didn't have any knowledge of learning."

The organizing that HPA did around the school issue was successful in terms of winning concessions from the school system, but in other ways it was disappointing. Counsel said he came out of the confrontations dismayed that "nothing really basic was happening. The people in the community really felt that it wasn't the type of thing that they could really get involved in and really bring changes over, because of the big power machinery that Dick Lee had.

"He had some of the greatest public relations men in the world, you know, in terms of selling the idea that New Haven was a model city and that there weren't any problems. And he built this paper empire around buying people off and moving people around. He even went so far as getting black ministers in the churches to be so-called leaders for his machinery."

What all this resulted in, said Counsel, was the city's receiving over $18 million "for a poverty program where none of it has really got to the community because the bureaucratic system sucked it up before it got there. My whole feeling," he said, "is that when a man stays in power for all that many years, he basically becomes a dictator."

Why, then, Counsel was asked, was he involved in yet another poverty program?

"Well, you see," he said, "you have to understand that the Hill Neighborhood Corporation is very unique. It's different from any of the Model Cities programs in the nation. When the Model Cities proposal was first written up here, it was written up in terms of no community participation *period* in the City of New Haven. But we changed that by going out in the community and organizing the community around the issues that we have learned from the mistakes of CPI and the other poverty programs that have been set up for black people—programs that have been complete failures.

"We felt that this time Model Cities should be *our* baby, and we should have a chance to prove to the nation that Model Cities can be a concept that works. Now, Model Cities was set up to be a failure by the bureaucratic system. But we see it in terms of the community level. We see that it can be a success in terms of really getting at the basic problems. I think this whole new approach that we have in New Haven can be an example throughout the country—that the people in the community are sophisticated and educated and efficient enough to really deal with the problem."

Counsel said the power structure had already interpreted the corporation as a threat and had started to place stumbling blocks in its path. The technical assistance was minimal; the red tape was endless. Why, he was asked again, if the situation was so conducive to pessimism, did he align himself with the operation?

"See," he said, "you have to understand that I'm involved in it because I believe in a Model Cities program that is basically controlled by the community, and we *do* have the control. And I'm saying that from the viewpoint of the community controlling it, I see great hope. But if it was controlled by the city administration, I would say forget it."

Did he think President Nixon and Vice President Agnew, both of whom had already showed a good deal of contempt for poor and black people, would let the community retain control?

"It'll be very interesting to see. If these guys pull community control out from under the people in the community, you know, then you really start chaos, and I don't expect that New Haven is *that* foolish. I think they have to play ball whether they like it or not. Because we feel that Model Cities is here to stay, and that it is to be controlled by the people. We believe in people-power. And not dictatorship."

People-power, said Counsel, was not achieved through the black organizations Mayor Lee had chosen to deal with in the past. "We deal with the nitty-gritty problems of the people. We believe in dealing with things *now*. We don't like delays and waiting, because we've waited over 400 years. From our viewpoint, we see that there hasn't been any change in New Haven, and there probably will not be any change until people really wake up, and start really understanding what's happening to them, and people start to get organized and educated around what the political structure does and how it affects them."

Would voting help? Would democratic politics help?

"No," said Counsel. "Democratic politics are dead. I say that it has not worked for over 400 years, and I don't see no great dreams that are going to make me believe that it is going to work in the next 400 years. Because it's too corrupt.

"Because what I want is people controlling their own destiny, and that has not happened."

XI

Hail and Farewell

Kids are dying . . .—Someone at the Democratic Town Committee nominating convention

RICHARD C. LEE sat in his polished black limousine in the front driveway of the Park Plaza Hotel, working on the speech he was going to deliver to the Democrats. Slowly and carefully he turned the crisp pages. They were bound in a thin three-ring notebook that he held under a reading lamp in the back seat of the official car. People walked by, stared at the limousine, recognized its occupant, and continued on into the hotel, where the Democratic Town Committee of New Haven was holding its nomination of candidates for the fall of 1969 election. Some of them walked over and tapped on the window and said hello to Dick Lee. The mayor knew them all by name.

It had been a long, hot summer, but not the usual kind. This time the heat had been produced largely by politics. Even before Lee had announced he was not running again, four Republicans had proclaimed their candidacies. Two of them were distinctly law-and-order men and a third was bordering on it, but the fourth, Paul Capra (one of those who had run against Fred Harris for the General Assembly back in 1966), was a cut above the average New Haven Republican.

Capra, a young assistant admissions director at Yale, said he stood for citizen participation. He had opened his campaign in a vacant lot in the middle of a neighborhood that was being destroyed to make way for the Route 34 project. He had said "New Haven suffers from an administration that has been in office for so long that it has forgotten that cities are for people, not monuments." And he had promised to "create for the citizens of New Haven a new environment founded on human concern rather than bricks and concrete." Capra, his partisans said, was a lot like John Lindsay of New York—a new breed of Republican. And when the Republicans had held their nominating convention, a week before the Democrats gathered for theirs, they had chosen Capra without hesitation.

Two Democrats had been so bold as to announce their candidacies, too, before Lee confirmed his retirement. One of them was a private investigator, state senator, and alderman; the other was Henry Parker, the black man who had been the head of the Black Coalition. Parker had charged that New Haven, under Lee, had paid too much attention to physical progress, and not enough to human need. Parker's statements and those of Capra sounded quite similar.

After Lee's announcement, the ball game changed. Another Negro, John C. Daniels, who had succeeded Richard Belford as the head of the Commission on Equal Opportunities, but who had tempered his criticism of the Lee administration in his campaign statements, entered the race, thus effectively confusing, if not splitting, the Negro vote. An alderman named Charles Gill was running. And the Democratic machine, under the town chairman, Arthur T. Barbieri, had chosen Bartholomew Guida, a realtor and insurance man and a member of the Board of Aldermen for 22 years, as its candidate. Guida had said virtually nothing in the campaign so far, and what he *had* said had amounted to little. When he announced his candidacy, he had said "A need for stability in all areas is ever present and the challenge for leadership and direction must be met with continued resolve and determination to bring forth a progressive and united city." He also had called for cooperation. During most of the pre-nominating period he had declined to engage in debates and question-and-answer sessions with his challengers. Guida was a shoo-in for the party's nomination, and he knew it. Arthur Barbieri had been denied power for so long—the better part of sixteen years, according to some accounts—that he had made sure that the next mayor, if he was going to be a Democrat, would be a faithful Democrat, one properly respectful of the apparatus that would help elect him. It was perhaps unavoidable that such a candidate could only be unimaginative, uncontroversial, and unexciting.

There had been charges that the Democratic convention would be a closed one; that Barbieri had engineered it so that only Guida could be nominated. And there had been denials that this was so. Partisans of Gill and Parker were at the meeting; they were going to make a fight, at least, at the first convention in so many years whose outcome would not be an absolute certainty.

Richard Lee was going to deliver the keynote speech. Some interpreted this as an indication that both Lee and Barbieri understood the need for party unity.

"It's a kind of a hail and farewell comment," said Lee as he closed the three-ring notebook, then opened it again. "It spells out in general terms what I believe in and what I've tried to do. It's positive. It's not negative. It just states what I believe in within the framework of the Democratic Party structure. And in a sense it's not really a keynote speech, which is what I've been asked to make. It's sort of a thank-you for everything. It's just about as honest an appraisal of what I feel as anything I've ever written. There's no subterfuge."

Was there a feeling of relief tonight; relief that the era was ending?

"Tonight? No, not tonight. Tonight is a nostalgic night."

Lee's police driver, Jerry McCormick, returned to the limousine from a scouting trip inside. Lee asked him who was there. McCormick listed some names. "What about the Negroes?" asked Lee. He wanted to know if Fred Harris or Ronald Johnson or Willie Counsel were there. Someone asked Lee whether it made any difference, and he said "No."

Soon a Democratic official brought word that the convention was ready to receive Lee. The mayor went inside to discover that the convention was not ready at all. Someone in his retinue said it was another of Barbieri's cheap tricks.

There were five or six hundred people in the hall, perhaps half of them displaying some form of banner, button, or molded plastic straw hat proclaiming their choice of nominee. Barbieri calmed the boisterous group and started to introduce Lee. Lee's allies held their breath in anticipation of the subtle digs they knew Barbieri would make at his enemy.

"While I have never invited a keynote speaker to any of the seventeen annual meetings of this convention called by me, I feel it is fitting that this man, who has established numerous precedents in city administration during his highly successful sixteen-year venture as mayor of the City of New Haven, should address us in this capacity. Dick Lee's vision and courage and, of course, his genuine love for his city, has blazed a trail for a better—"

Barbieri's voice was drowned out, momentarily, by a combination of boos and cheers.

"—We have grown accustomed to nominating him for the office of mayor, and not in having him assist us in the nominating process, as he is doing tonight. We are glad to have him with us to share with us perhaps some private thoughts on his stewardship and to offer some . . . advice to the nominees and to the Democratic Party. By his presence here tonight, Dick Lee has shown that he will actively campaign for the city ticket endorsed in this hall and assist in the transition from his administration to the new *Democratic* administration to be elected on November fourth."

[A Lee ally chalked up one subtle dig.]

". . . Ladies and gentlemen, our great mayor, Dick Lee." There was loud booing, followed by gradually rising applause. Lee waited patiently, his three-ring notebook with the speech in it before him, waiting for the noise to die down, waiting to begin his nostalgia. The booing went on for several minutes.

"Mister Chairman——" [catcalls and booing].

"——Officers of the Democratic Town Committee——" [more

catcalls] "——and ladies and gentlemen who are here tonight——"

["Let the mayor talk."]

"——some of you who are polite, some of you who are rude——" [catcalls and applause]

"——I have been mayor of the City of New Haven for sixteen years——" [a catcall]

"——If you'll keep your mouth shut, I'll finish my speech." [some applause, followed by a shout from a black man, "It'll be the *first* thing you ever finished!"]

"——If you want to go on outside, I'll talk to you when I get outside." [applause, from the white members of the audience]

"My comments tonight are comments of gratitude for what the Democratic Party has done for me, first in choosing me and then in supporting me in my campaigns for mayor these many years . . ." [Lee had skipped the first five pages of his prepared text, the nostalgic part.]

"We have learned many lessons together, you and I, and our city, immodestly if I may say so, has benefited much from our partnership. But now tonight your task is to choose another candidate. And our joint goal, going forward from tonight, is to provide new leadership in City Hall and at the same time to present a united party to our people.

"The problems of the community are too grave and too serious for our party to engage in battles which will divide us. Our party will only be able to move forward, to change with the changing conditions, to match deeds with needs if we will but only work together in a spirit of harmony and cooperation.

"It is an exercise in emotion for me to be here tonight, an exercise as well in control, for I see so many out here in front of me who have been with us all of these years, and then I think, as the roll is called within my heart, of those who once were with us, but now are no longer present. I have represented all of you, but I have represented them also.

"This is not a speech of goodbye. It is simply a statement of gratitude, for I will not appear again before a convention of the Democratic Town Committee as your mayor—" [light applause]

"Never again will this opportunity be mine." [catcalls]

"You have my heart tonight, even as I prepare to take leave in just four months of the assignment I have attempted to carry out these past sixteen years. As for the future, who can tell? Not you, nor I. Perhaps I shall return to you again soon, and should I, you may expect the same loyalty and devotion and leadership from me which I have given you in the past.

"I am grateful to the Democratic Party. I am grateful to all of you for all that you have done for me, and may the Lord in his wisdom tonight guide all of you in your decisions. And may the struggles which have gone on within our group cease. May our party once more be united.

"No one said it any better than Franklin Delano Roosevelt when he said, 'Let us move together, and let us move forward with strong and active faith.' I urge you in the same fashion to victory November fourth."

There was applause, and some booing, and then Lee left the ballroom and the nominating of candidates for the party's choice for mayor was begun.

Ronald Johnson had been one of those doing the catcalling. While some of the nominating speeches were going on, he, like many others at the meeting, repaired to the Park Plaza bar. He expressed contempt for the entire process. Why, then, he was asked, was he there?

"Well, to offset things a little," he said. He added that he was not for a black candidate any more than he was for a white candidate, "because it's going to be hard for any man, black, white, or otherwise, to make up for sixteen years of mistakes." It would take a lot more togetherness in the black community, he said, before black people would have any real reason to be interested in politics. "I don't think black people can do a hell of a lot, politically, other than the fact that they can go ahead and fuck and make a whole lot of babies twenty years from now. At this point we can't make it."

Johnson, whose conviction in the alleged bomb plot was still under appeal, said he was thinking of moving on. He said a lot of the original militants—people like Fred Harris, and himself, and Willie Counsel—were "sort of impositions on the people now. We did our thing initially, and now it's time for people to do their *own* thing, to carry on where we left off.

"See, you can bring people to a certain level, and you get to the point where if you continue to be who they think you are, who they think you should be, a leader in the community, what happens is the black people end up relying on you to make moves *for* them instead of making moves for themselves and being able to develop their own initiative and creativity. Deal on their own. If we stay here, everybody gets to the point where they say, you know, 'Let Ron and Freddie do it; let the HPA do it.'"

A lot of people were not there that night. Fred Harris wasn't on hand. He had been working as an assistant to the director of the Connecticut Mental Health Center, and a flap had occurred when the center had decided not to renew his contract. Once again, Harris' mere presence had been construed by some as a sign of danger. (Eventually, though, his contract was renewed.)

Peter Almond was there, as an observer.

Dr. and Mrs. William Ryan were not there. They had left New Haven in the summer and returned to Boston, where Dr. Ryan was to head a new graduate program in community psychology at Boston College. Dr. Ryan, who had said before that New Haven punished its dissenters by excluding them, acknowledged that to some extent he had been a victim of that punishment. "It could be interpreted that way," he said, although the offer of the Boston position had been a strong "pulling reason."

"You ultimately feel a sense of pressure and decide that you couldn't do what you wanted to do, and you decide to go elsewhere," he said. The pressure came from the knowledge that his license plate number was being copied down when he attended meetings; from "calls from downtown" to his superiors when he got involved in organizing a welfare rights group; from a promotion that Yale had promised him that dragged on and on. "Finally, when they approved it, I had already decided to leave Yale," he said. "I could see that they would tolerate me as a house radical, but that it wouldn't be possible to mount some meaningful programs. . . .

"It just got to the point," he said, "where New Haven was a frightening place to be."

Downstairs, in the Park Plaza lobby, Richard Lee was receiving well-wishers. Most of them complimented him on his tough attitude toward the catcallers. "Well, I tell you," he said to one of them; "I don't mind putting the wood to anybody." At one point he called his detractors "animals."

Someone asked him if he had been as nostalgic as he had planned.

"No," he said. "I think that my nostalgia disappeared in the heat of the evening. I'm a mercurial person, and when I'm confronted with a change in mood, I am able to adapt myself.

"I shortened the speech because it was too long. The moment I stood up there and saw all those people to be nominated, and, indeed, all that actual hostility—not necessarily toward me, but within the party—I just decided to substitute a knuckle ball for a fast ball."

What were the people angry about?

"It's just the ethnic development, I regret to say, in our cities, and I don't think it's anything more than that. I don't necessarily think they were angry at *me*. Some of it might have been that, but a good deal of it is people who think their time has come. This is a part of the problem that exists in urban America, and who knows more about it than a Jerry Cavanagh or a John Lindsay or a Dick Lee?

"Listen: I'm an old hand at adapting, and I sat there and I listened to the crowd going after Barbieri, and I realized that this wasn't the evening for this kind of speech, so I just changed."

Inside the convention hall, the partisans of Parker, Daniels, and Gill were still chanting and singing, although they certainly knew their cause was lost.

It was.

Guida, the machine's choice, won 52 of the ward delegates' votes, while Parker and Daniels got nine each and Gill got two. Later, Parker and Gill took the nomination into a primary. Despite the fact that Guida did little campaigning, he won the primary with 5,711 votes. Parker, the black candidate, got 3,795, and Gill got 2,472. Only 48 percent of the registered Democrats voted. An even bigger surprise was the fact that the turnout in the Hill, where the articulate black movement was at its most militant, was low, for Parker and for the other candidates as well.

The primary left Guida and Capra as the contenders in the November 4, 1969, mayoral election. Guida won, but by the tightest margin in eighteen years: 20,442 to 18,744. The Republicans won seven seats on the previously all-Democratic Board of Aldermen. There was talk, after the election, of a coalition of Parker and Capra forces for next time. *The Crow,* the Black Coalition's publication, published several articles hailing the outcome as "the Parker victory."

Even though the outcome of the mayoral nomination was a certainty, the Democrats did have some excitement with the "underticket"—the candidates for lesser offices, who were to be selected that evening. The party was devoted to ticket-balancing; with an Italian-American headed for the mayor's spot, the underticket had to be shuffled around a bit to please the ethnic voting groups. Some Italians had to go, and they had to be replaced by Irishmen and Negroes. When a Negro was nominated for the office of tax collector, a white man seconded his nomination and said, perfectly seriously, that the candidate was "a credit to his race."

A small group of young people moved toward the stage, where Arthur Barbieri was trying to maintain control over *his* first Democratic town convention in many years. "The people want to be heard," the young people chanted. Someone else, a delegate, waved a poster. "Be Smart; Elect Bart," it said.

"The people want to be heard."

A television cameraman aimed his film camera at the group. His light man lifted a portable spotlight into the air, aimed it at the demonstrators, and switched it on. When the light came on the chanting demonstrators shouted louder and they waved their fists in rhythm with the chant. When the light went out they stopped waving their fists, but the chanting continued.

Most of the demonstrators were black. They wore Afro haircuts; they looked strong, maybe mean. *"The people want to be heard."* Barbieri tried to talk into the microphone. He could not be heard. *"The people want to be heard!"* Barbieri's face twitched. He was sweating.

There was some scuffling at the edge of the stage. The demonstrators were trying to mount the platform and capture the microphone. The American flag fell down, slowly. No one tried to save it. The chanting continued. *"The people want to be heard!"* A policeman sprayed Mace into the face of one of the demonstrators. Two people were arrested. The ranking uniformed police officer there that night was Inspector Burton Gifford, who, until one and one-half years before, had been, like all other Negroes in the New Haven Police Department, a patrolman.

In his acceptance speech, which he delivered from behind a solid wall of policemen, Guida promised that after the election he would "meet immediately with leaders of all areas of the community, and with them discuss our problems openly, frankly, sensibly, and in orderly fashion. . . ." It sounded a lot like Richard Lee's promise, back in 1953, to form a Citizens Action Commission.

Guida's acceptance speech continued, and Democrats and non-Democrats gradually left the hall. Most of those who were still around after the first ten minutes were people carrying signs that said "Be Smart; Elect Bart." When Guida paused, and when there was applause, there was a minimum of booing, although there was some laughter when the candidate said "tonight the Democratic Party has made its choice in a free and open meeting." A few of the demonstrators were still around, though, watching the proceedings, and an onlooker asked one of them what the demonstration had been about. What had the people wanted to be heard about?

"Lead poisoning," the demonstrator replied. "We wanted to talk about lead poisoning. Kids are dying in the Hill because of lead poisoning. We wanted the candidates to know that. We wanted whoever's elected mayor to know that kids are dying in the Hill in New Haven, Connecticut, the so-called Model City, because of lead poisoning."

XII

"There Just Ain't No Easy Way"

> *... the question is, Where are the cities going?*
> *And nobody has that answer.*
>
> —Mayor Richard Lee

AFTER LEE'S ANNOUNCEMENT in July of 1969 that he would not run for reelection, the mayor had seemed more relaxed, less burdened, and more inclined to philosophizing than he had been in a long, long time. There was about his pronouncements, both public and private, a touch of nostalgia, of summing up. The phrase "Lee era" had begun to creep into the conversations of his colleagues, his friends, and even his enemies. And after the Democrats had selected his successor the phrase had become a permanent part of the vocabulary.

One morning a few days after the announcement, but some time before he actually left City Hall, Lee bounced into his office. He almost *literally* bounced; his step was springy, and he was wearing a brightly checked sport coat. He was met by what a secretary described as a very important telephone call. The caller was a man who wanted to build another hotel in downtown New Haven. Lee talked with the prospective landowner for a few minutes, hung up the phone, and turned to a visitor:

"What's really happening," he said, "is the increase in construction in New Haven, and the improvement, the *vitality* of the central city, and, of course, the construction of the coliseum—and with all that, more and more people are now literally coming back to downtown—to Central City, U.S.A. And this vindicates all our struggles and all of our attempts to restore the vitality in our commercial heart."

A secretary interrupted to tell the mayor of the death of a citizen of some prominence. The funeral was later that day. Lee made plans to change into a more somber suit. (Appearances at funerals were routine for Lee; it was said of him that he not only recognized the political value of attending a citizen's funeral, but that he also felt a genuine desire to console the mourners. On the other hand, Lee attended few weddings. Why attend a gathering, the reasoning went, where you were sure to be only the second most important living participant?)

Lee had said, in his announcement of retirement, that his mind had been made up for some time. Was that strictly correct?

"My mind was made up a *long* time ago," he said. "I actually reached the decision, literally, before I went into the '67 campaign. It was reinforced by a number of other things which happened, including the very real feeling that I had that not only was fourteen years time enough to serve, but sixteen years for a man in one job was more than enough.

"And the city really deserved a change in leadership. I'm not saying in *direction;* that remains to be determined by the man who succeeds me. But I have felt very strongly, and do feel now, that sixteen years is an impossibly long time for a man to be in a job like this, and I only stuck at it this long because there were a number of things which had to be done—things which, I think, if they aren't completed, at least they are under way. Some people will say that they knew what my decision was going to be. The truth of the matter is that I kept the decision to myself, and it was *my* decision, and not anyone else's. And it was a very personal decision, and one which I think, from my standpoint, is a positive one. There are other things to do in life besides running a city. Very few people have served sixteen years."

What, the mayor was asked, about those mayors—there had been several—who had turned in nearly quarter-centuries in other city halls across the country?

"Those were different years," said Lee, "and this is a different world. In those years, all you had to do was economize, keep the peace, and maintain the status quo. In 1969 it's a totally different ball game than it was in 1960, and this decade has probably been the most trying for mayors in America.

"This should be, properly, a beginning of real programs designed to lift the city and its people toward new goals, new ambitions. The war in Vietnam, we've been told, is going to draw to a close. The President has said troops are coming home. Well, let's hope that some of those 30 *billion* dollars which are now being poured every year into Vietnam can be rechanneled into the cities—and some of the great techniques which have been used to put a man on the moon can be turned now to solve this most basic problem, which is the urban center, which is modern civilization, which is the *city*. This is the kind of thing which I've been trying to do for many years and in which I've had some success. It might be called indifferent success, but certainly it's some success. And these are the things that can happen in the seventies; these are the things which *should* happen in the seventies."

The mayor was asked if he really believed that the money being spent on Vietnam would be diverted, after the war ended, to the cities.

"I don't know what they're going to do," he replied. "I don't have a crystal ball. But let me put it this way: They had just *better* do it, because the problems are so pressing, so urgent.[1] Even the

---

[1] A number of urban leaders, especially the more enlightened and pro-gressive mayors, had been broadcasting this theme during 1969, when it became apparent that it was not the national will to continue the hopeless war. A few days after Lee said this, however, the Nixon administration started discouraging the notion that the war money would be put into the cities. Daniel P. Moynihan announced that such funds would be soaked up by domestic and military programs already on the books or proposed. "I'm afraid that the peace dividend tends to become evanescent like the morning clouds around San Clemente," he said upon emerging from a conference at Nixon's California estate.

states have got to recognize more than ever before that the cities are corporate entities, and they'd better begin to pay attention to them. Because all the problems of each state in America are inevitably bound up with its cities. And this is the story of my life. I've been saying it so long. . . ."

Lee was reminded that he had said, before he announced his retirement, that if he decided not to run again, it would be because after sixteen years he had created "a momentum that can't be halted." Had he done that?

"Yes, I think so. I don't see how anybody can deny that." He pointed to a newspaper clipping on his desk. One of the many candidates swarming the streets for the Democratic nomination had said, in his announcement that he was in the race, that "We in New Haven are on the right track in our basic goals and plans, but there should be nothing sacred or static about what we have done. . . For New Haven's good health and continued growth, we can no more afford to undo or belittle what has already been done than we can afford to rest content with objectives accomplished."

Had the riot of 1967 affected his decision not to run?

"I would say that if I had any doubts about running, that it probably made me realize I *had* to run. That's just a guess. Those days are just a blur at this stage."

The mayor sighed and shifted his weight in the tall-backed swivel chair. He talked about polls—the Republicans had shortly before released one that said Lee's popularity had slipped—and he said that was "baloney," that he could have won the 1969 election if he had decided to run. "There's no political problem for me, as a candidate," he said. "My problem is *myself*. It's what do I want to do? And frankly, at this stage it's just a question of sixteen years." He pronounced the word "sixteen" slowly, in measured syllables.

"There were other mayors who came along, and who followed me—men like Ivan Allen in Atlanta and Jerry Cavanagh in Detroit. They patterned what they set out to do in a sense after what we were doing in New Haven. And now they've decided not to run again, and we're all stepping down together.

"And the question is, Where are the cities going? And nobody has that answer."

If any city did have the answer—if any city knew where it was going, and where urban America should be going, and how to get there—that city should have been New Haven.

New Haven was blessed with a liberal Democrat as its mayor. New Haven further blessed him with repeated political mandates and financial resources, and it refrained from active opposition to him long enough for him to demonstrate his ideas to the electorate and to other interested observers. New Haven and its mayor were blessed with unparalleled assistance from a Washington eager to invest in demonstrations that worked, and they were blessed with the invaluable interest and help of some segments of the "private sector," not the least of which was the Ford Foundation. By the end of the decade, New Haven should have known better than any other city where it was going.

But it did not. All that really could be said, as the end of the "Lee era" approached, and as the summing up started, was that there was no Model City, at least not yet.

If no Model City existed, and if unprecedented resources could not build one in sixteen years, then perhaps there were at least some tentative reasons why a Model City could not be built. Perhaps there were some lessons that could be drawn from New Haven's experience.

Before any realistic appraisal of New Haven's efforts can be made, the idea must be entertained that *no* city in America could have become a Model City, not with the resources that New Haven had or even with resources many times greater—for the simple reason that America does not have the will to do the job. America did not have that will even during the heyday of the Democratic liberals; by electing Richard Nixon and his very dangerous court jester, Spiro Agnew, America demonstrated that whatever will it *did* have had become evanescent like the morning clouds around San Clemente. The will, like the programs it sought to build, disappeared before it ever got started.

We may never know if a Model City is possible now. For America seems inclined to forever limit the energy she allots on fixing her cities. She prefers to spend her money and her will on things rather than people, on wars that cannot be won, on the development of supersonic airliners that should not be allowed to fly above human beings, on interstate highways, on sending men to the moon before seriously tackling some of the more elementary problems of the earth.

Confronted with civil disorder, she purchases not the talent and expertise and—to use an overworked but still exciting prospect— the technology to devise solutions. Rather she manufactures Chemical Mace and gives a small black can of it to every policeman, who is under some pressure to use it, for the argument is that temporary paralysis is more humane than a bullet, and the argument overlooks the fact that policemen are not supposed to use bullets, either, except as a last resort.

America builds stockpiles of ever more debilitating forms of tear gas, including some that she will not even use in her undeclared war, and she sprays them on her citizens who question her wisdom. She builds armored personnel carriers to transport her white National Guardsmen into the black ghettoes she still maintains. She makes rifles that will fire through the ugly brick walls of public housing projects which she built to contain colonies of the poor and the black, and that she now would like very much to abandon.

Confronted with the need for community action programs— programs that utilize the brains and talents of the poor and the black themselves—America appropriates a little money, only enough to insure that the programs stay alive for a few months. Then she chops the appropriation in half, then draws and quarters it. She gives millions of dollars to social scientists and public relations outfits to study the programs as they are dying, and they come back months or years later with the information that there is a need for more study—or, as in the case of one New Haven study, with the information that there was a lot of truth in the Kerner Commission report.

And when the program stands no chance of succeeding, America puts a black man in charge of it.

Willie Counsel, the black man who ran the Model Cities neighborhood organization in New Haven, observed once that when the poverty program started there, "it was a big, juicy Florida orange," and then the orange was squeezed by white men, who soon left. "And now the orange is dried up, and there's no more juice in it," he said. "And what happened is they put a black man in charge now. No money, now. They're going to spin programs off to the community. Programs with no money."

And then America wonders why people riot.

Confronted with intricate problems in housing, America does not wipe out the archaic building codes and the discriminatory practices of the contractors and the building trades unions and the real estate agents, nor does she enforce laws already on the books to eliminate segregation and discrimination. Nor does she build housing for her poor citizens; certainly she does not build housing for her poor citizens who need it the most, the large low-income families.

Confronted with problems in education, America does next to nothing to change the senile institution of education and its equally senile Establishment—an Establishment that renders even the youngest teacher senile in spirit. And the disaster of public education perpetuates itself.

Confronted with unemployment, America establishes a multiplicity of overlapping job-training programs that train people for jobs that do not exist, and probably never will—and in the meantime, a number of potential sources of employment that might serve as beginning points are neglected. The postal service is near collapse, for example. And America talks about the involvement of the "private sector," and she talks about businessmen doing the right thing for the profit motive, but even when the profit motive is enhanced by subsidies from public funds the businessmen do not do the right thing. They grind out publicity releases and they compose newspaper advertisements applauding themselves for doing the minimum, and when nobody is looking they do not even do that.

Confronted with dissent, even dissent remarkably close in quality and content to that which accompanied the birth of America herself, the nation responds with denial, evasion, and finally suppression. The action of Mayor Richard Daley of Chicago and his police force during the 1968 Democratic National Convention in brutally putting down dissent was more than a local phenomenon. The police action, and the filing of conspiracy charges against some of the protesters afterward, demonstrated the lengths to which America will go to put down dissent. And it was unlikely that the Chicago affair would remain localized for long.

In the summer of 1969 there was evidence that the next big target, the next group of Americans on whom open season would be declared, would be the Black Panthers. J. Edgar Hoover, in one of his frequent homilies, disclosed that among the "violence-prone black extremist groups," the "Black Panther Party, without question, represents the greatest threat to the internal security of the country." Before long policemen were hauling Black Panthers into jail all over the country, a number of them in New Haven. By the end of the year there was good reason to believe that there was a conspiracy among various local and national police agencies to incarcerate, incapacitate, or perhaps wipe out permanently the Black Panther Party.

Since many Americans might question a purge led by the men who tapped Martin Luther King's telephone, it was not too paranoid to wonder who the next big "threat" might be. Hoover supplied the answer in July, 1970: College students were organizing to "encourage the support of political candidates opposed to administration policies," he said. It was foolish to hope that the Justice Department, staffed by men who knew little and cared less about civil liberties, would restrain Hoover.

If there is some validity in the idea that America simply does not have the will to build a Model City, then neither New Haven nor Mayor Lee can be blamed for its failure. Lee must be pictured, and remembered, as a mayor who did as much as he could, within the context of the nation around him, his own intellectual and political limits, and his electorate.

There was some evidence, in the summer of 1969, that Lee was not alone in his inability to do more. A number of mayors—many of them, like Lee, liberal Democrats, and many of them, like Lee, men who had been responsible for making the office of mayor *important* for the first time in history—decided that year not to run for reelection. They gave various reasons for their retirement. Some said health was a factor; some said eight years, or whatever their term was, had been long enough. Whatever the reasons, it was obvious that many of them felt that some sort of an era had been ended, and they would just as soon sit out the next one.

Joseph Barr decided in 1969 not to seek a third four-year term as mayor of Pittsburgh. Commenting in a National Educational Television special on the troubles of City Hall, Barr noted that American mayors who had tried to do something with their cities were caught in a number of binds. "I watch my own mail," he said. His mail told him " 'You're a black racist' and 'You're a white racist.' Blacks feel that you have not done enough for them, and the whites feel that you have done too much. So you're caught in this turmoil presently in the political life. Fortunately, I think I chose a good year not to run."

Other mayors who were interviewed that summer and fall, as they were leaving City Hall, agreed in different ways that the American city had become the repository of most of the nation's domestic troubles and the forum for most of its confrontations, and that the job of mayor had become almost impossible. For many of those mayors, the central problem was the fact that the troubles were there in the cities, but the resources were not. Most of them were prohibited by law from levying the sort of taxes they thought they needed in order to operate their cities, and were denied by the legislatures the proper sort of state aid. (They used to worry about legislatures dominated by rural interests; after reapportionment they found that legislatures dominated by suburbanites who had fled the cities were just as bad, or even worse.) And the prospect of a Nixon Administration did not make these mayors feel that help was likely to be coming from Washington. As one retiring mayor put it, "If you think anybody with any integrity or any executive ability is going to hang around for four years and watch this guy screw up, then you're crazy."

Ivan Allen, who retired after eight years as mayor of Atlanta, observed that "Governments never accept a problem if there's a way to pass it along to some other government." And all the governments had been passing their problems along to the cities. "This is really where the buck stops," he said.

Arthur Naftalin, who headed the weak-mayor government of Minneapolis for eight years until his voluntary retirement in 1969, and who was succeeded by a man clearly of the law-and-order variety—a burglary detective who campaigned on a promise to take the handcuffs off the cops—said that the American mayor had emerged as a critical figure. But, he added, "that doesn't mean he has emerged as a more *effective* figure.

"He's got all the same old baggage, all the old inadequate machinery to work with, and he finds it increasingly impossible to provide the leadership that's expected of him."

One of the most articulate mayors who were departing from City Hall in 1969 was Jerome Cavanagh, a lawyer with no previous experience in elective politics who had become mayor of Detroit in 1961. His city frequently has been compared with New Haven in terms of its efforts to renew itself, and Cavanagh and Richard Lee often had been mentioned as examples of the new breed of "activist" mayors. But Detroit also was a city that had been wracked by one of the nation's most tragic riots, and as he left office Cavanagh was describing himself as worn out.

". . . after a while," he said, "you get punchy on a job like this. I hate to use the sports analogy—most politicians *do* use it—but it's almost like a fighter who answers the bell, you know: In the first few rounds you're coming out, right off that stool, and then by the tenth or twelfth round you're just dragging off that stool. And you find yourself almost wishing the bell wouldn't ring, forcing you into the center of the ring. There were days, some-times even weeks, in which that would happen in this job."

It happened, he said, partly because of the "impossibility of fulfilling the expectations that people have of the job. Just about all of our major present-day problems are centered in the mayor's office. The mayors have contributed, I think, to a very sharp definition of the problems that face the country. And in most instances they have also identified many of the solutions. But they don't have the resources to put the two together. This frustrates a mayor who is extremely active within his job, and at the same time contributes to the discontent generated by his holding office."

The frustration increased when President Nixon assumed power. The new administration soon indicated that it preferred to deal with the states, whose chief executives were, by and large, Republican, rather than with the big-city mayors, who were mostly Democrats.

Cavanagh recalled that Vice President Agnew had said that state government was " 'too important an institution to bypass.' In the abstract I would agree," said Cavanagh. "But the problems are so desperate in the cities that we can't afford to wage an on-the-job training course for state government over the next five or ten years and hope they'll begin to realize the desperation of the situation inside the cities.

"The state people are going through a stage that mayors went through ten years ago. They're dealing mainly in rhetoric. In the early sixties, the mayors were involved with all sorts of flourishing rhetoric, too, but they soon discovered that rhetoric just doesn't pay off. Out there in the streets you have to try and produce other things."

Nixon seemed determined to pursue his course with the states, however. Not long after Cavanagh uttered those words, Washington announced that the control of 82 federal job-training programs was being shifted from local community action organizations to state employment agencies. State employment agencies, as far as many students of urban problems were concerned, were mainly in the business of serving employers, rather than persons looking for work, and they were only slightly more attuned to the real needs of the nation's poor than were the state welfare departments. As

Mayor Cavanagh said of them: "They really don't know the gut problems down on the streets of a ghetto, or the problems of identifying, first, the people who need employment—which sounds easy but isn't—and then developing programs that not only provide job opportunities but also offer some hope and dignity."

During those years of state inaction, particularly during the Kennedy Administration and the first part of the Johnson term, said Cavanagh, the cities learned as well as, or better than, any other jurisdiction how best to spend money to eliminate poverty. "When I say 'the cities,' " he added, "I'm not just talking about the mayor. There's a great added dimension today in the cities that forms, either legally or extralegally, part of the whole picture of local government, and that is citizen participation. Some of the mayors had to learn it the hard way, but learn it they did."

Cavanagh's definition of citizen participation was one, he said, of "shared power, in that people should be able to control their own neighborhoods, particularly the poor neighborhoods. The wealthier neighborhoods have been doing it for years. They didn't *call* it 'maximum feasible participation' or 'citizen participation,' but that was what it was. The response of local city government has always been extraordinarily good to high-taxpaying, all-white neighborhoods, to homeowners' groups that were organized and wanted streets resurfaced and trees removed or planted, and parks built. Then everybody suddenly got very concerned about 'maximum feasible participation' when blacks and poor people started to say *they* wanted a voice in their own destiny, and in identifying what they wanted and felt they needed in their particular communities.

"Saul Alinsky was organizing a neighborhood group here a couple of years ago, and I invited him down to the office. Alinsky said to me, 'I was told by a lot of your people not to come down to see you because after an hour or two you'd have me in your pocket.' Or something like that. He and I understood each other well.

"I said, 'Flattery's going to get you no place, Saul.' But he in effect said, 'You know, you're killing us. I can't organize that neighborhood. Everytime somebody hollers, you're out in that neighborhood putting a park in,' or something like that. And I said, 'You're damn right. That's the way I survive. The way *you* survive is for me *not* to put a park in so you can organize the neighborhood against the so-called Establishment. That's *your* side of the street. I've got mine.'[2]

"There are, though, certain rules that the game has to be played by. There has to be a clear understanding that the responsibility for administering the program is vested in the mayor. He can't abdicate that responsibility. I used to bother a lot of people when I said categorically that if there ever was an impasse, it would be resolved by making a decision on it."

It would be easy, and correct, to say that no city in America, including New Haven, has yet come up with a viable, sustained program of citizen participation. Many mayors have bragged about the efforts they have made in that direction, but there is always a Saul Alinsky or a Fred Harris to point out that the people never did get control of their own programs. To some extent, the argument over citizen participation might seem to be a futile one: It does not exist, and probably will not exist, any more than does a viable, sustained program of democracy in America. Yet, like the fight for democracy, the fight for citizen participation—for "neighborhood participation," for "maximum feasible participation"

---

[2] Alinsky, the radical organizer, remembered the exchange a little differently. Advised of Mayor Cavanagh's recollection, he commented: "It was not anything even remotely along that line." Invited to Cavanagh's office, he said, "I just put my cards on the table and told him 'You're a new breed of mayor. It seems to me if you take a whole new course of action, you'd be doing fine.'" The suggested course of action involved making sure that people running the community action programs be selected by and from themselves. "Like most mayors, Cavanagh had been picking them," said Alinsky. "I said, 'Why not turn it over to them?' and so on, and he agreed. We walked out of his office and the press was there. They started asking me questions—I suppose they expected us both to come out of Jerry's office with black eyes—and Cavanagh had his arm around me, and I realized what was happening: the old smother treatment. So I said we had agreed that citizens should control their own programs, and so on and so forth. Cavanagh like to passed out and he started denying it. The people never did get control of their own programs."

—is going to go on, regardless of how mayors, governors, or Presidents feel about it.

Regardless of the intentions of the men who wrote the words "maximum feasible participation" into the Economic Opportunity Act of 1964, the result of the phrase, and of the aspirations it raised and the controversy it created, has been to convince vast numbers of Americans that what they had wanted all along was not impossible to achieve. Those Americans are going to participate, now, whether the phrase-writers and the law makers like it or not.

Such an effort should not have come as a surprise to some of the men who wrote the antipoverty legislation, since many of them were behavioral scientists, and behavioral scientists had been acquainted for some time with an idea called the "revolution of rising expectations." This is the notion that when people are completely subjugated they hardly ever revolt, but that when hope is offered to them—when their expectations are lifted by an event or a promise—they sometimes will stop at nothing in their efforts to get more, to get what they feel they deserve. In the case of Negroes, the expectations that were raised in the May 17, 1954, Supreme Court decision, and in the speeches of Presidents Kennedy and Johnson became goals that could not be set aside. In the case of "maximum feasible participation," the poor of America—or at least some of the more articulate among them—saw in federal law a promise that could not be retracted. In the case of New Haven, such physical manifestations of "progress" as the Oak Street Connector and the Chapel Mall, and, later, the Knights of Columbus building, provided daily visual evidence to the black and the poor that the city could be changed, just as talk of a "slumless city" and of the glories of citizen participation made some of the citizens hunger after the realities behind the words.

The idea of rising expectations has been around a very long time, but it was specifically applied to the problem of race relations back in 1947 by Professor Robin M. Williams, Jr., a sociologist. In a monograph titled *The Reduction of Intergroup Tensions,* published by the Social Science Research Council, Williams predicted pretty much what was to happen: With increased frustration and other factors, mass violence was possible.[3]

Of course, Williams' advice was ignored by almost everyone in administrative and policy-making positions, just as competent advice from that tiny minority of behavioral scientists who are qualified to give it has consistently been ignored. By contrast, the city-planning critics such as Jane Jacobs and the architectural innovators such as I. M. Pei were enjoying much greater acceptance of their ideas, undoubtedly because people who run things were finally convinced that an aesthetically pleasing environment was a salable commodity. The behavioral scientists have not yet been able to convince mayors, governors, or Presidents that the absence of racial and social tension is salable, or that it at least is worth the political risk that is involved in promoting it.

Williams' advice was ignored by the men who ran New Haven;[4]

---

[3] In discussing the revolution of rising expectations as it applied to American race relations, Williams wrote that "Militancy, except for sporadic and short-lived uprisings, is not characteristic of the most deprived and oppressed groups, but rather of those who have gained considerable rights so that they are able realistically to hope for more. A militant reaction from a minority group is most likely when (a) the group's position is rapidly improving, or (b) when it is rapidly deteriorating, especially if this follows a period of improvement." In listing the factors that might lead to mass violence, Williams included a "precipitating incident of intergroup conflict." Twenty-one years after the publication of his monograph, the National Advisory Commission on Civil Disorders assessed the mass violence that had occurred the previous summer and observed: "In virtually every case a single 'triggering' or 'precipitating' incident can be identified as having immediately preceded . . . the outbreak of disorder."

[4] Mayor Lee once said of behavioral science research: "It's almost like being a fighter pilot in World War I, flying a Spad or a Nieuport. You fly without a parachute; you fly the plane by the seat of your pants, or by the reaction in your gut. That's what you *do* in running a city today, in trying to develop programs to deal with people. No lengthy compendium or no social document of *x* pages written by theorists is of any major importance when you're dealing in a hard-nosed fashion on an eyeball-to-eyeball basis with the nitty-gritty problems of the inner city." Milton Brown, of CPI, said his agency read the scientists' output, but "In most instances it's concocted by people who have a theoretical understanding of the problem" which is limited by their whiteness. "I don't give a damn how social-scientist-oriented you are," Brown said; "unless you are a person who has understood and lived with and experienced some of these problems, I don't believe you can effectively relate to them. This is why I don't spend too

it was ignored for a long time by the men who ran Yale University; it was ignored by several Presidents of the United States; and it continues to be ignored by most of the nation.

New Haven perhaps deserves particular blame for ignoring the phenomenon of rising expectations as it developed there. A city administration sharp enough to get bagsful of money from Washington, sharp enough to entice conservative businessmen into risky redevelopment schemes, sharp enough to be on so many occasions the first and the prototype, should have been sharp enough to recognize, cope with, and even welcome and promote the involvement of the citizens in the planning and execution of programs designed to turn their expectations into reality. Such involvement, if it did nothing else, at least would have shown the citizens how painfully difficult the process of change was.

When militancy finally developed in New Haven, especially through the formation of the Hill Parents Association, Mayor Lee and his colleagues ignored it. At first, the city was surprised, then hurt, that a group of citizens had found it necessary to question what had been done for them.[5] The new breed of militants were not easily co-optable; that was apparent. So the city ignored them, and when that no longer worked, the city frustrated them, refused to allow them any power, and, in the end, demonstrated by its actions that it apparently wanted to suppress them with "law and order." Even the mild militancy expressed by the city's own agency, its Commission on Equal Opportunities, was ignored and then put down.

The militants were cut back at every turn. They were deprived of an opportunity to negotiate calmly and peacefully for their

much time digesting that—stuff." Melvin Adams, the development administrator, said, "I read three-page articles."

[5] Bernard M. Shiffman, who worked for CPI for its first five years, before becoming the deputy administrator of the New York City Human Resources Administration, observed in an interview that politicians (he was talking about the Johnson Administration, but the idea could be applied to any jurisdiction) "really don't understand the dynamics of people acting in groups. They don't understand a very simple notion, and that is that they can't expect people to have gratitude for things that are justly theirs; for giving them what actually belongs to them."

demands, and they were forced, instead, to precipitate crises; in New Haven, as in most other cities, they had to get part of what they wanted through creating fear. And they knew what is won through fear will not stay won long, for the people with power will take it back as soon as their fear subsides; as soon as the crisis is over; as soon as summer turns into autumn.

The militants had no choice but to become more militant, for the evidence was abundant that the traditional avenues through which change might be promoted were closed to them. They had to conclude that New Haven was a racist institution, a collection of components that were, in themselves, small racist institutions— City Hall, the white business community, Yale, the establishment of justice, the educational system, the white homeowners, the Redevelopment Agency, CPI. All of these institutions, the militants said, had been practicing, were practicing, and would continue to practice the sort of racism that the National Advisory Commission on Civil Disorders had found and identified as an "explosive mixture" which had been accumulating in American cities since the end of World War II. The commission had discovered racism that was brought on and compounded by out-and-out discrimination in employment, housing, and education; by the white exodus from the central cities; by the continued maintenance of black ghettoes.

To these general ingredients, the militants and the not-so-militants in New Haven could add others: The evidence before their very eyes that when the Establishment *did* want something— such as a highway or a shopping mall—it got it. But when something equally important was wanted by a sizable portion of the population that had heretofore been powerless, and the Establishment did not want it, then it did not happen. A highway was a sword thrust at poor people who lived in its path; a revitalized business community was an attempt to lure and satisfy the white suburbanites once they had driven into the city on the new highway. But real citizen participation in a program of social change was a non-negotiable item. Community Progress, Incorporated, said the militants, was a device to get private and public funds and to dispense a minimum of safe, tried-and-true services, which then were heralded as revolutionary by its own mimeograph machines.

Even a matter as simple and as black and white as lead poisoning, the issue on which "the people" wanted to be heard at the Democratic town convention, became a controversial one, and a crisis was required to involve the leaders of what once had been called the Model City in an effort to save children's lives. The controversy showed, about as clearly as it could be showed, the tragic way in which New Haven, the once imaginative, innovative, and sensitive city, had slipped from its position of leadership and become merely typical of urban America.

The city that once had wooed middle-class citizens of Wooster Square with color sketches of rehabilitated town houses; that once had excited Presidents, Secretaries and foundation executives with promises of slumlessness; that had founded Head Start— this city, in the summer of 1969, could not figure out a way to keep children from eating the poison that peeled off the walls of their slum homes.

In that summer it became apparent that horrifying numbers of children, many of them from the Hill, were becoming victims of poisoning from lead-based paint. A pediatrician said New Haven had a higher reported incidence of lead poisoning than any other city.

City Hall did nothing other than to assure the citizens that it was doing all it could. Funds were short, it was said.

A march on City Hall was held. More cases were reported. The Redevelopment Agency—that body once known for its hustle, its sophistication, its ingenuity—insisted that it was doing all it could. Finally, months after the matter had reached the crisis stage, the agency became involved. Even then, the critics said its involvement was token. It was difficult to tell whether the critics were correct or not—whether they continued their criticism just out of force of habit. But it did not matter. In a city where communications are not encouraged, where dissent is considered a manifestation of a conspiracy on the part of crackpots and Communists, and where negotiations are impossible until a crisis is produced and then allowed to get out of hand, the critics have every right and obligation to distrust everything that issues from the government.

And they had every right to believe that the government was racist. Fred Harris was asked what he felt was keeping New Haven from being a Model City. He answered, without hesitation: "The same thing that's keeping every other city from being a Model City, and that's racism. Just like everyplace else, it filters out of the people in the different areas where they're working—in city planning, in politics, in housing discrimination, jobs, education, the whole bit."

Their belief that New Haven was an incurably racist institution led the militants, and many of their followers and sympathizers, to dismiss as futile another institution without ever trying it—the vote. Blacks in New Haven had never got themselves together to the degree that they could become a potent force at the ballot box. Undoubtedly, this was because Lee kept running and getting re-elected, and even for those who disliked him, he was always the lesser of two evils. But even after he decided not to run again, and as two black candidates started campaigning for the post, attempts to register black voters (and to get those already registered as independents to identify themselves as Democrats so they could participate in the party's primary) were largely unsuccessful.[6] Some of the militants said voting simply was not worthwhile. "My feeling," said Fred Harris, "is that the only good I see coming out of elections and stuff like that is that campaigns can bring

---

[6] Prior to the September 1969 Democratic primary, pro-black politicians estimated that about 4,000 of the city's 33,000 independent voters were Negro, and they tried to get them enrolled as Democrats so they could vote for black candidates. Only about 800 persons, white and black, decided to identify themselves as "new" Democrats, however. New Haven politicians, including black ones, estimated before the 1969 elections that there were about 16,000 Negroes who were eligible to vote, about 8,000 of whom were registered, and only about 4,000 of whom actually voted regularly. Of the 60,000 persons eligible to vote in New Haven as of November 1969, it was estimated that about 25,000 were Democrats, 6,000 were Republicans, and the rest were independents. The politicians' rule of thumb in New Haven was that there were about 23,000 Italians registered to vote, 11,000 Jews, and 11,000 Irish.

people together—people who have never been involved before."

Harris' attitude was not unique to New Haven. All through the urban centers of the North, Negroes have refrained from using their voting power, and from forging coalitions with sympathetic whites at election time, and as a consequence they have been saddled with less than perfect representation. Until such time as they do at least give the vote a try, they have got to share the blame for the condition of their cities.[7] And the white radicals, many of whom (especially the younger ones) seem to have decided that the ballot box is just another obstacle placed by the Establishment in the way of their as yet unfinished revolution, have got to share the blame, too.

Richard Lee was billed as a man out to save a city. He obviously took delight in being recognized as a new-breed mayor (maybe the *first* of the new breed), a man trying to do something that had not been done before. But he was also a politician, and there is only one thing that really influences a politician in America, and that is a vote. There is no record that the black or otherwise oppressed voters of New Haven mounted any kind of a sustained effort to impress Lee with their voting power.

It was not difficult to blame Lee, as many inside and outside of New Haven have done, for his paternalism, for his protectiveness of the programs he had initiated, for his unwillingness, or perhaps his inability, to change—to share power with a new, populist ethnic politician of a sort he had not seen before, a man like Fred Harris. It was even easier to blame Lee when it developed that it was not just his personal dislike of Harris that held him back—for Lee

---

[7] As of the fall of 1969 the state with the most elected black officials was New York. There was a tie for second place between Michigan, a state fairly progressive in matters of political action, and Alabama—a state where, until very recently, a black man could get his head blown off for trying to vote. A coalition made up of black voters and a broad spectrum of whites in Atlanta failed to elect a black mayor that time around, but it also defeated a law-and-order candidate and turned down a law-order-and-justice candidate in favor of one who said he believed in justice. And a black man was elected vice mayor in Atlanta. With the exception of Cleveland and Gary, and, finally in 1970 in Newark, there were few examples of such political sophistication on the part of black voters in the North.

also refused to share power with a much more moderate alternative, the Black Coalition, when it came along. Many politicians would have welcomed an organization like the Black Coalition—broadly representative of the black community; willing to be reasonable at a time when some persuasive militants were shouting that only Uncle Toms were reasonable; potentially helpful politically; a source of power, votes, confidence, and assistance. But Lee and the leaders of the city, with the exception of Kingman Brewster at Yale, apparently failed to understand the significance of the Black Coalition; they ignored it, too.

So it was easy to blame Lee. But the record is very short on evidence that the citizens of New Haven tried—until, perhaps, it was too late—to tell Richard Lee that they wanted him to do anything but what he had been doing.

For so many years, since 1953, New Haveners really *had* been content to "Let Dick do it alone." It was only as the end of the sixties approached—a decade that was a very painful one, full of expectations that had been raised for everyone, then dashed by assassins' bullets, by rioting that many of the nation's leaders refused to understand, and by a war that refused to end by itself—that a significant percentage of the people in New Haven began to complain. Then, and only then, did they start looking for someone on whom to blame their own inaction of previous years. The logical target was Richard Lee.

Peter Almond disagreed with Lee on many subjects and on many occasions. He had been "radicalized" by what Lee had allowed to happen in the Hill. But Almond, like many others who became radicalized, could not find it within himself to blame Lee entirely. He spoke of this one night in the summer of 1969, a few days before Lee announced his decision not to run. Almond's job at Yale was in aestivation; he was headed for California, where he would grow a bushy mustache and spend a little time thinking about his future. (His immediate future, it later turned out, would be to work in John Lindsay's campaign for reelection as mayor of New York City.)

"I don't think you can blame Lee," said Almond, "because he's doing the best he can to respond to the problems as he understands them. He is shaped by his own past, his own view of New Haven and the world. It's easy to try to blame him, and that is just what keeps us from making significant progress. I think that in the end, history will say he started something great. It was only a contribution, though, to a whole chain of events in an entire era, and what he did has to be picked up and continued and given new interpretation and new meaning.

"Lee still identifies the problems of the city as the crucial ones that face this society, and these days that is a bold thing for a politician to do. One has to credit him even *now,* because when he speaks for the life of the city, he is speaking for the same city that Willie Counsel and Fred Harris are talking about. So he hasn't shut himself off entirely from what's going on . . ."

It would be "very healthy," Almond continued, "if some of the significant private institutions in the city, which for so long supported Lee and Lee's leadership, began to go their own ways, began to follow their own leads and their own instincts about what is right and what has to be done. That would provide the base for the challenge that Lee needs, that New Haven needs, to make itself better. This is what has been missing for so long, because Lee did in fact co-opt the New Haven Establishment to back him, whether it was the CAC, or the CPI board, or Redevelopment, or just through his careful development of relationships with the Establishment. And I include the private business leadership, the banking community, the WASPs, the various industries in town, and, most important of all, Yale.

"In trying to understand what's wrong with New Haven right now, you have to understand that there is one man who is in office for sixteen years. And then you have a problem because he is *now* committed to ideas which were really formed when he was just getting into office—in 1953. So the problem is that the man becomes a prisoner of his experience and his memory, and he has only so much energy to commit to new ideas, and his ideas, which were indeed the most bold ideas of the mid-fifties, took us into the sixties. They led the way in terms of what cities can do to solve their problems.

"And here we are in 1969, faced with truly complicated problems which, yet, in New Haven are so much more complicated because they're always seen in contrast with what a guy did fifteen, sixteen years ago. It seems to me the assumption in the political system is that you have new people all the time who either set things back badly, or they challenge the system to do new things. Here you had just one guy with ideas which were strong ones. He wasn't just an average politician; he was a real leader; he really *took* the place.

"But now he can't relate to the new conditions and the new issues. That doesn't reject the man for what he once did. It speaks for the uniqueness of the city that continued to stay with him."

Mitchell Sviridoff, sitting in his comfortable office high in the magnificent Ford Foundation building in New York, kept up with what was happening in New Haven, even though he had been gone since 1966. The foundation still had money invested in the city's progress, and not long before it had produced the intramural document, critical of CPI, that *The Register* had published all over its front page. Sviridoff kept in touch, too, by telephone with people like Mayor Lee, his old friend, and Milton Brown, the current head of CPI. And people from New Haven often walked into his office to talk over some program they were developing, usually with the financial assistance of the Ford Foundation.

What of the premise, he was asked, that if any city in America could properly rebuild herself, New Haven should be that city?

"Well," he replied, "I don't agree with the premise, first of all, that any city can do it by itself. The problems which the city faces—and New Haven's no exception—are *national* problems that only national policy can cope with.

"As an example: What can *any* city do about the problem of migration of the uneducated, oppressed, unskilled, unurbanized black poor of the South? That's a problem that has to do with the new industrial revolution and the problems that this population faces cannot be dealt with through city policy alone. It has to do with welfare policy, which is a national policy; it has to do with employment policy, which is national policy; it has to do with economic policy, which is national policy. And even housing has to do primarily with national policy.

"Now, cities *can* do better. Some cities have done better than other cities. I think New Haven, until very recently, was doing much better than other cities; was making better use of federal programs than other cities. But to look to a mayor, and to look to a city, to solve complex problems of a national character, is to look for the impossible."

A lot had happened in New Haven in and around the summer of 1967. There was the disturbance, of course, but before that there had been some blatant evidence that the city was not geared to accept citizen participation. The Ford Foundation report on CPI, which *The Register* had made public in 1968, was written in 1967, just before the violence.

"But that was not the turning point in New Haven," said Sviridoff. "I think New Haven at a certain point started to go downhill. I think at a certain point it lost its momentum. At a certain point it lost its initiative as a city, and I wouldn't take that report that the foundation did as a turning point. I would take that period *generally*.

"Let me give you the characteristics of the period: Robert Dahl characterized the New Haven strategy as an executive-centered strategy. That was an accurate characterization. And even though CPI was independent of the city, I always publicly acknowledged that it was part of the executive coalition. I never pretended that it was anything but that.

"Now, there came a time when participation, or maximum feasible participation, as it was described in the Economic Opportunity Act, became very important, as a national issue and as a local issue. New Haven, because of its long history—and a successful history—of an executive-centered strategy, had difficulty making that adjustment. No question about that. And that was a factor.

"Second factor: There came a time somewhere in late '65— which happened to coincide with the time I was planning to leave, although that was a pure coincidence—when federal funds began to get cut back. That complicated the problem.

"Then there was a time—and all of these things happened roughly in the same period—when the talent began to leave New Haven. Each of these factors fed the others. Participation was an issue; the need for a drastic change in strategy; the cutback in federal funds; the exodus of talent—and all of this acted as a depressant on the mayor, both psychologically and physically.

"And these fed one another, and this led to a loss of morale; a loss of initiative; a loss of momentum; confusion. And that was the turning point. From the city of the first half of the sixties and the second half of the fifties, it lost the pre-eminence it had had."

The riot, said Sviridoff, more or less put the cap on the city's confusion, although, he added, the riot itself was not a major factor in New Haven's decline. "You can have a good city and still have a riot," he said. "The question is whether you could have prevented those complications from setting in, or whether any city could sustain momentum, avoid the difficulties that beset New Haven starting sometime in '65 and '66."

What could have made the outcome different? Would things have been better if Sviridoff had stayed in New Haven?

Sviridoff paused and rearranged some papers on his desk for a moment. "I would like to think so, but who knows? Some people have told me that if I had stayed, maybe it might have been different. I had a relationship with the mayor that my successor did not have, couldn't possibly have. I had relationships in the community, and lines out in the community, that were really quite unique. I spent most of my life there, practically all my life, and I'd been in the business practically all my adult life—the business of social change and social reform. I would *like* to think that I was sensitive enough to the need for change, even in the executive-centered strategy, that I could have influenced change early enough to have averted what has now beset New Haven.

"I'm not talking about averting the rise of black militants. That was inevitable, even under the best of circumstances. But to have averted a breakdown in relations between the black community and the white community, and to have stayed where I think New Haven was for several years: one step ahead of the social revolution, and not several steps behind it.

"And that's what happened, by the way. I think that up until the point we're talking about, New Haven *was* a solid step ahead of the social revolution. But after that period, New Haven had fallen several steps behind."

Although the conflict between citizen participation and the executive-centered strategy was one of the factors in the city's loss of momentum, Sviridoff said, he did not necessarily advocate total citizen control of agencies and programs. Nor, he said, would participatory perfection be accomplished through the regular channels of representative government. "If you leave to the Board of Aldermen what the city should be like, it would not be a city that the participatory advocates want. And so what the participatory advocates talk about is really something more than what the elective process produces.

"We're really talking about what some people call 'a piece of the action,' what others calls a sharing of power. It takes more than what the elective process produces, because the elective process produces at its most extreme a winner-take-all situation. And Dick Lee, for a long time, was a winner-take-all politician.

"Those who win the winner-take-all kind of victory are not power-sharers, as a rule. And Dick Lee wasn't a power-sharer. Power-sharing is a fine art, which no mayor has figured out how to do. And there just ain't no easy way. It means, in some cases, creating community-based corporations and delegating authority to those corporations. It means maybe decentralizing your school system and delegating a measure of authority and control to a locally-based group. It means setting up economic development corporations and putting some of your wealth into those corporations. It means allowing new leaders from the new groups—in this case, the black groups—to emerge as leaders; it means providing them with the instruments for the development of leadership.

"That's why I think Pat Moynihan missed the point in *Maximum Feasible Misunderstanding*. I think that's the great achievement of the antipoverty program. It's not what's done in terms of program; it's what's done in terms of producing new leaders from this group, and making it possible for the leaders to emerge, to acquire experience and sophistication so that they in fact *can* share power.

"I think this is where Mayor Daley is wrong and where John Lindsay has been right. I think this is where the city of New Haven was slow in adjusting to new needs and new pressures."

Did Sviridoff think New Haven would regain its position, a solid step ahead of the social revolution?

"No. I don't see that happening."

America had a brief moment of insight. For a few years in the sixties, just long enough to be part of her history, there was a fragment, a glimpse of what might have been done. In New Haven, the moment lasted longer than in most cities, mainly because New Haven started first. But the moment came, eventually, in other cities—in Detroit and Minneapolis, Philadelphia and Atlanta, Los Angeles, Fresno, San Francisco, Louisville, Charlotte, Boston, even Newark.

During that moment, resources were available. There was money, and there was talent, and there was an eagerness on the part of some of the nation's powerful men to use those resources to see if things could be changed. Because America cares, first of all, about things, the resources first were used on things. Men tore down the old things that offended their eyes and noses; they restored some of those old things that were still pleasing, and they built some new things. The new things often were neither as handsome nor as well-constructed as the old things, but they were called progress. They lovingly restored Wooster Square, and they selfishly ignored the Hill. And then, as Mayor Lee and a lot of other veterans of New Haven's rebirth like to put it, the bulldozer uncovered the problems of people.

Maybe not by design at all, maybe only by mistake, America raised the expectations of some of her citizens who previously had been taught to expect nothing. A Supreme Court decision in 1954, an inaugural speech in 1961, a march in Washington in 1963, a President saying "We shall overcome" in a southern accent, phrases like "New Frontier" and "Great Society," legislation that promised equality—these raised the expectations of people all over the nation. And at the local level, there were expressways, office towers, shopping malls, architecturally pleasing parking lots, and talk of "people-programs" and "human renewal" that would be accomplished on the same grand scale, and with the same fervor, as the physical programs. And there were phrases, too, like "maximum feasible participation" and "citizen participation" and "control of your own destiny." These things happened everywhere, not just in New Haven. Only in New Haven they happened on a grander scale.

At about the time the nation was on the verge of learning something, of learning both how difficult the task would be and how absolutely necessary it was to try to do it anyway, the era ended. It ended with cutbacks in money, with rebellions of the white lower-middle-class, with riots, with phrases like "law and order" and "black capitalism," a fantasy; with observations that all ghettoes looked alike.

The era closed before America learned how to build decent housing at low cost; before she learned how to involve suburbia in a problem it had to be involved in; before she learned how to provide education for her children; before she learned how to utilize men's skills; before she learned how to build public and quasi-public agencies that could break the patterns established by the old institutions of welfare; before she learned how to provide her mayors, the men at the center of all the struggle, with the resources they needed to do the job she demanded of them. She refused to provide the most important resource—the will to do it. The era closed before America allowed a single example of citizen participation to be fairly tested.

What America had left at the end of that remarkable decade, and what New Haven had left at the end of the era of Richard Lee, was a great deal of architecture that probably will not stand the test of time and a handful of half-completed and tentative models of programs, projects, and agencies, of theories and hypotheses that there had been no time or money or will to execute or test. The bureaucracies that were to run those projects, that were to test those theories, were still there, going through the motions, turning out the paperwork that once was handled on the telephone, Xeroxing in quintuplicate agreements that once were made verbally by gentlemen who were trying to accomplish the same exciting and somewhat majestic goals. The bureaucracies remained, but the spirit was gone, and may never return. The absolute best that could be said for the experiment in liberal democracy and citizen participation was that it was "not proven." And for the experimenters—and particularly Richard Lee of New Haven—it could be said that they had done, probably, the best that they could and a lot better than most everyone else. Given the apathy and skepticism of the public and the incredible lack of national leadership, sympathy, and resources, Lee and the handful of people like him were quite successful in at least starting something—in creating expectations—even as the Sixties ended and the cold, dangerous grayness of the Seventies started to spread across the land, snuffing out expectations and excitement and threatening, even, to choke dissent and freedom of speech.

And yet, the expectations continued. Expectations that had risen before, only to be smashed and suppressed, kept on rising. Bruised, battered, made cynical and bitter, people somehow retained the expectation that it was within the national will to do something about our predicament; to create, maybe in some other era, the Model City.

Bibliography

Abrams, Charles, *The City Is the Frontier* (New York: Harper & Row, 1965).

City, a bi-monthly review of the urban scene published by the National Urban Coalition, Washington.

Clark, Kenneth B., *Dark Ghetto: Dilemmas of Social Power* (New York: Harper & Row, 1965).

Coleman, James, *et al., Equality of Educational Opportunity,* a report to the U.S. Department of Health, Education, and Welfare (Washington: U.S. Government Printing Office, 1966).

Coles, Robert, *Children of Crisis* (Boston: Atlantic Little-Brown, 1967).

Daedalus, the Journal of the American Academy of Arts and Sciences; especially the issues of fall 1965 through winter 1966, devoted to the Negro American, and fall 1966, devoted to cities.

Dahl, Robert A., *Who Governs? Democracy and Power in an American City* (New Haven: Yale University Press, 1961).

Hearings Before the National Commission on Urban Problems, Vols. 1–5; hearings on conditions in Baltimore, New Haven, Boston, Pittsburgh, Los Angeles, San Francisco, Denver, Atlanta, Houston, Dallas-Fort Worth-Arlington, Miami, New York City, Philadelphia, Detroit, St. Louis, East St. Louis, and Washington (Washington: U.S. Government Printing Office, 1968).

Jacobs, Jane, *The Death and Life of Great American Cities* (New York: Random House, 1961).

Jacobs, Jane, *The Economy of Cities* (New York: Random House, 1969).

Kaufman, Herbert, and Sayre, Wallace, *Governing New York City: Politics in the Metropolis* (New York: Russell Sage Foundation, 1960).

Killian, Lewis, and Grigg, Charles, *Racial Crisis in America: Leadership in Conflict* (Englewood Cliffs, N.J.: Prentice Hall, 1964).

Lowe, Jeanne R., *Cities in a Race with Time: Progress and Poverty in America's Renewing Cities* (New York: Random House, 1967).

Marx, Gary T., *Protest and Prejudice* (New York: Harper & Row, 1967).

Metz, Don, and Noga, Yuji, *The New Architecture in New Haven* (Cambridge: MIT Press, 1966).

Miller, William Lee, *The Fifteenth Ward and the Great Society: An Encounter with a Modern City* (Boston: Houghton Mifflin, 1966).

Moynihan, Daniel P., *Maximum Feasible Misunderstanding: Community Action in the War on Poverty* (New York: The Free Press, 1969).

Myrdal, Gunnar, *An American Dilemma,* twentieth anniversary edition, two volumes (New York: McGraw Hill, 1964).

Osterweis, Rollin G., *Three Centuries of New Haven* (New Haven: Yale University Press, 1953).

Rainwater, Lee, and Yancey, William L., *The Moynihan Report and the Politics of Controversy* (Cambridge: MIT Press, 1967).

Report for Action, a report of the Governor's Select Commission on Civil Disorder (State of New Jersey, 1968).

Report of the National Advisory Commission on Civil Disorders, March 1, 1968 (Washington: U.S. Government Printing Office, 1968).

Rights in Conflict: The Violent Confrontation of Demonstrators and Police in the Parks and Streets of Chicago During the Week of the Democratic National Convention of 1968, a report by Daniel Walker, director of the Chicago Study Team, to the National Commission on the Causes and Prevention of Violence (New York: Bantam-*New York Times* edition, 1968).

Talbot, Allan R., *The Mayor's Game: Richard Lee of New Haven and the Politics of Change* (New York: Harper & Row, 1967).

"Toward a Social Report," U.S. Department of Health, Education, and Welfare (Washington: U.S. Government Printing Office, 1969).

Violence in America: Historical and Comparative Perspectives, a report to the National Commission on the Causes and Prevention of Violence, June 1969, prepared by Hugh D. Graham and Ted R. Gurr, two volumes (Washington: U.S. Government Printing Office, 1969).

Watters, Pat, *The South and the Nation* (New York: Pantheon, 1969).

Wilson, James Q., editor, *Urban Renewal: The Record and the Controversy* (Cambridge: MIT Press, 1967).

Index

343